This book is to be returned on or before
the last date stamped below.

Introducing Psychology

History of Psychology

Grange
BOOKS

This edition published in 2005 by Grange Books
an imprint of Grange Books Plc
The Grange
Kingsnorth Industrial Estate
Hoo, Near Rochester
Kent ME3 9ND
www.Grangebooks.co.uk

ISBN: 1-84013-801-7

Printed in China

Editorial and design:
The Brown Reference Group plc
8 Chapel Place
Rivington Street
London
EC2A 3DQ
UK
www.brownreference.com

FOR THE BROWN REFERENCE GROUP PLC
Editors: Windsor Chorlton, Karen Frazer, Leon Gray, Simon Hall, Marcus Hardy, Jim Martin, Shirin Patel, Frank Ritter, Henry Russell, Gillian Sutton, Susan Watt
Indexer: Kay Ollerenshaw
Picture Researcher: Helen Simm
Illustrators: Darren Awuah, Dax Fullbrook, Mark Walker
Designers: Reg Cox, Mike Leaman, Sarah Williams
Design Manager: Lynne Ross
Managing Editor: Bridget Giles
Production Director: Alastair Gourlay
Editorial Director: Lindsey Lowe

CONTRIBUTORS

Consultant:
Ann L. Weber, PhD
Professor of Psychology,
The University of North
Carolina at Asheville

Authors:
Sarah-Jayne Blakemore, PhD
Mental Processes and Brain
Activation, INSERM (National
Institute of Mental Health and
Medical Research), Lyon, France
Brain-imaging Techniques

Joseph M. Boden, PhD
Lecturer, Department of
Psychology, University of
Southern Queensland, Australia
Functionalism & Psychoanalysis

Christopher D. Green, PhD
Associate Professor of
Psychology and Philosophy,
Department of Psychology,
York University, Ontario, Canada
Ancient Greek Thought

David Hardman, PhD
Department of Psychology,
London Guildhall University, UK
Cognitive Psychology

Katherine Hay
Cross-cultural Psychology

Peter Jones
Gestalt Psychology

Evelyn B. Kelly, PhD
Adjunct Professor of
Education, Saint Leo
University, Florida
Early Psychology

Robert Kurzban, PhD
Psychologist, Department
of Anthropology, University
of California, Los Angeles
*Nature and Nurture &
Evolutionary Psychology*

Sven L. Mattys, PhD
Lecturer, Department of
Experimental Psychology,
University of Bristol, UK
Psycholinguistics

Gary B. Nallan, PhD
Associate Professor of Psychology,
Department of Psychology,
The University of North
Carolina at Asheville
Beginnings of Scientific Psychology

Dany Nobus, PhD
Senior Lecturer in Psychology
and Psychoanalytic Studies,
Brunel University, London,
UK, and Visiting Professor of
Psychoanalysis, Boston Graduate
School for Psychoanalysis
*Psychoanalysis & Nonwestern
Theories of the Mind*

William Steele
Science Writer and Editor,
Cornell University News Service
*What is Psychology? Behaviorism,
Cognitive Psychology, Computer
Simulation, & Research Methods*

Oliver Turnbull, PhD
Center for Cognitive
Neuroscience,
School of Psychology,
University of Wales, UK
Neuropsychology

Andy Wills, PhD
Lecturer in Cognitive
Psychology, School of Psychology,
University of Exeter, UK
Behaviorism

Keith Woods, MSc
Clinical Psychologist,
New Zealand
Phenomenology and Humanism

Contents

About This Set

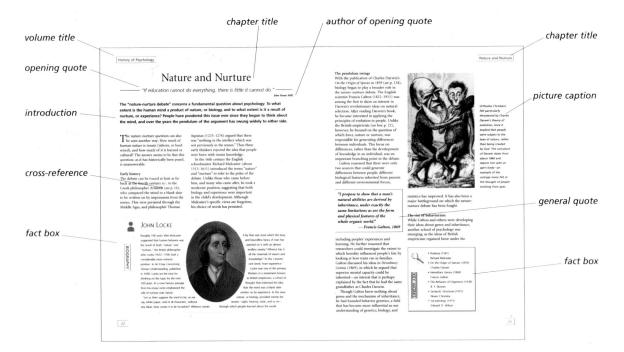

volume title

opening quote

introduction

cross-reference

fact box

chapter title

author of opening quote

chapter title

picture caption

general quote

fact box

These pages explain how to use the *Psychology* encyclopedia. There are six volumes in the set, each one illustrated with color photographs and specially commissioned artworks. Each volume has its own contents list at the beginning and a glossary at the back explaining important terms. More information, such as websites and related reference works, are listed in the Resources section, also found at the back of each volume.

To find articles on a particular subject, look for it in the set index at the back of each volume. Once you have started to read a relevant chapter, cross-references within that chapter and in the connections box at the end of the chapter will guide you to other related pages and chapters elsewhere in the set.

Every chapter has several color-coded fact boxes featuring information related to the subject discussed. They fall into distinct groups, which are described in more detail in the box opposite (p. 5).

The diagram above shows the typical elements found within a chapter in this set. The various types of fact box are explained more fully in the box shown opposite.

THE SIX VOLUMES

History of psychology (Volume One) takes a look at psychology's development throughout history. It starts in ancient Greece when concepts of "mind" existed only as a topic of philosophical debate, looks at the subject's development into a separate field of scientific research, then follows its division into various schools of thought. It also explores the effects of scientific developments, discusses recent approaches, and considers the effects of new research in nonwestern cultures.

The brain and the mind (Volume Two) analyzes the relationship between the mind and the brain and looks at how the brain works in detail. The history of neuroscience is followed by a study of the physiology of the brain and how this relates to functions such as thinking. Chapters tackle the concept of the mind as an intangible and invisible entity, the nature of consciousness, and how our perceptual systems work to interpret the sensations we feel. In a chapter entitled Artificial Minds the volume explores whether or not machines will ever be able to think as humans do.

Thinking and knowing (Volume Three) looks at how the brain processes, stores, and retrieves information. It covers cognitive processes that we share with animals, such as associative learning, and those that are exclusive to people, such as language processing.

Developmental psychology (Volume Four) focuses on changes in psychological development from birth, throughout childhood, and into old age. It covers theories of social and intellectual development, particularly those of Jean Piaget and Lev Vygotsky. It also covers social and emotional development and how they can be improved and nurtured.

Social psychology (Volume Five) studies people as unique individuals and as social animals. It analyzes the notions of personality and intelligence as well as considering how people relate to and communicate with each other and society, and the social groups that they form.

Psychologists using a variety of approaches work in different fields (developmental, social, or abnormal, for example), but all study the brain, trying to figure out how it functions and how it influences people's behavior, thoughts, and emotions.

Abnormal psychology (Volume Six) asks what is abnormality? It shows how the number and types of abnormalities recognized as mental disorders have changed over time and examines specific disorders and their causes. It also looks at diagnosis of disorders and treatments, which can be psychological (talking cures) or physical (drugs and surgery). The social issues associated with abnormality and how society deals with people who have mental disorders are also explored.

KEY DATES
Lists some of the important events in the history of the topic discussed.

KEY POINTS
Summarizes some of the key points made in the chapter.

KEY TERMS
Provides concise definitions of terms that appear in the chapter.

KEY WORKS
Lists key books and papers published by researchers in the field.

FOCUS ON
Takes a closer look at either a related topic or an aspect of the topic discussed.

EXPERIMENT
Takes a closer look at experimental work carried out by researchers in the field.

CASE STUDY
Discusses in-depth studies of particular individuals carried out by researchers.

BIOGRAPHY
Provides historical information about key figures mentioned in the chapter.

PSYCHOLOGY & SOCIETY
Takes a look at the interesting effects within society of the psychological theories discussed.

CONNECTIONS
Lists other chapters in the set containing information related to the topic discussed.

What Is Psychology?

"...seeing behavior and mental processes from multiple viewpoints."

Philip G. Zimbardo

Long before written history, people wondered both about the world around them and about themselves. Wondering how people's minds worked, what made people love or hate, and how people learned language eventually gave rise to the science of psychology.

Until as late as the 19th century only philosophers considered questions about the "mind," and for many it was the same as "soul" and thus beyond understanding (*see* pp. 10–15 and 16–21). The first real efforts to study mental processes scientifically were made by physiologists, who were interested in the workings of the brain and nervous system. Psychology only emerged as a distinct discipline when Wilhelm Wundt created the first laboratory, in Leipzig, Germany, in 1879. Just four years later G. Stanley Hall set up a similar laboratory at Johns Hopkins University in the United States.

In its early years psychology was guided as much by what people believed as by objective facts. Those with certain beliefs about how the mind worked or how it should be studied formed "schools" of thought, and the ideas of these schools often spilled into popular culture, creating larger movements in society.

Structuralism (*see* pp. 30–39) was based on Wundt's experimental work. It took a mechanistic approach to understanding mental processes by analyzing them into component parts—termed mentalism.

Functionalism (*see* pp. 40–45) grew out of the writings of William James. It held that understanding the mind's structure was less important than understanding its purpose or function.

Gestalt psychology (*see* pp. 46–51) arose in 1910, challenging structuralism's focus on parts by suggesting that the mind dealt with the experience of wholes. Gestalt psychologists mainly studied visual

This is an example of an inkblot test. People shown these stimuli are asked to describe what they see; their answers often reveal something about their personality. For many people this test encapsulates the essence of psychology —it tells us something about ourselves we would not otherwise have known.

perception but extended their ideas into other areas such as therapy—which tried to deal with all aspects of the patient's life, and was the basis for modern "family therapy."

Psychoanalysis (*see* pp. 52–65) was based on the work of physician Sigmund Freud, who claimed that unconscious mental processes caused neurotic anxiety and mental illness. His explanations for many behaviors were applied as social policy.

Behaviorism (*see* pp. 74–89 and 22–29) was founded by John B. Watson in the 1920s and further developed by B. F. Skinner. Both argued that psychologists should study only observable behavior, rejecting other approaches that claimed to identify inner processes. Behaviorism had a wide effect in education and spilled over into social policy, promoting the idea that learning grew from repetition and that most human misbehavior could be controlled by proper "reinforcement."

Humanistic psychology (*see* pp. 66–73) embraced the ideas of phenomenology and was a reaction to psychoanalysis and behaviorism. It proposed that people were neither controlled by unconscious processes nor shaped by conditioning but had free will and could solve their own problems. Carl Rogers used these ideas to develop an approach to therapy in which the therapist helped patients find their own solutions, giving rise to various forms of group therapy, "encounter" groups, and self-help movements.

The study of psychology and its various schools had a huge influence on society.

Freud's belief that many problems were caused by the repression of sexual feelings may have supported the liberalization of social attitudes in the 1920s. Behaviorism provided an authoritarian view of society in which people could be "corrected," and an individual could be manipulated by society. In contrast, humanism provided a system of value based on the individual's worth that appeared to undermine theories of competition in society.

Cognitive psychology (*see* pp. 104–117) arose in the middle of the 20th century as a revolution against the limitations of behaviorism. Psychologists returned to studying the workings of the mind but found ways to do so by objectively measuring outward behavior. It also linked psychology more closely with science and led to a belief in a more egalitarian view of humankind in which there were generic cognitive abilities of which all were capable, whatever their learned experience.

In the 1990s the most significant change in psychology was probably an expanding interdisciplinary approach. Many psychologists worked closely with physiologists, trying to link behavior with new knowledge about the biology of the brain and nervous system. New tools for imaging the brain (*see* pp. 96–103) made it possible for researchers to see which parts of the brain were active during various mental activities. Where people had once theorized about perception or problem solving, it became possible to see how changes in sensory input altered mental processing.

Evolutionary psychology (*see* pp. 134–143) is one of the newest fields and has a growing influence on other disciplines. Advances in science meant psychologists could examine the influence of genetics on behavior, leading some psychologists to suggest that behaviors that encourage survival may be inherited in the same way as physical characteristics.

Psychology has also grown through its links with other disciplines. Examples of cross-disciplinary collaboration include

One of the major issues in psychology concerns the effect of early life experiences on the development of the individual. How do children learn, and what causes problem behavior in later life? Questions such as these can be tackled from many different perspectives.

work with computer scientists to build computer models of mental processes (*see* pp. 126–133); work with linguists to study how people learn to speak, read, and write (*see* pp. 118–125); and work with anthropologists to see how culture influences people's behavior (*see* pp. 152–161), and to compare and contrast the thought processes, social attitudes, and behaviors of people in different societies in an effort to understand how society and the roles it assigns—based on factors such as race, gender, or social class—influence behavior (*see* pp. 144–151). Cognitive science combines cognitive psychology, neurophysiology (*see* pp. 90–95), and computer science, and has almost become a discipline of its own.

So, after what many see as false starts and digressions, psychology has evolved into an orderly experimental science (*see* pp. 162–163) in which less importance is placed on the traditional schools. Traces do remain, however, especially in applied psychology. Psychotherapists, for example, may use behavior modification methods, the client-centered therapy of Carl Rogers, or psychodynamic therapy (the modern form of psychoanalysis). Some even describe themselves as "eclectic," meaning they will use whichever method works. Researchers may adopt one label or another, but concentrate on collecting data and understanding the mind without trying to advance a particular theory. They are categorized more by the things they study than by theoretical camps.

PHILOSOPHICAL AND CULTURAL BACKGROUND (see pp. 10–15; 16–21; 152–161)

570–500 B.C. Pythagoras proposes a dualistic view of body and immortal mind (soul). pp. 10–11
540–480 B.C. Heraclitus discusses the *psyche* and *thumos*. p. 11
500–428 B.C. Anaxagoras develops his theory of *nous* (rationality). p. 11
492–432 B.C. Empedocles suggests a theory of perception. p. 11
460–377 B.C. Hippocrates proposes various medical theories, preferring

observation to abstract reason. p. 15
470–399 B.C. Socrates disputes that there is no objective truth. p. 12
428–348 B.C. Plato develops his theories of Platonic forms and of the tripartite psyche. pp. 12–13
384–322 B.C. Aristotle writes *De Anima*, discussing the faculties of the psyche. pp. 14–15 He also studies behavior, developing ideas that lead to empiricism. p. 17

200 B.C. Bharata discusses Rasa theory in *Natyasastra*. p. 148
100 B.C. Julius Caesar writes essays on grammar. p. 118
A.D. 400–1450 The Middle Ages. Religion and superstition rife. p. 17
600s Buddhism develops. p. 147
700s Muslim Arabs establish asylums for the mentally ill. p. 17
1200s Thomas Aquinas rejects the possibility of innate ideas. p. 22

Buddhism spreads in Japan. p. 147
1247 Bethlehem Hospital founded in London, England. p. 18
1400s First European hospital for the insane established. p. 17
1400s–1500s The Renaissance. Church power curtailed and studies of the mind revitalized. p. 17
1506 Croatian Marco Marulik first uses the term *psychology*. p. 18
1500s–1600s Rapid growth in

science. First philosophy academies emerge. p. 119
1581 Richard Mulcaster publishes *Positions*, introducing the terms "nature" and "nurture." pp. 22–23
early 1600s René Descartes suggests that body and mind are separate. pp. 18 and 9.
mid-1600s Baruch Spinoza develops psychophysical parallelism. p. 18 Akbar of India tests the

SCIENTIFIC BACKGROUND (see pp. 16–21; 30–39; 96–103)

A.D. 1700s and 1800s Physiology, physics, and chemistry develop. p. 30
1801 Thomas Young proposes a theory of color perception. p. 31
early 1800s Ernst Weber relates physical stimuli to mental experience.
mid-1800s Gustav Fechner studies perceptual thresholds. Johannes

P. Müller and Hermann Helmholtz study perception and sensation. pp. 21 and 31
1803 John Dalton devises a table of atomic weights. p. 35
1840s Dr. Harlow reports on the case of Phineas Gage. p. 91
1842 Hermann Helmholtz studies

nerves and nerve fibers. p. 31
1856 Helmholtz proposes an empirical theory of perception. p. 31
1861 Pierre-Paul Broca studies the effect of a brain lesion on speech in his patient Tan. pp. 92–93 and 118
1874 Carl Wernicke makes further discoveries about aphasia. p. 125

1880s Charles Sherrinton suggests a link between brain metabolism and blood flow. p. 100
1882 Jean-Martin Charcot opens a neurological clinic and practices the clinicoanatomical method. p. 92
late 1800s Scientists realize that the cortex of the left hemisphere is

involved in language functions. p. 93
1906 Ramon y Cajal proves that the nervous system is composed of individual neurons (nerve cells).
1924 Hans Berger makes the first EEG recording. pp. 97–8
1930s Berger discovers and studies alpha waves. p. 97

STRUCTURALISM (see pp. 30–39)

A.D. 1858 Wilhelm Wundt becomes Hermann Helmholtz's assistant.
1862 Inspired by Weber and

Fechner, Wundt gives the first lectures on psychology, establishing it as a distinct discipline. p. 32

1873–74 Wundt publishes *Principles of Physiological Psychology*, outlining his model of

the brain. p. 36–37
1879 Wundt founds the first psychology laboratory and uses

introspection to study sensation and perception. He also develops his theories of elementalism and

FUNCTIONALISM (see pp. 40–45)

A.D. 1867 William James studies physiology under Helmholtz.
1875 James teaches psychology.

1890 James outlines the notion of self and identifies consciousness in *Principles of Psychology*. p. 42

1896 John Dewey publishes "The Reflex Arc Concept in Psychology." p. 43

1902 Dewey publishes *The Child and the Curriculum*. p. 41
1904 James Rowland Angell

publishes *Psychology: An Introductory Study of the Structure and Function of Human Consciousness*. p. 44

GESTALT PSYCHOLOGY (see pp. 46–51)

A.D. 1910 Max Wertheimer studies the phi phenomenon. p. 46
1912 Wertheimer, Wolfgang

Köhler, and Kurt Koffka publish "Experimental Studies of the Perception of Movement." p. 46

1917 Köhler studies insight in chimpanzees. p. 27
1920 Wertheimer and Köhler

found *Psychological Research*. p. 46
1923 Wertheimer publishes the "Theory of Form." p. 48

1927 Rudolf Arnheim visits the Bauhaus. p. 50
1929 Wertheimer teaches at

PSYCHOANALYSIS (see pp. 52–65)

A.D. 1869 Eduard von Hartmann writes *Philosophy of the Unconscious*.
1885–1886 Freud studies under Jean-Martin Charcot, who is using hypnosis to treat hysteria. p. 53
1890s Freud works in Vienna with

Joseph Breuer developing a "talking cure" for hysteria. p. 53
1894 Freud publishes "The Psychoneuroses of Defense." p. 53
1900 Freud publishes *The Interpretation of Dreams*. pp. 53

1906 Jung uses word association to access the unconscious. p. 56
1909 Freud publishes the case of Little Hans. p. 57
1911 Adler breaks with Freud to study goals and parenting. p. 58

1913 Jung develops a theory with an emphasis on symbolism. p. 59
1918 Melanie Klein begins to apply psychoanalysis to children. p. 58
1919 Freud discusses *thanatos*. p. 54
1920s Anna Freud develops ego-

psychology; Klein and Anna argue over child psychoanalysis. pp. 58–59
1926 Klein moves to London and develops play therapy. p. 62
1927 Erik Erikson begins training under Anna. p. 58

BEHAVIORISM (see pp. 74–89)

A.D. c. 1900 Ivan Pavlov studies reflexes in dogs. pp. 25 and 75.
E. L. Thorndike studies learning in animals using puzzle boxes and proposes the "Law of Effect." pp. 25 and 75

John B. Watson studies learning in rats. p. 76
1903 Pavlov publishes his findings on classical conditioning. pp. 74–75 Thorndike publishes the first edition of *Educational Psychology*.

1911 Thorndike publishes *Animal Intelligence*. pp. 25 and 81
1913 Watson publishes "Psychology as the Behaviorist Views It." pp. 25 and 76
1914 Watson publishes his

influential textbook *Behavior*. p. 76
1920 Watson and Rosalie Rayner publish *Conditioned Emotional Reactions*. p. 79
1920s Behaviorism becomes the dominant school. p. 39

1925 Watson publishes *Behaviorism*, establishing rat research as a useful model for human behavior. p. 76
1928 Watson publishes *Psychological Care of Infant*

PHENOMENOLOGY AND HUMANISM (see pp. 66–73)

A.D. 1913 Edmund Husserl outlines phenomenological approach. p. 66
1940s Charlotte Bühler outlines

four basic human tendencies. p. 67
1942 Carl Rogers outlines the idea of self-actualization in *Counseling*

and *Psychotherapy*. pp. 69–71
1945 Maurice Merleau-Ponty publishes The *Phenomenology*

of *Perception*. p. 66
1951 Abraham Maslow employed at Brandeis University. p. 67

1954 Maslow develops his hierarchy of human needs. p. 68
1957 Albert Ellis opens the Institute

LANGUAGE, COMPUTERS, AND COGNITIVE PSYCHOLOGY (see pp. 118–125; 126–133; 104–117)

A.D. 1921 Jean Piaget publishes his first article on intelligence in *Journal de Psychologie*.
1936 Alan Turing introduces the idea of the Turing Test. p. 127
1948 John von Neuman compares the brain with a computer, and Karl S. Lashley argues that behaviorism cannot explain language. p. 105 Norbert Wiener discusses feedback in *Cybernetics*. p. 105

1949 Max Newman builds the first electronic computer. p. 126
1956 Jerome Bruner, George Miller, and Herbert Simon revive interest in studies of the mind. p. 84 Conference on information theory held at M.I.T.. Noam Chomsky presents his paper "Three Models of Language," providing a starting point for studies of thinking. p. 106 Simon, Allen Newell, and J. C. Shaw

demonstrate the Logic Theorist at Dartmouth. p. 129
1957 Chomsky publishes *Syntactic Structures*. pp. 27 and 119 Frank Rosenblatt builds the Perceptron. p. 132. Simon, Newell, and Shaw develop the General Problem Solver. pp. 112 and 130
1959 Chomsky attacks behaviorist approaches in his "Review of Skinner's Verbal Behavior."

1960 Center for Cognitive Studies founded at Harvard.
1960s Wolfgang Köhler shows that chimpanzees can use insight to solve problems. p. 27 Alexander Luria introduces the idea of a functional system formed by several brain regions. p. 94
1965 Bruce Buchanan develops the expert system DENDRAL. p. 131
1966 Wason develops his

selection task. p. 142
1969 Marvin Minsky and Seymour Papert's criticism stalls research into neural networks. p. 132
1970s Psycholinguists test Chomsky's theory, discovering that speech production involves a division of labor within the brain. p. 122
1971 First version of HEARSAY developed. p. 131

EVOLUTIONARY PSYCHOLOGY (see pp. 134–143)

A.D. 1859 Darwin publishes *On the Origin of Species*. pp. 23; 134
1860s Gregor Mendel studies inheritance in pea plants. p. 135
1869 Francis Galton publishes *Hereditary Genius*. p. 23

1871 Darwin publishes *The Descent of Man*. p. 138
late 1800s Social Darwinists use theories of natural selection to justify social oppression. p. 24
1900 Mendel's work rediscovered

and interpreted. p. 135
1920s Genetic determinism used to justify social policies. p. 24
1930s–1940s The Nazis use eugenics to justify murder. p. 24
late 1950s Noam Chomsky

suggests people are born with systems for language. p. 27
mid-1960s John Garcia suggests some behavior is inborn. p. 26. Keller and Marian Breland suggest much behavior is instinctive in *The*

Misbehavior of Organisms. p. 26 Harry Harlow concludes not all behavior is learned. p. 27
1966 George Williams discusses traits in *Adaption and Natural Selection*. p. 137

effects of isolation on language learning. p. 123
1690 John Locke publishes *An Essay Concerning Human Understanding*. p. 22
mid-1700s U.S. psychiatry develops and Dr. Benjamin Rush promotes moral therapy. pp. 16 and 20
1741 Johann Kaspar Lavater first uses facial expressions to diagnose mental illness. p. 17

1790s Franz Gall introduces phrenology. pp. 37 and 91–92
1793 Philippe Pinel promotes humane treatment. pp. 18–19
1796 First patients admitted to The York Retreat in England. p. 19
1813 Samuel Tuke reports on bad treatment in asylums. p. 19
mid-1800s John Connolly insists on changes in the treatment of the mentally ill. pp. 19–20

late 1800s Western psychologists and anthropologists classify cultures on a scale ranging from modern to primitive. p. 154
1883 Emil Kraepelin begins writing *Classification of Disorders*. p. 21
1900s Colonization drives weakens endogenous psychologies in Africa and Asia. p. 147
1905 Alfred Binet and Théodore Simon devise the intelligence test.

1920s Anthropologist Bronislaw Malinowski highlights the cultural specificity of behavior. p. 160
1940s Claude Lévi-Strauss decides the notion of a primitive mind is a myth. Some psychologists begin to view endogenous psychologies as on a par with western views. p. 147
1970 Stanley Sue finds traditional psychotherapy excludes sections of the U.S. population. p. 153

1980s Wolfgang M. Pfeiffer and A. Kleinmann claim it is impossible to understand culture-bound disorders using western approaches. p. 158
1994 David Matsumoto suggests individualistic societies are less concerned with people's social responsibilities. p. 156
Today Cross-cultural perspectives are more influential; psychiatry and psychology separate disciplines. p. 21

1936 Walter Freeman pioneers prefrontal lobotomy.
1939–1945 World War II. Doctors link brain injuries to the loss of abilities. pp. 90–95 and 105.
1950s Physiologists define the brain as a vast parallel processing system. Brenda Milner identifies the role of

the hippocampus in memory. p. 93
1950s Hospitals routinely use EEG to detect brain abnormalities. p. 97
PET is developed. p. 100
1949 Donald Hebb carries out research on neural networks.
1953 onward H. M. is studied to document memory deficits caused

by an operation for epilepsy. p. 94
1960s Roger Sperry carries out split-brain experiments. p. 93
1968 David Cohen carries out MEG scans of the brain. p. 98
1970s Elizabeth Warrington describes selective losses of categories of knowledge. p. 94

1972 Godfrey Hounsfield and Allan Cormack invent CT scanning. p. 101
1975 First MEG experiment carried out using visual stimuli. p. 98
late 1980s Functional MRI brain imaging is developed. p. 102
Marta Kutas and Steven Hillyard discover the N400 wave. p. 99

1990s Functional brain scans become widely available. p. 91
late 1990s Andreas Kleinschmidt uses fMRI to study brain activity during perceptual switches. p. 103
2001 Burkhard Maess uses MEG to study brain activity when subjects hear unharmonic chords. p. 99

---

association. pp. 32 and 34–35
1881 Wundt founds a journal for psychological research. p. 32

1892 Edward Bradford Titchener receives his doctorate from the University of Leipzig. p. 31

1898 Titchener champions structuralism. p. 38
1912 Titchener publishes

The Schema of Introspection.
1929 E. G. Boring publishes *History of Experimental Psychology*,

supporting structuralism. p. 39
1920s Structuralism declines as behaviorism becomes popular.

Calkins elected as the first woman president of the American Psychological Association. p. 45

1907 James publishes *Pragmatism; A New Name for Old Ways of Thinking*. p. 41

1904 James publishes *Does Consciousness Exist?*
1925 Harvey A. Carr proposes that

behavior is adaptive in *Psychology: A Study of Mental Activity*. p. 45
1920s Functionalism absorbed into

other areas of psychology such as intelligence testing and educational and clinical psychology.

Frankfurt University, Germany. p. 47
1930–31 Karlfried von Dürckheim lectures at the Bauhaus. p. 50

1933–35 Wertheimer, Köhler, and Koffka flee Nazism. p. 49
1935 Koffka publishes *Principles*

of Gestalt Psychology. p. 51
1954 Rudolf Arnheim publishes *Art and Visual Perception; A Psychology*

of the Creative Eye. p. 50
1947–1969 Fritz and Laura Perls develop Gestalt therapy in the

United States. p. 51
Today Gestalt approaches largely absorbed into other areas.

1930s Margaret Mahler integrates psychoanalysis and developmental psychology. p. 61
1935 Anna publishes *The Ego and the Mechanisms of Defense*. p. 65
1939 Heinz Hartman and Ernest

Kris develop Anna's ideas. p. 59
1940s Erich Fromm develops humanistic psychoanalysis. p. 65
1947 Dorothy Burlingham and Anna establish training center. p. 65
1950 Erikson discusses his society-

oriented version of ego psychology in *Childhood and Society*. p. 58–59
1950s–1960s Ego psychology criticised for its approach. p. 59
1950s Jacques Lacan places the emphasis on language and

anthropology. pp. 60–61 and 63
1971 Heinz Kohut develops self-psychology, and introduces the idea of the narcissistic selfobject. p. 61–62
1973 Fromm publishes *Anatomy of Human Destructiveness*.

1980s Stephen A. Mitchell develops the integrated relational model and introduces the relational matrix. pp. 63–64
Today Psychoanalysis continues to be popular.

---

and Child. p. 76
1935 B. F. Skinner distinguishes between classical Pavlovian and operant conditioning. pp. 25–26
1938 Skinner discusses operant conditioning in *The Behavior of*

the Organism. p. 85
1948 Skinner publishes *Walden Two*: a fictional account of a utopian society based on behavioral conditioning. p. 80
1953 Behavior modification therapy

is based on Skinner's *Science and Human Behavior*.
1962 Anthony Burgess publishes *A Clockwork Orange*. p. 85
early 1970s Aversion therapy becomes popular. p. 85

1971 Skinner publishes *Beyond Freedom and Dignity*. p. 80
1972 Bob Rescorla and Alan Wagner devise the Rescorla-Wagner rule, a mathematical equation for learning in rats. p. 87

1985 James McLelland and David Rumelhart develop the delta rule for computer learning. p. 87
1999 Maria Pilla and colleagues publish their findings on cocaine addiction in rats. p. 88

---

for Rational Living. pp. 69 & 72
1959 Rollo May, Arnest Angel, and Henri Ellensberger introduce

existentialist psychology to the United States. p. 69
1961 First edition of *Journal of*

Humanistic Psychology published.
1963 Rogers founds the Center for the Studies of the Person. p. 69

1968 Maslow publishes *Toward a Psychology of Being*.
1969 May writes *Love and Will*. p. 69

Today Phenomenology and humanistic psychology continue to be influential.

1973 MYCIN is developed. p. 133
1974 The "backpropagating" version of the Perceptron revives interest in neural networks. p. 133
1976 Neisser criticizes the linear programming model of cognitive psychology in *Cognition and Reality*.
1976 Richard Duda develops the expert system PROSPECTOR. p. 131
1980 Newell argues that intelligent actions can only be produced by a

symbol-processing device. p. 112
1980s Cognitive neuropsychology emerges as a discipline. p. 94
1982 *Vision* by David Marr is published, suggesting that cognition can only be understood if the laws and principles governing complex metal activity are understood. p. 116
1983 In *The Modularity of the Mind*, Jerry Fodor suggests the mind consists of various

information-processing devices. p. 114. Howard Garner publishes *Frames of Mind: The Theory of Multiple Intelligences*. p. 114
Newell presents SOAR, a program that provides a unified theory of cognition. p. 130
1986 David Rumelhart, James McClelland, and colleagues develop connectionist models, providing new insights into the way in which

information is remembered. p. 113
1987 The first international conference on neural networks.
1990s Antonio Damasio studies the effects of emotion on cognition. p. 95. Advances in imaging techniques allow psychologists to pin down neurological and anatomical processes. pp. 94–95
1994 Mike Oaksford and Nick Chater show that probability

influences reasoning. p. 116
1996 Emphasis on the statistical nature of language learning. p. 118
1997 Deep Blue beats Garry Kasparov at chess. p. 131
1999 Gerd Girgenzer introduces the idea of mental shortcuts in *Simple Heuristics That Make Us Smart*. p. 116–117
Today Cognitive movement remains dominant.

1970s William D. Hamilton studies kin selection in bee colonies. p. 135
1975 Edward O. Wilson discusses genetic influence in *Sociobiology: The New Synthesis*. pp. 28 and 136
1976 Richard Dawkins publishes

The Selfish Gene. p. 135
1979 Donald Symons publishes *The Evolution of Human Sexuality*. p. 28
1980s Evolutionary psychology emerges as a discipline. p. 28
1983 John R. Anderson suggests

human behavior is evolutionarily fitted to the environment. p. 116
1985 Leda Cosmides discusses cheater detection. pp. 115 and 138
1988 Martin Daly and Margo Wilson publish *Homicide*. p. 136

1994 Steven Pinker publishes *The Language Instinct*. p. 28, and Robert Wright publishes *The Moral Animal*. p. 138
1995 Buss publishes *The Evolution of Desire*. p. 142

1996 First center for evolutionary psychology opens. p. 138
1997 Pinker publishes *How the Mind Works*. p. 140
2002 Evolutionary perspectives becoming more influential. p. 143

Ancient Greek Thought

"The universe has psyche and is full of gods."

Thales

In the western world the earliest evidence of a systematic exploration of the idea of the mind dates back to ancient Greece. The main figures involved included the philosophers Plato and Aristotle and the physicians following the medical tradition of Hippocrates. For them the key issues were the basic nature of the mind (what it was made of) and its various functions and parts. They also made some discoveries about the relation between the mind and the brain.

Before the 19th century, when the two disciplines separated, psychology was considered part of philosophy. The earliest known philosophers lived in Miletus, a city in the region of Ionia in western Asia Minor (modern Turkey). We don't know a great deal about their ideas, but we do know that they thought about the nature of the world and what they called *psyche*, a concept that was only loosely related to what we think of as the "mind" today.

Thales (lived about 585 B.C.), Anaximander (about 610–547 B.C.), and Anaximenes (lived about 550 B.C.) tackled two of the key questions of the time: identifying the basic element of the world and finding out why the universe moved on its own. Thales believed water was the basic element, Anaximander said that there had once been something called "the unbounded" out of which all other elements had been extracted by the action of the spinning universe, and Anaximenes thought the basic element was air. They all believed that the universe had a psyche, which was the force that caused things to change. Thales also considered magnets to have psyche because they could make other objects move.

Metempsychosis

In 546 B.C. the Persians took control of Ionia, forcing many Greeks to emigrate. One such emigrant was Pythagoras (about 570–500 B.C.), who established a school at Croton (now in modern Italy). None of

his writings survive, so we know little of what he taught, but his pupils attributed their findings to him for many years after he died. Some of the ideas connected with his name—including "Pythagoras's theorem" in geometry—were probably not known to the philosopher himself.

Pythagoras's pupils believed that all things could be reduced to numerical relationships—even abstract ideas such as justice were associated with a number. This focus on number and proportion led to a belief in the harmony of the cosmos. Pythagoras saw mathematics as a means of purifying the psyche and liberating it from its imprisonment in the body, which may have been the earliest claim that the psyche had cognitive powers (powers of thought). The Pythagoreans also believed

This map shows the lands around the Aegean and Ionian Seas in the fifth century B.C. This was a golden age for the Greek city-states, but it was also a time of war. The two main conflicts set Greeks against Persians and most of the Greek city-states (led by Athens) against Sparta.

that the psyche was immortal, passing at death from one body to the next—some human, some animal—in an endless series of lives, a doctrine known as metempsychosis (or reincarnation).

Heraclitus

Although many Greeks moved from Ionia, Heraclitus (about 540–480 B.C.) stayed in Ephesus (now in modern Turkey). He believed that the matter out of which a thing was composed did not alone define its existence; its essence was formed by an underlying structure. A river, for instance, remained the same, although its waters changed constantly. This underlying structure governing the organization of the cosmos was called *logos*, which translates as "plan," "reason," or "word."

> *"One would never discover the limits of psyche, should one traverse every road, so deep a logos does it possess."*
> — *Heraclitus*

Heraclitus also had much to say about the psyche. First, wetness was bad for it: "For psyche it is death to become water." This statement led some people to conclude that Heraclitus believed the psyche was made of fire. Second, the psyche was a mysterious object that one could never know fully. Third, psyche and strong emotion were opposites: "It is difficult to fight *thumos*, for whatever it wishes it buys at the price of psyche." *Thumos*, often translated as "spirit," was another important psychological term used by the Greeks, who thought it the cause of courage, indignation, anger, and other action-oriented emotional states. Heraclitus also believed that the psyche was immortal, at least in noble people.

Heraclitus inspired many enthusiastic followers, but he also provoked sharp criticism. After his death philosophical thinking turned mainly toward more abstract questions such as: Are there many things in the world or just one? Do things move, or are they forever still? Are things in distinct locations in space, or are they in one and the same place?

The cosmos

Anaxagoras of Clazomenae (about 500–428 B.C.) spent most of his adult life in Athens. He developed a theory about *nous*, which was a kind of rationality or intellect. Originally, *nous* just meant the ability to think, but Anaxagoras expanded the meaning of the term to include the rationality of the cosmos as a whole—the principle that kept the world orderly.

Empedocles of Acragas (about 492–432 B.C.) said that the cosmos was composed of four elements: fire, air, earth, and water. He also proposed an influential theory of perception. He claimed that all material objects continually gave off "effluences" (tiny copies of themselves), and that these were picked up by the sense organs and transmitted to the heart, where they became known to the individual.

Democritus of Abdera (born about 460 B.C.) believed that all things were made of tiny, indivisible atoms. The smallest and smoothest of these atoms were those in the psyche, which explained the rapidity of perception and thought.

SOCRATES AND PLATO

During Anaxagoras's lifetime Athens became the cultural and economic center of the Greek world. Traveling teachers

KEY DATES

Thales (lived about 585 B.C.)
Anaximander (about 610–547 B.C.)
Anaximenes (lived about 550 B.C.)
Pythagoras (about 570–500 B.C.)
Heraclitus (about 540–480 B.C.)
Anaxagoras of Clazomenae (about 500–428 B.C.)
Empedocles of Acragas (about 492–432 B.C.)
Democritus of Abdera (born about 460 B.C.)
Hippocrates of Kos (about 460–377 B.C.)
Socrates (about 470–399 B.C.)
Plato (about 428–348 B.C.)
Aristotle (384–322 B.C.)

called sophists (from the Greek for wisdom) came to the city to teach everything from mathematics to literature and politics. Athens was a democracy, and rhetoric (the art of eloquent public speaking) became a valued skill. Indeed, some of the sophists held it in higher esteem than truth itself.

This golden period ended when Athens lost a long war against Sparta. The city went into decline and lost its democratic form of government. During Athens' darkest days there was one man who

> *"Do we learn with one of our aspects, get worked up with another, and with a third desire the pleasure of eating, sex, and so on, or do we use the whole of our psyche for every task we actually get going on?"*
>
> *— Plato*

would roam the marketplace, engaging people in debate about the nature of virtue, truth, justice, and goodness— usually showing them that they were not as knowledgeable about such things as they thought. This man was Socrates (about 470–399 B.C.), a native of the city. A small group of young men gathered about him to learn, even though he told them: "All that I know is that I know nothing."

In 399 B.C. Socrates was put on public trial for "impiety" and "corrupting" the young men of Athens by turning them away from the gods and encouraging them to criticize the government. He was sentenced to death and was forced to kill himself by drinking poisonous hemlock.

Some of Socrates' followers wrote accounts of the debates in which they had heard him

take part. One of these followers became a great philosopher in his own right: He was Plato (about 428–348 B.C.), another Athenian. Plato's writings were far-ranging and arguably the most influential works in the history of Western philosophy. During the course of his career he developed an elaborate theory of the psyche that was unlike anything that had preceded it. To understand this theory completely, we must also know a little about his theory of knowledge (*see* box opposite).

Plato's theory of the psyche

Plato's theory of the psyche changed and developed throughout his life. In his early works he wrote about the possibility of improving one's psyche through learning and of the psyche being the source of human morality. Later he wrote that the psyche was "something you value more highly than your body," and that it was "in command" of the body, being the seat of all knowledge. Knowledge was not learned through experience, but was innate. Experience brought this inborn knowledge to consciousness, through a process of recollection (*anamnesis*). Elsewhere Plato said that the psyche was immortal, and that the death of the body freed the psyche to be with the Forms that one could only glimpse, via philosophy, for as long as the psyche is trapped in the body.

Plato's theory of the psyche became more complex in later years. In the *Republic* he argued that the psyche was made of three distinct parts: the intellect, which he called the *logistikon*; the emotional part, called *thumos*; and the seat of appetites and desires, called the

Born in Athens, Plato was one of the greatest ancient Greek philosophers. His ideas influenced philosophy right up to the 20th century. After the execution of Socrates he traveled widely before founding the Academy in Athens in about 387 B.C.

PLATONIC FORMS

How do we come to know things? How do we know, for example, that a horse is a horse? Plato believed that there is something that all horses have in common, something that enables us to identify them as horses. This something is not the horses' similarity in appearance, because they appear in many different colors, shapes, and sizes. Plato believed that there must, somewhere, be an "Idea of Horse" that all horses "reflect" in some way. The same went for abstract ideas such as virtue and justice—all just acts are just because they reflect the Idea of Justice. These Ideas are known today as Platonic "Forms."

Plato explained his theory of Forms using an allegory: Imagine some prisoners chained in sitting positions in a cave, facing a wall. A fire is lighted outside the cave, and between the fire and the prisoners statues of people and various animals are paraded back and forth, casting shadows on the cave wall. The prisoners have lived their entire lives in the cave, so they believe the shadows to be reality. If one of them were freed, however, and turned around to look out of the cave, at first he would be dazzled by the light of the fire; but as he approached the statues, he would come to see that they were real, and that the shadows were merely their images.

Similarly, Plato argued, the things around us in the world are like distorted shadows of the true Forms. In order to know the Forms, we cannot depend on just looking straight ahead, as it were. Instead, we have to explore further by thinking about the essence of each

A 19th-century illustration of Plato's cave allegory, which he used to demonstrate that there was a reality behind the material world. He called this reality the world of ideas, or Forms.

thing—the essence of what it is to be a man, to be a horse, or to be just or good. For Plato, thinking about the Forms was the core of what it was to be a philosopher; it was the same as if the prisoners broke their chains, walked out of the cave, and encountered reality directly.

---

epithumetikon. In the best psyche, Plato argued, the *logistikon* ruled, harmonizing the needs of the three parts through the use of reason. If the *epithumetikon* took over, however, the person would be dominated by appetites and desires. The *thumos* was the "action" part of the psyche that turned thoughts into deeds. It was also thought to be responsible for indignation, anger, courage, and the like.

The senses

In his later work *Timaeus* Plato gave an extended account of the senses and how he believed perception to work. The eyes, he said, continually gave off a "visual stream of pure fire" that made vision

possible. According to Plato, the different sensations of touch were caused by the different geometric shapes of things. Earth was hard because it was formed from cubes that had "wide bases" and so resisted our touch. Fire was made of four-sided pyramids that were sharp and so caused pain when touched. Air was made up of eight-sided figures, and water of 20-sided figures. Having so many sides, they easily slipped around each other and out of people's grasp when touched.

Plato also set out in *Timaeus* his ideas about human physiology and illness, including mental illness. He believed they were caused by bodily imbalances, poor upbringing, and bad training.

This detail from a fresco, or wall painting, called School of Athens by Raphael (1483–1520), shows Plato (left) with Aristotle (right) surrounded by other philosophers.

ARISTOTLE

Many students at Plato's school, the Academy, became successful philosophers. None, however, would have as much influence on western culture as Aristotle (384–322 B.C.). In 336 B.C. he founded his own school, the Lyceum, in Athens.

Aristotle's book on the psyche is the earliest surviving work on the subject. In Greek it was called *Peri Psyches*, but today it goes by its Latin title *De Anima* or the English *On the Soul*. In the book Aristotle considers what life is about and discusses how the psyche and the body combine to produce a living being.

Aristotle worked from a series of analogies. First, he compared the relation between the psyche and the body to that between a finished house and the pile of bricks from which it was made. He also compared the relation to that between a lump of wax and a pattern stamped into it. In a third analogy Aristotle said: "If some tool, say an ax, were a natural body, its substance would be being-an-ax [that is, having the capacity to chop], and this

would then be its psyche." In a fourth analogy he said: "If the eye was an animal, then sight would be its psyche…. Just as pupil and sight are the eye, so, in our case psyche and body are the animal."

What did Aristotle mean? Consider the wax. The impression is a form (a pattern of organization) that has been taken on by some matter (the wax). Aristotle believed that all things could be analyzed as a certain kind of matter given a certain form. He believed that the same approach could be used to analyze the relation of the psyche to the body—the psyche was the form (or the organization) given to the matter of the body. Together, psyche and body made the living thing.

Faculties of the psyche

Aristotle variously described the faculties of the psyche. At one point he stated: "We say that a thing is alive if, for instance, there is intellect or perception or spatial movement, and rest or indeed movement connected with nourishment, and growth, and decay." At another time he wrote that "the psyche comprises cognition, perception, and belief. It also comprises appetite, wishing, and desire in general. It is the source of locomotion for animals and also of growth, flourishing, and decay." Later, he said that the psyche has five faculties: nutrition, perception, desire, locomotion, and intellect (*nous*).

Aristotle believed that the psychic faculties were arranged in a ladder or hierarchy. The psyches of the simple life forms had only the most basic faculties, while those of the more complex life forms had more sophisticated faculties. Nutrition was basic to life and was the only faculty plants had. To be an animal, a living thing had to have the faculty of perception: sight, touch, taste, smell, hearing, and sight. Aristotle also proposed a "common sense" in which the various kinds of sensation were combined into a single, integrated mental image. If an animal had perception, it also had imagination and desire. He believed that imagination was a voluntary movement of the sense organs, causing them to respond as though they were perceiving.

Locomotion was the next highest rung on the ladder, and Aristotle attributed it only to some animals. Finally, he considered just a few animals to have "the thinking faculty and intellect, such as man and any other creature that may be like him or superior to him." Aristotle also believed that the mind had nothing "written on it" in advance, so knowledge could be inscribed on it by experience.

GREEK MEDICAL TRADITION
Followers of the medical tradition of ancient Greece also had much to say about the mind, sometimes in opposition to the philosophers. Hippocrates of Kos (about 460–377 B.C.) is known as the father of medicine. Many hundreds of documents are attributed to him, although most are the work of his disciples. Together they are called the Hippocratic Corpus, and they show a preference for observation over abstract reason and for concrete explanations rather than metaphysical (supernatural) ones. Neither did Hippocrates and his followers believe, as many did, that disease was a punishment sent by the gods. For instance, epilepsy was called the sacred disease, but Hippocrates believed it was caused by the brain.

In many of the writings health was related to a balance between competing or opposing elements, such as hot and cold. It was also considered vitally important to maintain the correct balance between the four bodily fluids called the humors: blood, phlegm, yellow bile, and black bile. Imbalances were thought to cause specific diseases and mental problems. This doctrine of the humors formed the basis of medical care well into the Middle Ages and is still in our modern vocabulary: Too much blood caused one to be "sanguine," too much phlegm made one "phlegmatic," too much yellow bile made one "choleric" (angry), and too much black bile caused one to be "melancholic."

The ideas of Hippocrates and Aristotle influenced scientific thinking for the next 2,000 years, laying the foundations for studies of biology, anatomy, physical and emotional health, and disease.

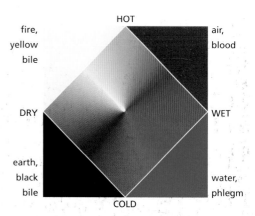

Medical theory in ancient Greece was based on maintaining a balance between opposites and the four humors. Each of the humors, or bodily fluids, was related to one of the four basic elements (earth, fire, water, and wind).

CONNECTIONS

• Early Psychology: pp. 16–21
• The Mind: Volume 2, pp. 40–61

• Perception: Volume 2, pp. 62–85
• Consciousness: Volume 2, pp. 110–139
• Personality: Volume 5, pp. 94–117
• Intelligence: Volume 5, pp. 118–141

Early Psychology

"All mental illness is rooted in brain disease."

Roy Porter

Today psychology is the study of behavior and mental processes, while psychiatry is a branch of medicine concerned with the treatment of mental illnesses. Originally, however, they were both branches of philosophy, only becoming distinct disciplines late in the 19th century.

In the western world the earliest recorded theories on philosophy, which encompassed psychology and attempts at healing, date back to the ancient Greeks (*see* pp. 10–15). The word psychology comes from two Greek words: *psyche*, meaning "mind" or "soul," and *logos*, meaning "word" or "reason." The word psychiatry, also Greek in origin, comes from *psyche* and *iatros*, meaning "to heal."

The Greek physician–philosopher Hippocrates (about 460–377 B.C.)

proposed that illnesses were caused by an imbalance of body fluids, or humors—blood, phlegm, yellow bile, and black bile. This was known as humoral theory. Madness was thought to be caused by an excess of black bile (*melan chole* in Greek), and the word melancholy still refers to extreme sadness. In some parts of the world humoral theory was considered valid until the end of the 19th century.

The Greek philosopher Aristotle (384–322 B.C.) was interested in the

KEY DATES

400 B.C. Hippocrates proposes that an imbalance of body fluids causes madness.

about 350 B.C. Aristotle studies human and animal behavior, developing ideas that lead to empiricism.

A.D. 400–1450 In the Middle Ages behavior was generally viewed from a religious, rather than a scientific, standpoint.

1506 Croatian humanist and Latin author Marco Marulik first uses the term psychology.

Early 1600s French philosopher René Descartes suggests that body and mind, or rational soul, are separate structures that influence each other.

Mid-1600s Baruch Spinoza introduces the concept of psychophysical parallelism.

1600s English philosophers Thomas Hobbes (1588–1679) and John Locke (1632–1704) propose that the mind is empty at birth and is molded by the environment.

Mid-1700s English philosopher David Hartley (1705–1757) proposes a secular (nonreligious) framework for human behavior. U.S. psychiatry develops from British models. U.S. doctor Benjamin Rush believes in moral therapy and institutes reforms in the care of the mentally ill. After his death he is called the "Father of American Psychiatry."

Late 1700s Hospitals for the mentally ill (asylums) are developed by Philippe Pinel, who demands that shackles be

taken off his patients at the Bicêtre in Paris, France.

1813 The Tukes, a rich and influential English Quaker family, produce a damning report about bad management and inhumane treatment at asylums, particularly the famous one known as "Bedlam" in London, England.

Mid-1800s German scientists Johannes Mueller and Hermann Helmholtz (*see* p. 31) begin systematic studies of perception and sensation. John Connolly and the doctors of Bedlam insist on changes in treatment.

Phrenology (the art of skull-reading) starts as a science but soon becomes a popular parlor game, sparking widespread interest in the brain and behavior (*see* p. 37).

1841 First professional group established in England: Medical Officers of Asylums and Hospitals.

Late 1800s Austrian physician Sigmund Freud develops psychoanalysis based on free association (*see* pp. 52–57).

1870s German psychologist Wilhelm Wundt founds the first psychological laboratory at the University of Leipzig (*see* pp. 33–34). He also publishes the first journal of experimental psychology. Psychology and psychiatry thus become separated from philosophy and begin to achieve recognition as sciences in their own right.

1900s Psychology and psychiatry both develop into strong professions that work together for the benefit of patients.

behavior of both people and animals. His direct methods of observing the natural world led to the development of empiricism. Empiricism is knowledge based on observation, and Aristotle was the first westerner to apply this process to the study of the natural world, including human behavior and illness.

Later, Greek practitioners working in Rome under the Roman Empire advocated quiet, useful occupation and drugs as remedies for mental illness.

The Middle Ages

During the Middle Ages (about the 5th to 15th centuries) western scholars studied human behavior from a religious, rather than a scientific, viewpoint. They were more interested in nature than medicine, and in Europe there were few advances in the field for almost 2,000 years.

People who were seen to behave unusually were thought to be possessed by evil spirits or influenced by witchcraft, and sufferers were usually considered to have sinned in some way. Treatments aimed at releasing these evil spirits, and the medieval sweat house was a building where a smoldering fire of leaves smoked out demons and "treated" those afflicted. Magical or religious rituals were also popular. Suffers were declared deviant, mad, or lunatic. While some were cared for by religious orders, many were forced to become beggars and vagrants. It was left to Muslim Arabs to keep the Greek

CASE STUDY

PSEUDOSCIENCE

During the Middle Ages people with mental illness were thought to have *stigmata diaboli* (marks of the devil). Supposedly they were physical marks, but the interpretation of what one looked like was greatly subjective. Many people found to have these marks were subsequently executed by being burned at the stake or drowned. By the 19th century stigmata were being used as a way of diagnosing mental illness.

Swiss theologian Johann Kaspar Lavater (1741–1801) first advocated the use of facial expressions to diagnose mental illness. This technique was also used to detect criminals. Guillaume Duchenne (1806–1875), a French neurologist, created a complete book of facial expressions with photographs of different kinds of "looks" and descriptions of what they denoted. Known as physiognomy, this technique used all kinds of devices to measure the emotion on people's faces, and doctors would pronounce people insane merely by examining their faces. For a while after photography had been developed, doctors also used photographs of faces as standards of insanity.

traditions alive, and they continued to make significant advances in medicine, establishing the first asylums for the mentally ill in the eighth century. The first European hospital for the insane was only established in the early 15th century.

The birth of psychology

Between the 14th and 17th centuries (a period known as the Renaissance) studies of the mind and brain anatomy were revitalized. Instead of studying

By the 17th century those who cared for the mentally ill were called mad-doctors, although they had little training, and their treatments were often barbaric. In 1788 the British king George III suffered at the hands of both his court physician and the mad-doctor Francis William, a clergyman. His plight was depicted in the film The Madness of King George *(1995).*

Eighteenth-century French physician Philippe Pinel demands that shackles and chains be removed from the mentally ill at the Bicêtre Hospital in Paris, France.

animals, thinkers turned their attention to human behavior and anatomy. Marco Marulik, a Croatian humanist, first used the term psychology in 1506.

The French philosopher René Descartes (1596–1650) suggested that the body and the mind (or rational soul) were two separate structures that strongly influenced each other. He held that the workings of the body were mechanical, but that the rational soul was neither

> *"Until the close of the 18th century, madhouses were not primarily medical institutions; most [were] religious or municipal charities"*
> — *Roy Porter, 1997*

physical nor mechanical—it interacted with the body through the brain and was the seat of wisdom. This dualistic concept of the relationship between mind and body continues to influence ideas today.

The Dutch philosopher Baruch Spinoza (1632–1677) believed that mind and body did not interact but coordinated their actions because they were influenced by the same stimuli. This idea became known as double aspect theory and led to the theory of psychophysical parallelism (the

idea that the brain process and the mental process coexisted, and could vary without affecting one another). Scholars attempted to apply these philosophical principles to the practice of medicine.

MADHOUSES

In Europe from the 17th century onward all those who were seen as being outside normal society were confined together in institutions called madhouses. This included people who were mentally ill or handicapped and those who were criminals and vagrants.

Set up by churches or charities, madhouses were more like prisons than hospitals. Volunteer physicians might sometimes visit to purge the inmates by administering tonics made from herbs and shrubs such as ipecac, which induces vomiting, but most of the people there were shackled, chained to walls, or put in straitjackets. The oldest and most famous of these madhouses, the Hospital of St. Mary of Bethlehem in London, England, was a horrific place of cruelty, neglect, whips, chains, and filth. Bethlehem was shortened to Bethlem or Bedlam, a word that came to mean "uproar."

In 1793 French physician Philippe Pinel (1745–1826) was given responsibility for the Bicêtre, an institution for mentally ill men in Paris, France. Disgusted at the inhumane treatment inmates habitually received there, Pinel demanded that everyone in the asylum be unshackled, given pleasant rooms, and allowed to exercise in the grounds. He believed that if the inmates in these institutions behaved like animals, it was because they were treated so cruelly, a view that challenged the conventional assumption that insanity caused people to become like animals. A

> *"Before the 19th century the treatment of the mad hardly constituted a specialized branch of medicine."*
> — *Roy Porter, 1997*

devout Roman Catholic, Pinel promoted moral treatment and a humane approach. He categorized insanity into melancholia, mania, idiocy, and dementia, and also recognized partial insanity. He did away with treatments like purging and bleeding in favor of discussions with the patient and a program of activities.

Pinel had a great influence on the Bicêtre and also on Salpêtrière, a similar institution for women. His writings were widely influential and were translated into English, Spanish, and German. Moral treatment also developed in other countries. In Florence, Italy, for example, Vincenzo Chiarugi (1759–1820) implemented radical changes in the organization of mental institutions.

The Tukes

While psychology remained a branch of philosophy, a new science was starting to emerge that was later to be named psychiatry. Shocked at mismanagement and cruelty in an asylum at York, England, in 1796 an outraged Quaker community built a charitable retreat based on quiet, comfort, and a supportive atmosphere. The Tukes, a rich family of tea merchants who ran the institution, paved the way for widespread changes in attitude.

William Tuke (1732–1822) likened his retreat to a place for children and believed that patience would be rewarded by improvements in the patients' mental health. This reflected a major new development: For the first time there was the hope of a cure for mental illness. In 1813 Samuel Tuke (1784–1857) delivered a stinging report to a parliamentary committee that had been set up by the British government to look at madhouses. He described how the treatment at Bedlam was a hell of scandals and mismanagement, and contrasted it unfavorably with the methods and philosophy of the York Retreat. With the success of the Tukes' efforts the notion

---

EXPERIMENT

MAD-DOCTORS

In the 17th century people with mental illnesses began to be placed in institutions known as madhouses. They quickly became associated with cruelty, filth, and corruption, the most infamous example being Bedlam (Bethlehem) in London, England. The physicians put in charge of these establishments became known as mad-doctors or lunatic-doctors.

In the 19th century seven innovative mad-doctors changed the scene forever. They turned mad-doctoring—which until then had been held in poor esteem—into a respected profession, and their ideas helped lead to various reforms in the treatment of the mentally ill. John Haslam

(1764–1844), an apothecary (chemist) at Bedlam, began to study the nature of those deemed insane. John Connolly (1794–1866), who had been the overseer at Bedlam, first pioneered nonrestraint. W. A. F. Browne (1805–1885) was an active and persistent reformer of the system in Scotland. Sir Alexander Morrison (1779–1866) became a visiting physician and was the first to carry out consultations with the inmates. Samuel Gaskell (1807–1886) and Sir Charles Bucknill (1817–1897) were proponents of noninstitutionalization, encouraging home care whenever possible. Henry Maudsley (1835–1918) criticized the traditional asylum in his *Journal of Mental Science*.

that mental illness was a medical condition requiring skilled treatment began to gain a wider acceptance than it ever had before.

American psychiatry developed from British models, and the York Retreat influenced well-known asylums in Boston, Hartford, and Philadelphia. However, Benjamin Rush (1746–1813), a founding father of American medicine, believed in using physical restraint and fear as a form of moral therapy. He also advocated venesection (bleeding) as an effective method of calming insane people.

Science and humanity

As a result of changing attitudes to mental illness, madhouses were renamed asylums during the early 1800s. Psychiatrist John Connolly (1794–1866) was superintendent of a large asylum in Middlesex, southern England, and strove to make it a place of respite and rest "where humanity shall reign supreme." He supported non-restraint and encouraged staff to write case histories to record the patients' psychological and social backgrounds.

Before asylums were reformed, scenes such as this 1880 drawing of the men's gallery at "Bedlam" (properly known as the Hospital of St. Mary of Bethlehem) would have depicted the mistreatment and abuse of patients. It was only as the public learned not to fear mental disorders that patients began to be treated with greater respect and care.

Connolly bridged psychiatry and psychology in his support of phrenology, a movement incorporating both psychiatry and studies of behavior (*see* p. 37). Developed initially by Franz Joseph Gall (1758–1828), phrenology held that the brain was the organ of thought and will, and that the contours of the bumps on the skull determined personality. Although phrenology is now regarded as a pseudo-science, it was an important stage in the development of psychiatry and the humane treatment of the mentally ill.

Also emerging at this time was the idea that mental illness originated within the person, possibly in the brain. There was a sharp rise in the number of books on mental disorders, and in the number of practicing physicians, who were known as mad-doctors or "alienists."

An act of parliament passed in England in 1808 gave local authorities permission to levy taxes to build lunatic asylums for what were termed "the mad poor." Several commissions inspected these places, but mad-doctors were still not given a distinct status. The first professional group, the

Medical Officers of Asylums and Hospitals, only came into being in 1841. In 1853 this British association published the *Asylum Journal*, a magazine that later changed its name to the *Journal of Mental Science*. By this time interest in the nature and treatment of mental illness was growing, and there was widespread optimism that it might be curable.

In 1883 the German psychiatrist Emil Kraepelin (1856–1926) began his book *Classification of Disorders* in which he classified mental illnesses into categories that he considered treatable and those that he considered incurable. He continued to refine his classification system and was working on the ninth edition of his book when he died. His ideas were extremely influential during the early 20th century.

SCIENCE AND PSYCHOLOGY

Psychology and psychiatry remained closely linked until the mid 19th century, when German scientists Johannes P. Mueller (1801–1888) and Hermann Helmholtz (1821–1894) began the first systematic studies of perception and sensation, examining mental activity using scientific methods of observation. But it was not until the late 1800s that Wilhelm Wundt (1832–1920), a philosopher trained in medicine and physiology (*see* pp. 30–39), published the first journal of experimental psychology in Germany, establishing psychology as a distinct discipline based on careful observation. The work of these and others helped separate psychology from philosophy and from psychiatry, which was steadily developing its own identity.

The best-known approach in psychiatry is psychoanalysis, which was developed by Sigmund Freud (1856–1939). Originally a therapeutic strategy, it is also a theory of mental disorder and an approach to understanding human nature. Freud believed that forces buried deep in the subconscious mind determined behavior, and that repressed feelings caused personality disturbances, self-destructive

> *"Restriction of the individual's aggressiveness is the first and perhaps the severest sacrifice which society requires of him."*
> — *Sigmund Freud, 1933*

tendencies, and physical problems. Later, psychoanalysis developed to include scientific research into personality, developmental and abnormal psychology, and psychotherapeutic techniques.

Crossover and interaction

Today psychology and psychiatry are separate disciplines. Psychologists study normal and abnormal behavior, typically obtaining an academic degree and then moving on to further specialized training. Psychiatry is a medical speciality— psychiatrists specialize in disorders of the mind and brain and have earned a medical degree. They are also licensed to prescribe and administer drugs and other medical therapies.

There are still many areas of crossover, however. In 1879 the term "clinical psychology" was introduced to describe analysis carried out in a clinical setting such as a hospital, and clinical psychologists who work as therapists in mental health centers often train under experienced psychiatrists. Psychologists and psychiatrists will also cooperate to help their patients cope with all kinds of problems and mental illnesses.

CONNECTIONS

- Ancient Greek Thought: pp. 10–15
- Psychoanalysis: pp. 52–65

- The Mind: Volume 2, pp. 40–61
- What Is Abnormality?: Volume 6, pp. 6–19
- Mental Disorders: Volume 6, pp. 20–67
- Mental Disorders and Society: Volume 6, pp. 142–163

Nature and Nurture

───── *"If education cannot do everything, there is little it cannot do."* ─────

John Stuart Mill

The "nature-nurture debate" concerns a fundamental question about psychology: To what extent is the human mind a product of nature, or biology, and to what extent is it a result of nurture, or experience? People have pondered this issue ever since they began to think about the mind, and over the years the pendulum of the argument has swung widely to either side.

The nature-nurture question can also be seen another way: How much of human nature is innate (inborn, or hard-wired), and how much of it is learned or cultural? The answer seems to be that this question, as it has historically been posed, is unanswerable.

Early history

The debate can be traced at least as far back as the fourth century B.C. to the Greek philosopher Aristotle (*see* p. 14), who compared the mind to a blank slate to be written on by impressions from the senses. This view persisted through the Middle Ages, and philosopher Thomas Aquinas (1225–1274) argued that there was "nothing in the intellect which was not previously in the senses." Thus these early thinkers rejected the idea that people were born with innate knowledge.

In the 16th century the English schoolmaster Richard Mulcaster (about 1513–1611) introduced the terms "nature" and "nurture" to refer to the poles of the debate. Unlike those who came before him, and many who came after, he took a moderate position, suggesting that both biology and experience were important in the child's development. Although Mulcaster's specific views are forgotten, his choice of words has persisted.

JOHN LOCKE

BIOGRAPHY

Roughly 100 years after Mulcaster suggested that human behavior was the result of both "nature" and "nurture," the British philosopher John Locke (1632–1704) took a considerably more extreme position. In *An Essay Concerning Human Understanding*, published in 1690, Locke set the tone for thinking on the topic for the next 200 years. In a now famous passage from his essay Locke emphasized the role of nurture over nature:

"Let us then suppose the mind to be, as we say, white paper, void of all characters, without any ideas; how comes it to be furnished? Whence comes it by that vast store which the busy and boundless fancy of man has painted on it with an almost endless variety? Whence has it all the materials of reason and knowledge? To this I answer, one word, from experience."

Locke was one of the primary thinkers in a movement known as British empiricism, a school of thought that endorsed the idea that the mind was a blank slate written on by experience. In this view nature, or biology, provided merely the senses—sight, hearing, taste, and so on—through which people learned about the world.

The pendulum swings

With the publication of Charles Darwin's *On the Origin of Species* in 1859 (*see* p. 134), biology began to play a broader role in the nature-nurture debate. The English scientist Francis Galton (1822–1911) was among the first to show an interest in Darwin's revolutionary ideas on natural selection. After reading Darwin's book, he became interested in applying the principles of evolution to people. Unlike the British empiricists (*see* box p. 22), however, he focused on the question of which force, nature or nurture, was responsible for generating differences between individuals. This focus on differences, rather than the development of knowledge in an individual, was an important branching point in the debate.

Galton reasoned that there were only two sources that could generate differences between people: different biological features inherited from parents and different environmental forces,

Orthodox Christians felt particularly threatened by Charles Darwin's theory of evolution, since it implied that people were subject to the laws of nature, rather than being created by God. This caricature of Darwin dates from about 1860 and depicts him with an ape's body—an example of the outrage many felt at the thought of people evolving from apes.

> *"I propose to show that a man's natural abilities are derived by inheritance, under exactly the same limitations as are the form and physical features of the whole organic world."*
> — *Francis Galton, 1869*

including peoples' experiences and learning. He further reasoned that researchers could investigate the extent to which heredity influenced people's fate by looking at how traits ran in families. Galton discussed his ideas in *Hereditary Genius* (1869), in which he argued that superior mental capacity could be inherited—an interest that is perhaps explained by the fact that he had the same grandfather as Charles Darwin.

Though Galton knew nothing about genes and the mechanism of inheritance, he had founded behavior genetics, a field that has become more influential as our understanding of genetics, biology, and

statistics has improved. It has also been a major battleground on which the nature-nurture debate has been fought.

The rise of behaviorism

While Galton and others were developing their ideas about genes and inheritance, another school of psychology was emerging, as the ideas of British empiricism regained favor under the

KEY WORKS

- *Positions* (1581)
  Richard Mulcaster
- *On the Origin of Species* (1859)
  Charles Darwin
- *Hereditary Genius* (1869)
  Francis Galton
- *The Behavior of Organisms* (1938)
  B. F. Skinner
- *Syntactic Structures* (1957)
  Noam Chomsky
- *Sociobiology* (1975)
  Edward O. Wilson

PSYCHOLOGY & SOCIETY

BIOLOGICAL APPROACHES AND POLITICS

Many of Darwin's and Galton's contemporaries met their ideas with hostility, and even today biological approaches to understanding human behavior are the focus of intense controversy. To understand why, it is important to grasp how the swing of the nature-nurture debate influenced political thought at the beginning of the 20th century. At that time, a growing emphasis on nature rather than nurture gave birth to three movements that had serious political consequences: social Darwinism, biological determinism, and eugenics.

In the late 19th and early 20th centuries social Darwinists held that social groups were subject to the forces of natural selection in the same way that individuals were under Darwin's theory—that is, they believed that stronger groups of individuals would eventually outcompete and replace weaker groups of individuals. They applied this idea to all kinds of groups, including nations, races, and ethnicities.

In the political arena social Darwinism was used to justify the oppression of particular groups, such as the poor or minorities. In economics business leaders used the idea to support the notion that governments should not intervene in business, arguing that allowing firms to compete freely enabled the best firms to survive. They did not believe this was evil or immoral because it was, in the words of one such businessman, "merely the working out of a law of nature."

Biological determinism, also known as genetic determinism, was the idea that genes alone determined a person's fate. In other words, an organism would develop in the same way regardless of the environment in which it was placed. Some politicians in the 1920s and early 1930s used this argument to justify reduced government spending in areas such as welfare and education. If destiny was determined by genes, the genetic determinists argued, then no amount of spending would have any improving effect on the lives of the poor. Neither was there any point in spending money trying to educate the so-called uneducable.

Eugenics was the idea that people could improve the genetic quality of the human race by controlling who was allowed to reproduce. Eugenicists believed that only members of "superior" social groups should be permitted to have children: In this way the human race would gradually improve. These arguments were sharply criticized in the 1930s and vehemently rejected when the Nazis used them to justify genocide (mass murder).

The problem with these approaches is that science can only describe the way things are. But some people exploited the findings to provide moral judgments or political decisions. Philosopher G. E. Moore (1873–1958) pointed out that it made no sense to say that a scientific finding was "good" or "bad" and coined the term "naturalistic fallacy" to refer to arguments of this type.

This 1934 rally of the German Nazi party was one of many held in the city of Nürnberg. The Nazi leader, Adolf Hitler, was an enthusiastic supporter of eugenics, which he saw as a way of eliminating Jews, black people, and homosexuals.

behaviorists (*see* pp. 74–89). In contrast to Galton's belief in the power of heredity to shape character, the father of behaviorism —U.S. psychologist John B. Watson (1878–1958)—put the emphasis on experience. Thus behaviorism sought to explain virtually all aspects of behavior, both animal and human, in terms of laws of learning, of which the behaviorists proposed two kinds: classical conditioning and operant conditioning.

Physiologist Ivan Pavlov (1849–1936) discovered classical conditioning by accident (*see* p.75). He was studying dogs' digestive processes when he noticed something peculiar: While he was in the process of delivering food to the dogs, they would begin to salivate even before the food had arrived. Investigating more closely, he discovered that by ringing a bell

> "Give me a dozen healthy infants and my own specified world to bring them up in, and I'll guarantee to take any one at random and train him to become any kind of specialist I might select—doctor, lawyer, artist, merchant-chief, and yes, even beggar and thief, regardless of his talents, penchants, tendencies, abilities, vocation, and race of his ancestors."
> — *John B. Watson, 1924*

just before feeding time, he could condition the dogs to salivate when they heard the sound even if no food was delivered. The dogs had formed an association between the ringing of the bell and the food, where previously there had been none.

Psychologist E. L. Thorndike (1874–1949) contributed to a different theory of learning called operant conditioning (*see* p. 75). He suggested that animals tended to repeat actions that produced a positive result, a rule he called his "Law of Effect."

According to this rule, behaviors that were rewarded were repeated, while behaviors that were punished were not.

In one experiment Thorndike placed a hungry cat in a cage with a simple latch and a piece of fish outside. At first the cat tried to reach the fish through the cage bars, then it moved around inside the cage until it accidentally hit the latch and could escape to eat the fish. After repeating this procedure numerous times, the cat learned to open the latch right away: The positive reward of food eliminated the behavior of moving around the cage.

Psychologist B. F. Skinner (1904–1990) extended Thorndike's work, using his famous "Skinner box" (*see* p. 81). He also believed that an organism's current behavior was a result of repeating those behaviors that had been rewarded in the past. In Skinner's experiments animals such as rats or pigeons were rewarded for engaging in certain behaviors that the

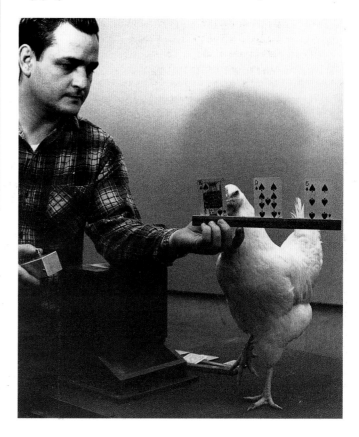

A researcher uses operant conditioning techniques to teach a chicken to select a particular playing card. By rewarding the chicken with food for choosing the desired card, it can gradually be trained to select a complex sequence of cards.

researcher was trying to encourage. This was a gradual process, but eventually the animals could be trained to perform complex sequences of behavior. This type of operant conditioning is the primary means by which animals are trained to perform tricks in circuses or films.

Both these behaviorist learning theories fell on the "nurture" side of the nature-nurture debate because they emphasized experience as the source of behavior. Classical conditioning assumed that an animal could learn to associate any two stimuli with one another, and that "nature" merely provided the senses and the ability to make these associations. Operant conditioning assumed that any behavior could be shaped with the proper rewards and punishments. Both suggested that biology's contribution was merely an innate sense of what was rewarding. Thus little was assumed innate, and it was experience that was thought to fill the organism's brain and shape its behavior.

The decline of behaviorism

Opponents of behaviorist theory believed that animals were more than blank slates. They thought that if they could show that animals were born with some "writing" already filled in, then these theories would have to be revised. In particular, if they could show that animals formed some associations more easily than others, it would suggest that more was innate than merely the ability to learn associations.

That is precisely what scientist John Garcia and his colleagues demonstrated in a series of experiments with rats in the mid-1960s. Garcia gave his rats a little tube to drink from, which dispensed a solution with a distinctive flavor that the rats had never tasted before. Whenever the rats drank from the tube, a light came on, and there was a little "click" sound. Each time this happened, the rats were exposed to x-rays that made them temporarily ill.

If the behaviorists were correct, the rats should have come to associate all three conditions—the light, the click, and the taste of the solution—with feeling sick.

They should, in short, have learned to avoid all three. But that is not what happened. Instead, the rats learned to avoid the solution, but not the light or the click, suggesting that they associated being sick with the novel taste, but not with the light or the sound.

This was exactly what Garcia expected to find. Rats in their natural environments need to learn which foods, based on their taste, are good to eat, and which are poisonous. To do this, they learn to avoid any new food that makes them sick. As Garcia playfully suggested in his report of the experiment, the rats did not blame the light or the click for making them sick,

> "...it is our reluctant conclusion that the behavior of any species cannot be adequately understood, predicted, or controlled without knowledge of its instinctive patterns, evolutionary history, and ecological niche."
> — K. & M. Breland, 1961

but concluded that "It must have been something I ate." The behaviorists did not view rats' thoughts as necessary to learning, believing that conditions like illness after certain stimuli changed the rats' behavior without requiring any conscious thought processes.

Misbehavior

At around the same time, two former graduate students of B. F. Skinner, the husband-and-wife team Keller and Marian Breland, published a now classic paper that signaled the beginning of the end for behaviorism. In "The Misbehavior of Organisms" (a lighthearted reference to their mentor's famous book *The Behavior of Organisms*) the Brelands gave numerous examples of experiments in which the organisms being studied did not behave as behaviorist theory predicted.

In one case they trained a raccoon to drop coins into a metal box. First, it was

Cognitive psychologists try to understand which structures in the brain enable people to learn about the world around them. For example, the work of linguist Noam Chomsky showed that people are born with the capacity to learn language, but that their environment is responsible for the specific language that they learn.

rewarded for simply picking up the coins, which presented no problem. Then the experimenters rewarded it for dropping the coins into the box. Despite the potential for reward, however, the raccoon resisted letting go of the coins once it had them. Instead, the Brelands reported that it preferred "rubbing them together (in a most miserly fashion)." It appeared that the raccoon had mistaken the coins for food. These and other cases in which animals did not conform to behaviorist theory led the Brelands to conclude: "It seems obvious that these animals are trapped by strong instinctive behaviors."

In the 1950s and 1960s evidence against behaviorism continued to accumulate. For example, the behaviorists held that rewarding organisms for past behavior was both necessary and sufficient for producing future behavior, but the results of several experiments contradicted this.

Wolfgang Köhler (1887–1967) showed that chimpanzees did not need their behavior reinforced or rewarded to solve some problems. Instead, they could use "insight," working out the solution by careful perception of the problem, rather than by trial-and-error learning.

Similarly, in his work with monkeys, Harry Harlow (1905–1981) showed that rewarding certain behaviors was not always effective. He separated newborn monkeys from their natural mothers and provided tham with an artificial "mother" made from hard, uncomfortable wire but equipped with a feeding tube and nipple. Despite being fed (that is, rewarded) by this "mother," the monkeys showed no tendency to become attached to it or spend any nonfeeding time near it. In contrast, a nonfeeding doll made of soft, fluffy material proved rewarding to the motherless babies because it was comforting to touch and hold.

The cognitive revolution
A critical turning point in the nature-nurture debate came in the late 1950s with the work of linguist Noam Chomsky (*see* pp. 119–123), who argued that behaviorist learning principles could not account for language learning. Instead, he claimed that humans had a language "organ": a distinct part of the brain specifically for learning language. According to Chomsky, the particular language children learned depended on their environment, but the ability to learn that language was innate.

A second important idea that Chomsky developed was the concept of "universal grammar." He argued that although each language is different, there are certain properties that they all have in common. The similarities in languages, he said, were a result of the innate language organ (the areas of the brain that produced speech) that all people shared. This organ was only capable of learning languages with certain grammatical rules, which meant that all the world's languages were constructed from the same set of possible rules.

Chomsky's work marked the start of what came to be known as the cognitive revolution (*see* pp. 104–117), in which cognitive psychologists viewed the mind as a kind of computer—a machine that took in information from the world, processed it, and then generated behavior. The rise of cognitive psychology changed the tone of the nature-nurture debate once again. There was an acknowledgment that there had to be innate learning mechanisms in people's heads that enabled them to learn about the world; Chomsky's work on language had made that clear. Thus cognitive psychologists sought to describe other learning mechanisms that people were born with.

Sociobiology

With the cognitive revolution nativism, or the belief that nature plays an important role, once again became respectable. In 1975 Edward O. Wilson, a Harvard biologist and an expert on ant behavior, published a book entitled *Sociobiology*. In it Wilson proposed that the social behavior of all animals, including people, was based on genetics. Although he thought that only about 10 percent of human behavior was genetically induced, his views created a firestorm of protest, and at one academic conference someone even poured a pitcher of water over him.

Despite the adverse reaction to Wilson's work, others also tried to use biology as a way of understanding human psychology. In 1979 anthropologist Donald Symons published *The Evolution of Human Sexuality*, a look at how the process of evolution by natural selection might have shaped human sexual behavior.

During the 1980s and 1990s a new discipline emerged called evolutionary psychology (*see* pp.134–143). It took many of the ideas of sociobiology, but added in others from cognitive science (studies of the human mind and how it works). Evolutionary psychologists no longer saw nature, or individuals' genetic makeup, as a set of restrictions on human behavior. Their model for behavior was the computer, and they saw evolution as a force that built information-processing systems, enabling each organism to interact adaptively with its environment. Thus they viewed nature as an enabler. Genes (inherited codes) were not seen as "determining" an organism's destiny. Instead, they constructed the organism jointly, together with the environment.

Psychologist Steven Pinker built on Chomsky's insights in his book *The Language Instinct* (1994). By referring to

the language organ as an instinct, he called attention to the way in which he thought natural selection built information-processing systems that enabled people to learn new ideas. Accumulating more and more information-processing systems through natural selection, said Pinker, made people increasingly flexible. This did not mean that the evolutionary approach left no room for learning, for Pinker also emphasized that language had to be acquired by using an innate mechanism specifically designed to learn language.

Recall Garcia's experiments (*see* p. 26). An evolutionary interpretation of his results would be that natural selection has resulted in a rat brain that is designed to learn which foods are good to eat. In the same way people have numerous learning mechanisms, each designed for a specific task or adaptive problem.

Many people continue to be hostile to biological approaches to human behavior, which are sometimes seen as resurrecting the ideas of social Darwinism, genetic determinism, or eugenics (*see* box p. 24). Sociobiologists and evolutionary

Steven Pinker's influential book The Language Instinct *was published in 1994. In it he explained that babies are not born talking because language structures in their brains are not fully developed and because language has to be learned. Language by its very nature is shared: No gene would be able to encode 60,000 words—the average vocabulary of a high school student.*

HERITABILITY

When organisms differ from one another, the variations can come from two sources: differences in the genes or differences in the environments in which the organisms developed. Heritability can be used to measure just how much the differences between individuals in a population are due to differences in their genes. The concept can be understood by considering two simple experiments.

If you had a large number of genetically identical pea seeds and planted them in different soils, small differences in the soil would cause the pea plants to grow to different heights. This fact emphasizes how the environment can affect growth, and from this you could conclude that some differences are due to environmental factors. The height of the plants has low heritability since the differences in height are largely due to nongenetic factors.

Now suppose you took a large number of genetically different peas and planted them all in the same soil. In this case any discrepancies you observed would be due to differences in the peas' genes. If there were still big differences in the heights of the plants, you would conclude that the trait of height had high heritability, or a high degree of genetic influence in that particular soil.

Heritability refers to a population, not to individuals, and it is important to realize that it can change depending on the environment. If you took the genetically different peas and put them in different environments, in some cases there might be big differences in height, and in other cases there might be small differences in height. This would show that genetic differences can express themselves differently depending on the environment.

psychologists specifically and explicitly reject these ideas, but the destructive political movements of the 19th- and 20th-centuries have continued to make people resistant to biological explanations for social behaviors.

Untangling the debate

One reason the nature-nurture debate has raged for so long is partly because there is no single issue at stake. With ample research to build on, it now seems likely that there is no absolute answer to the debate. Instead, modern genetic research focuses on two key questions.

The first question has its roots in the work of Charles Darwin and Francis Galton, and concerns the origins of differences. Behavior geneticists try to discover why differences exist between people, the origins of these differences, and whether they are due to variations in peoples's genes or in their environments. The question is complicated because they do not know what any individual person's genes are, and differences in genes do not always express themselves the same way: Environment can have a profound effect on genetic differences (*see* box above). Behavior genetics is often confused with

genetic determinism. Some recent books taking behavior genetics approaches have said that differences between people are inevitable because of differences in genes. That is not true. What behavior genetics can do is to tell us a little about the source of differences between people.

The second question has to do with the way in which an individual's genes interact with the environment. Every aspect of an individual is thought to be the product of both genes and the environment. It is also thought to be impossible to divide that person's traits into "environmental" and "genetic" components because every organism's genes interact with the environment in a complex way to build that organism.

CONNECTIONS

- Behaviorism: pp. 74–89
- Cognitive Psychology: pp. 104–117
- Psycholinguistics: pp. 118–125
- Evolutionary Psychology: pp. 134–143
- Learning by Association: Volume 3, pp. 44–63
- Language Processing: Volume 3, pp. 114–135
- Nature or Nurture: Volume 5, pp. 142–163

Beginnings of Scientific Psychology

"Physiological psychology is first of all psychology."

Wilhelm Wundt

In the 18th and 19th centuries developments in sciences such as chemistry and physics led to the emergence of psychology as a scientific discipline. One of the scientists who was influenced by these advances was Wilhelm Wundt (1832–1920), who introduced introspection as a research tool for the study of the mind and set up the world's first psychology laboratory.

From the earliest written records of human thought we know of people's interest in psychology. It seems that people have always been interested in their own minds and behavior—an interest that includes questions about how the mind works and why we do the things we do.

Psychology only began to make the transition from speculation to science in the late 19th century, however, as researchers investigated how the mind works. The emphasis shifted again in the early 20th century, as psychologists focused their scientific investigations on understanding people's behavior.

THE SCIENTIFIC CONTEXT

There were huge advances in science during the 18th and 19th centuries, especially in the fields of physiology (how bodies work), physics, and chemistry. As effective experimental techniques developed, many of the latest scientific theories were published and applied to technology and contemporary life. There were also major advances in medicine, and medical breakthroughs led to a dramatic fall in the death rate.

Science became a part of people's lives in a way that it never had before. Science, scientists, experimentation, and the laboratory became fascinating to many people and a popular subject of conversation among the more educated classes. The subject advanced both as a basic laboratory enterprise and as a way of improving people's lives through the application of scientific findings.

Before the late 19th century psychology was a branch of philosophy, but the new emphasis on science meant that people began to view the subject in a different light. Wilhelm Wundt (*see* box p. 32) was the first person to use scientific principles to investigate psychological processes, and his main method of investigation was introspection, a technique that required researchers to observe and record their perceptions, thoughts, and feelings. Experiments supplemented their findings. Wundt founded the first psychology laboratory and the first journal for psychological research. Due to his efforts psychology became a science, and as a

This portrait of Lucy Lutwidge dates from about 1858. It was taken by her nephew Charles Dodgson, known as Lewis Carroll (1832–1898), the author of Alice in Wonderland. *Lucy's interest in science was typical of many educated families in the 19th century.*

result, he is known as the founder of scientific psychology. His achievements, however, should be seen in the context of other scientific pioneers, such as Gustav Fechner and Herman Helmholtz.

Fechner and Helmholtz

The German scientist Gustav Fechner (1801–1887) was the founder of the field of "psychophysics": a term that can be defined as the application of the principles of physics to mental processes. Fechner used mathematics and physics to understand the mind, quantifying the mathematical relationship between different levels of stimuli and the mind's perception of them. For example, Fechner conducted research in which various levels of sound intensities were presented to volunteers; their reaction times were measured as they attempted to indicate when they first heard each stimulus. After calculating the average reaction times he discovered distinct patterns, one of which he called the auditory perceptual threshold—that is, the average minimum intensity necessary for people to hear a sound. Fechner's experimental research influenced Wundt and other psychologists.

Another important German scientist was Hermann Helmholtz (1821–1894), who was interested in physiology, physics, sensation, and perception. Helmholtz developed a theory of color perception, which had initially been proposed by Thomas Young (1773–1829) in 1801. This theory (ultimately called the Young-Helmholtz three-color theory) became widely accepted and still helps explain many of the facts of color perception, especially the way in which cells in the retina of the eye process colors.

This photograph of the scientist and philosopher Hermann Helmholtz dates from about 1847. He was born in Potsdam (in Germany) and graduated from the Friedrich Wilhelm Medical Institute, Berlin, in 1843. He is best known for his statement of the law of conservation of energy.

Helmholtz was also interested in the speed of neural (nerve) impulses. Other scientists had assumed that neural impulses were instantaneous or perhaps too fast to be measured. Helmholtz conducted empirical research (based on observation) on the topic using motor nerves (which impart motion) in frogs. He found that the speed of the neural impulse was 90 ft. (19m) per second. Helmholtz studied sensation and perception as well. He wanted to understand how sensory information was processed by the brain: in other words, how external stimuli such as light and vibrations made their way into people's minds as sight and sound. One of his main conclusions was that these sensations from the external world only made sense in the brain after being organized in a logical way. This view anticipated modern-day theories known as "top-down" processing," which refer to processes that are driven by a person's knowledge and experience (*see* p. 107).

Both Fechner and Helmholtz were part of the tradition emerging in the 19th century that the principles of science should be used to study mental activity.

KEY DATES

1855 Wilhelm Wundt receives his doctorate, University of Heidelberg.

1879 Wundt founds the world's first psychology laboratory at the University of Leipzig.

1881 Wundt founds the world's first journal for the publication of psychological research.

1892 E. B. Titchener receives his doctorate, University of Leipzig.

However, these two scientists were both physicists, not psychologists. It was Wundt who created psychology as a separate branch of the sciences.

Animal and human psychology

In 1862 Wundt gave a series of lectures on animal and human psychology at the University of Heidelberg. It was the first course ever taught in scientific psychology, and it firmly separated psychology from physiology and philosophy for the first time. Wundt taught that psychology should be experimental and scientific. He believed that many psychological phenomena, such as perception and sensation, were measurable. However, he suggested that psychology had limitations because it could not explain complex human functioning such as higher mental processing or social interaction. His lectures were published a year later.

Wundt believed that human behavior resulted from a complex interaction between motivations and other subtle, often unknown influences. He said that these elements could not be measured because none of them directly caused behavior on their own. Wundt stated that human behavior was not measurable in the same way that physical phenomena such as electricity were measurable. In

> *"The first step in the investigation of a fact must be a description of the individual elements of which it consists."*
> — *Wilhelm Wundt, 1902*

other words, Wundt believed that psychology was an interaction between the measurable and the unmeasurable.

This position marked a clear separation of psychology from physiology, physics, and chemistry. Today most psychologists would disagree with Wundt's views. They believe that psychology is as rigorous a science as any other, with quantifiable effects that are clearly measurable.

WILHELM WUNDT

BIOGRAPHY

Wilhelm Wundt was born in 1832 in the small village of Nekarau in Germany. He came from a strongly Christian family. Wundt became a scientist but never saw any contradiction in being both scientist and Christian, believing that science and religion were both ways of understanding the world and were not mutually exclusive. This may explain how he was able to conduct scientific work without the need for demonstrating indisputable findings.

In 1855 Wundt received a doctorate in physiology from the University of Heidelberg, where he taught physiology and later psychology (1862). He wrote many books, of which the most important was *Principles of Physiological Psychology* (1873–1874). In 1875 he was appointed professor at the University of Leipzig, where he founded the world's first psychology laboratory in 1879. Two years later he founded the first journal for the publication of psychological research. At first it was called *Philosophical Studies*, but it was later renamed *Psychological Studies*. Wundt's systematic investigation of psychological phenomena was a prime factor in establishing psychology as an experimental science.

PSYCHOPHYSIOLOGY

Wundt made important advances in psychophysics, and he is recognized as one of the first true psychophysiologists. Psychophysiology investigates how people and nonhuman animals sense the external world and how they perceive information from sensory data, and today it is considered to be a branch of psychology. Psychophysiologists accept that the senses, such as vision and hearing, send sensory information to the brain, where the process of perception occurs; but they try to determine how much of what we know is due to the sense organs themselves, and how much is due to the brain and its perceptual processing.

Introspection

Wundt developed systematic methods to measure the basic elements of sensation and perception. The science of physics relied on techniques of inspection (observation) to study physical phenomena; Wundt sought to develop introspection to study people's mental phenomena. Introspection literally means "looking within," since participants examined their own thoughts.

The subjects in these experiments were called observers, and they were trained to report their thoughts and feelings. They would be presented with a stimulus, such as a shape or color, and had to report their thoughts in response to that stimulus. The difficult part was that they were supposed to separate their knowledge from their memories of the stimulus object, so that they could give an objective report of their immediate thoughts and feelings. This proved difficult, so observers required extensive training.

Flaws in introspection

Unfortunately, introspection proved to have flaws as a scientific method. By its very nature it was unverifiable, for there was no way to determine whether the observers were reporting their true thoughts and feelings. There were also difficulties in obtaining reliable and valid data from different observers in different laboratories. So by today's scientific standards the data from introspection experiments were unreliable.

Other psychologists commented that the observers could only report their conscious thoughts and feelings. People

This design for a general laboratory dates from 1822. It reflects the vast increase in public support for the new scientific discoveries of the 19th century.

have other thoughts and feelings that are unconscious (people are unaware of them), and they were left out of the introspection reports.

Wundt was aware of the flaws in his introspection research and acknowledged that the process of introspection interrupted the natural thinking process. After all, it is not natural to think about every thought as you are thinking it. He spent his career revising his introspection methodology and trying to improve it.

The Leipzig laboratory

In 1875 Wilhelm Wundt accepted a position as full professor at the University of Leipzig, which is considered to be the historical home of experimental scientific psychology. It was his intention to establish a psychology laboratory there, but that was not immediately possible,

---

METHODS OF KNOWING

FOCUS ON

People come to "know" something in several different ways. With the method called tenacity something is considered to be true because it has always been true; such beliefs are called tenacious beliefs. With the authority method something becomes true because a respected authority has told us it is true—the authorities we may listen to include political and religious leaders. With the method called empiricism we know something is true because we have experienced it via our senses.

Philosophers use the method called rationalism, which relies on logic and reason to reach a conclusion. But the most reliable and valid way of knowing something is the scientific method, in which scientists use controlled laboratory investigations to establish knowledge. Science is self-correcting because it allows for verification and change based on the results of experiments conducted in laboratories. When psychology became a science, psychologists also began to use controlled investigations.

since the university could not give him the laboratory space he needed. For this reason Wundt did not teach psychology in his first year at Leipzig.

In addition to this resources problem Wundt found himself in a difficult situation with a colleague: Johann Zoellner, an astrophysicist. Zoellner was interested in supernatural phenomena. After the American spiritualist Henry Slade visited Leipzig in 1877, he became convinced that Slade had supernatural powers. Wundt disagreed with Zoellner, both in conversations and in published writings, suggesting that scientists would be poor judges of supernatural ability because they had little familiarity with deception. As a result, Zoellner viewed Wundt as an enemy of the spiritual world.

Despite these initial problems, Wundt was eventually awarded space for his psychology laboratory. Research began there in 1879, and studies focused on three primary areas of study: sensation, perception, and psychophysics.

Many students wanted to study with Wundt, and those who did included some of the pioneers of U.S. psychology, such as G. Stanley Hall (1844–1924), James McKeen Cattell (1860–1944), and Edward Bradford Titchener (*see* p. 38)

WHAT DID WUNDT STUDY?

Although introspection had its limitations, Wundt used it effectively to conduct psychological research. He studied the psychophysics of light and

A 19th-century illustration of the University of Leipzig, where Wilhelm Wundt established the world's first psychological laboratory. He was a professor there from 1875 to 1917.

color at his Leipzig laboratory and examined broad questions of sensation and perception, such as how the brain turned electrical activity in the eye into images. He also investigated hearing, including research on frequency (pitch), beat, tone, and tone intervals.

Wundt also investigated the topic of attention, which plays an important role in perception. Attention is an awareness of the here and now; but an individual cannot consciously experience all available events and information at any one time, so attention is selective. Wundt believed that the mind could attend to events that happened both sequentially (one after the other) and simultaneously (at the same time). This meant that attention was possible in several modes of processing, a theory confirmed by later research in cognitive psychology (*see* pp. 104–117).

Elementalism

Wundt also developed a theory called elementalism, which has endured in psychology to the present day. He thought psychologists should analyze conscious processes and divide them into elements (that is, smaller parts and processes). This

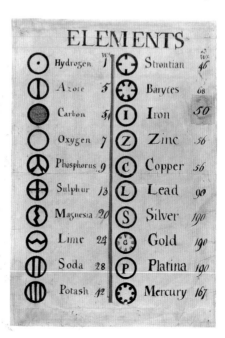

English chemist John Dalton (1766–1844) stated that all elements (the basic building blocks of the physical universe) were composed of tiny, indivisible particles called atoms. The atoms of different elements have different weights, which Dalton set out in the table shown here. His work influenced Wilhelm Wundt's theory of elementalism.

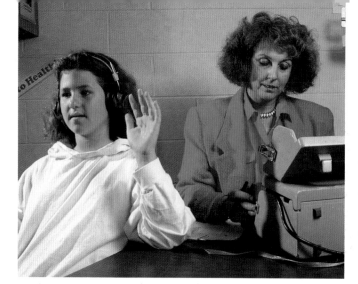

A school nurse checks a student's hearing in a reaction-time experiment. The student responds as quickly as possible to a stimulus.

Wilhelm Wundt (far right) with some of his coworkers in the laboratory he founded at the University of Leipzig, Germany.

theory was influenced by John Dalton's theory of the atom and the development of the periodic table of elements by Dmitry Mendeleev (1834–1907).

According to Wundt, the elements of consciousness were connected, and these connections could be determined by research. If laws could be discovered, people could understand how connections were made and how they worked. This theory persists in modern psychology with different terms: Wundt was discussing what we now call neural networks in the brain and how they communicate via neural pathways (*see* p. 132).

Timing of mental processes

Wundt extended the concept of elementalism to the belief that certain mental processes took a fixed amount of time to complete. He believed that when the same thought was repeated constantly, the connection between its elements became more developed with each use. This helped explain a result Wundt found repeatedly in reaction-time experiments. In these experiments a subject responded as quickly as possible to a stimulus, and the response time was measured carefully.

Wundt found that people got better at a task after practice, but that after a certain point they reached a fixed fastest-response time. For example, if subjects were asked to tap a button as quickly as possible when they saw a green object, after some practice they became faster at tapping the button.

But at a certain point they no longer showed improvement, no matter how much more practice they had.

Wundt was the first person to carry out such psychological research, suggesting that it might yield information about how the brain functioned and how the mind worked. In modern-day psychology researchers still conduct reaction-time experiments, and they still continue to reveal important information about cognitive (thought) processes in the brain (*see* pp. 104-117).

The concept of association

In one of his studies Wundt showed that the mind was designed to perceive the world at different levels of experience. He demonstrated this with a memory task. People were asked to look briefly at a number of random letters of the alphabet and then recall as many letters as possible. The results showed that they could recall an average of four letters, and that with practice they could increase the total to six letters.

Wundt then presented words to his subjects, who recalled a similar number of words as they had previously recalled letters, even though each word had more

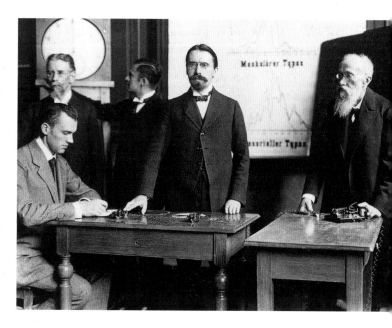

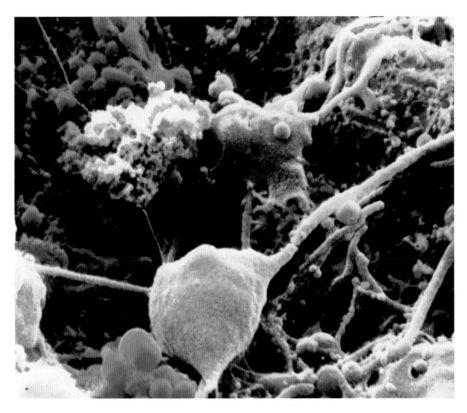

This photograph shows glial cells (red-orange), neurons, or nerve cells (large and gray), and the slim appendages linking the neurons together (axons and dendrites). When a neuron "fires," it releases chemical neurotransmitters from the terminal branches of the axon; these chemicals stimulate adjoining dendrites and may cause the associated neurons to fire. Some neurons have single dendrites, some have two, and others have multiple links to other neurons—in much the same way as Wundt envisaged.

than one letter. This suggested that when people organized the information (letters) into larger units (words), it enabled them to deal with more information. Later this process became known as "chunking."

Drawing on data like these, Wundt suggested laws of association. First, there was fusion or blending of feelings. He used the word "feelings" to refer to many things, from emotions to sounds. Second, Wundt believed that two or more feelings could merge to form a single feeling, even though they were independent initially. He also believed that similar things were more likely to be associated.

Brain and nerve cell theories

Wundt's most important book was called the *Principles of Physiological Psychology* (1873–1874), and it described his view of how the brain worked. In Wundt's model brain activity was rooted in chemical activity. He thought the brain to be a complex organ of fluid chemicals, which

were sometimes more active in one region, and sometimes in another. He believed that the entire brain constantly shared in the same chemical-mental activity.

In modern neuroscience it is now believed that there are different "systems" at work in the brain at all times. The interrelationship between these chemicals is intricate and not yet well understood. Wundt, therefore, made important contributions to neuroscience. Although his view of the brain was not correct in all the details, it was basically on target, and his work has continued relevance to contemporary neuroscience research.

Wundt also came up with a theory on the structure of the nervous system, speculating that there had to be a chemical component to the conduction of nerve impulses, which he referred to as the chemical process. He believed that nerve cells sent out three types of chemical processes to other cells. Unipolar (or one-ended) cells could send out only one type, bipolar (or two-ended) cells could send out two types, and multipolar cells could send out multiple chemical processes. Unipolar cells were the least common, while bipolar and multipolar cells were the important centers of physiological activity for human life. According to Wundt, it was the connections that bipolar and multipolar cells made that allowed for behavioral complexity. The technology available to Wundt was not as advanced as that available today, but much of what he believed has turned out to be correct (*see* photograph, left, and p. 131). Research has revealed that the interrelationship between nerve cells is more complicated than he had assumed, however.

Modern-day nerve cell theory takes a biochemical approach to understanding nervous system activity. Nerve cells, or neurons, receive information from the senses (sight, hearing, sound, smell, and touch) and control conscious and unconscious movements of the body, transmitting information via electrical impulses. Multiple connections allow for neural control of complex behavior, just as Wundt anticipated.

WUNDT'S MONUMENTAL OUTPUT
Wundt published more than 53,000 pages of theory during his lifetime—a total that excludes revisions of his most important publications. Although his psychological

PHRENOLOGY

FOCUS ON

Founded by Franz Josef Gall (1758–1828) and further developed by Johann Kaspar Spurzheim (1776–1832) and George Combe (1788–1858), phrenology became popular in the 19th century. It appeared to use scientific techniques but has been wholly discredited by scientific research, although it enjoyed great popular appeal into the 20th century.

Phrenology was based on the idea that all mental faculties were located in specific regions of the brain. These regions influenced the shape of the skull, which meant that mental abilities and character traits could be determined by studying the shape of the skull. For

This phrenological head is based on Gall's map of the 26 principal "organs," or faculties. other phrenology enthusiasts made several adaptations.

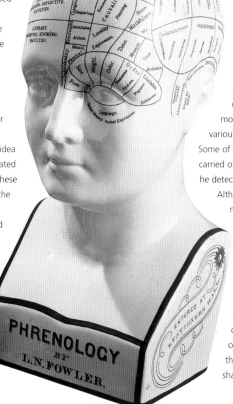

example, if a person had a good memory, the area of the brain responsible for the function of memory would be enlarged, and that would be noticeable on that person's skull. Gall and other phrenologists drew detailed diagrams of the brain on models of the skull, labeling the various structures and their functions. Some of these earlier studies were carried out in prisons, and Gall claimed he detected several "criminal" traits. Although Wundt believed that mental activities occurred in certain places in the brain, he opposed phrenology because he believed that these places were not definite. He thought that mental activity occurred throughout the brain, with certain areas more active at certain times. He did not believe that brain tissue could affect the shape of the skull.

research formed the bulk of his work, he also wrote about topics such as logic and ethics. The famous psychologist William James (1842–1910) declared that formulating an argument against Wundt's theories was futile, since he was constantly revising or discrediting his own work, or developing another field of research altogether. So impressive is the scope of Wundt's work that it can also present scholars with a problem in determining the final form of many of his theories.

Wundt's legacy

It was Wundt's use of experimental methodology that finally separated psychology from philosophy, while his opposition to reductionism (the belief that psychology could more properly be explained by physical sciences) kept psychology distinct from physiology. Thus the rich history of psychology as an independent scientific discipline really began with his work. Introductory psychology textbooks often downplay Wundt's importance, but many people now consider this a serious misreading of his influence. Psychology textbooks that discuss its history more appropriately tend to devote a chapter to Wundt.

In the 1920s a new school of psychology, behaviorism, became popular (*see* pp. 74–89). Behaviorism rejected the study of the mind in favor of the study of behavior, and it dominated American psychology until at least 1960. But more recently the study of the mind has become a focus once again (*see* pp. 104–117), so Wundt's work is being appreciated by a new generation of psychologists.

STRUCTURALISM

Edward Bradford Titchener (1867–1927), a student of Wundt's, popularized the scientific study of the psychology of the mind in the United States. Titchener was an Englishman who studied with Wundt at the University of Leipzig. He received his Ph.D. from Leipzig in 1892 and subsequently moved to Cornell University, where he established a productive

Edward Bradford Titchener received his Ph.D. from the University of Leipzig in 1892. From 1898 he was the leading proponent of structuralism in the United States.

psychology laboratory. He learned the scientific methodology of introspection during his studies with Wundt and brought it to America.

The focus of Titchener's work was on mental events—especially the contents of mental events. In Titchener's view the fundamental task for psychological research was to discover the nature of conscious elements. He wanted to analyze thoughts into their component parts so that he could discover the underlying structure of the mind. As a result, he decided to give his theories of psychology the label of structuralism.

In contrast with Titchener's view, Wundt thought that complex mental phenomena could not be studied by

introspection. Titchener, however, strongly disagreed, firmly believing that all mental phenomena could be scientifically studied in the laboratory.

One of the first important textbooks about the history of psychology, the *History of Experimental Psychology*, was written by E. G. Boring (1886–1968), one of Titchener's students. The first edition was published in 1929 and the second edition in 1950. This publication was very favorable to Titchener and helped spread his reputation, but it incorrectly claimed that Titchener and Wundt were in agreement about the use of scientific methodology as a means of studying all mental phenomena. Boring was a loyal structuralist and agreed with Titchener.

> *"All of the sciences have the same sort of subject matter, there can be no essential difference between the raw materials of physics and the raw materials of psychology."*
> — *E. B. Titchener, 1921*

Many doctoral students studied with Titchener at Cornell University. In his 35 years there 50 doctoral candidates received the degree under his mentorship, one-third of them women. Titchener exercised his authority by selecting the topics for the doctoral research of these students, thus influencing the content of the field among these young scholars.

Structuralism dominated American psychology for several decades. The father of behaviorism, John B. Watson, claimed that structuralism and its methodology were unacceptably subjective. He argued that psychology could only achieve objectivity if its subject matter was

SCHOLS OF THOUGHT

FOCUS ON

Groups of psychologists who held specific beliefs about how the mind worked or about how it should be studied formed groups that became known as schools.

Structuralism was the first school of thought in the history of psychology, defining it as the study of the structure of the normal human adult mind. Titchener founded structuralism and was its most famous advocate and spokesperson, and the school dominated American psychology from about 1895 to 1920.

Meanwhile, critics of structuralism began to form a new school of thought called functionalism (*see* pp. 40–45) in which the U.S. psychologist William James was a leading figure. Functionalism defined psychology as the study of the functions of the mind—but while it challenged structuralism, it never replaced it.

John B. Watson challenged both structuralism and functionalism, establishing behaviorism as the dominant school of thought in U.S. psychology. Behaviorism (*see* pp. 74–89) defined psychology as the study of behavior, and it dominated U.S. psychology from about 1920 to 1960.

There were two important European schools of thought—Gestalt psychology (*see* pp. 46–51) and psychoanalysis (*see* pp. 52–65). Gestalt psychology defined psychology as the study of how people understood their perceptual experiences as a whole (*gestalt* is German for "whole"). Max Wertheimer, Wolfgang Köhler, and Kurt Koffka were its leading proponents. Psychoanalysis defined psychology as the study of the unconscious mind. Its leading proponent was Sigmund Freud.

In the 1960s Carl Rogers and Abraham Maslow established humanism (*see* pp. 66–73)—defining psychology as the study of personality and human growth, and challenging behaviorism in U.S. psychology. It was the cognitive psychology movement (*see* pp. 104–125), however, that ousted behaviorism and became the leading school of thought in the U.S. It defined psychology as the study of the mind as an information processor.

behavior rather than the mind. But even behaviorism owed a debt to Wundt's work, as both a foundation for scientific psychology and a school of thought that could be appreciated—and questioned.

CONNECTIONS

- Behaviorism: pp. 74–89
- Cognitive Psychology: pp. 104–117

- Computer Simulation: pp. 126–133
- History of the Brain: Volume 2, pp. 6–19
- The Human Computer: Volume 3, pp. 6–23
- Storing Information: Volume 3, pp. 88–113

Functionalism

——— "...broadly speaking, American psychology today is functionalistic." ———

Edwin Boring

The school of functionalist psychology began in the late 19th century, shortly after psychology separated from philosophy as a distinct scientific discipline. Functionalism refers to an approach to studying psychology, rather than a particular theory, and functionalists believe that psychological processes should be viewed in terms of their particular purpose, or function.

Before functionalism most of psychology was based on observation and description. Functionalists believed that this was not enough to make psychology a useful science. To be useful, they believed that psychology must show what purposes mental processes served and how they helped an individual function. The creation of functionalism is usually credited to William James, one of the first (and still most famous) U.S. psychologists, although other famous functionalists include John Dewey, James Angell, Harvey Carr, and one of psychology's first pioneering women, Mary Whiton Calkins.

The origins of functionalism

Prior to functionalism the most common method or approach in psychology was structuralism (*see* pp. 30–39). Structuralism (or structural psychology) was concerned with identifying and describing mental processes (primarily consciousness) using a method known as introspection, devised by Wilhelm Wundt (*see* p. 32). Structuralists also wanted to break consciousness down into its individual parts, believing they could only understand how a mental process worked when each part was identified.

According to the structuralists, an introspectionist had to be carefully trained and follow strict procedures, which limited how easily introspection could be used. Many researchers found the method too difficult and unpredictable. Scientists also found that the results reported by introspectionists differed depending on the person: One person's experience was not like another's. For a method to have scientific validity, it had to give the same result whoever used it.

Another reason why people found structuralism a limited way of studying psychology was related to the old philosophical problem of the mind-body split. For centuries philosophers had debated the relationship between the mind and the body, discussing whether they were separate entities, or whether the mind was part of the body. Early psychologists such as Wundt believed that the mind was not a physical entity, and that the mind and body were separate but working in parallel. Changes in the mind

William James advocated the comparative study of peoples in other cultures as a way of understanding the human mind and behavior. Studies of the Inuit, for example, show how they have adapted physically and psychologically to life in a cold environment.

ADAPTATION

The work of Charles Darwin on adaptation and evolution (*see* pp. 134–138) was a major reason for scientific interest in the purpose of natural processes. Darwin proposed that many animals' physical features and behaviors were adaptive—thus animals behaved in the way they did because it helped them survive and function in their environment. Over time organisms that had inherited the tendency to engage in adaptive behaviors were the most successful in surviving, reproducing, and passing this tendency on to their offspring. The idea that behavior had a purpose (and that animal behavior was worth studying) was popularized by Darwin and became a central belief of the functionalists.

corresponded with changes in the body, but neither could influence the other (the mind could not influence the body, and the body could not influence the mind).

This view did not make a great deal of sense to some. It certainly seemed as though the mind controlled the body, and the body also seemed to influence the mind at times—for example, when the body was tired or hungry, that could have an effect on mood. Structuralists claimed that this interaction was an illusion; but the idea that mind and body interacted was a powerful one, and many were determined to explore whether it was true.

By the late 19th century descriptive science had given way to practical science. Instead of observing and categorizing nature, most scientists were interested in the purpose of natural processes and hoped that the knowledge they gained could be put to good use. By the early 20th century introspection had also had its day, since it was no longer seen as a sufficiently objective method.

William James
William James (1842–1910) was born in New York City and was the older brother of Henry James, the famous novelist. He trained at Harvard as a physician (although he never practiced) and later taught physiology and eventually philosophy at Harvard.

William James' early years were unsettled and marked by ill-health. It was not until his mid thirties that his life as a creative and original thinker began. His writings on psychology and philosophy were immensely influential in the English-speaking world.

James based his philosophy on the notion of pragmatism (also the title of one of his most famous philosophical works), which refered to the use that could be made of knowledge and ideas. An idea was only worthwhile if it had some particular purpose. James had previously applied the standard of pragmatism to his psychological theories, which were concerned with the purpose of different psychological processes rather then being descriptive.

James' interest in the usefulness of mental processes became the basis of the functionalist movement. In his classic work the *Principles of Psychology*, first published in 1890 (*see* box p. 42), James

- *Principles of Psychology* (1890) William James
- "Reflex Arc Concept in Psychology" (1896) John Dewey
- *An Introduction to Psychology* (1901) Mary Whiton Calkins
- *The Child and the Curriculum* (1902) John Dewey
- *Psychology: An Introductory Study of the Structure and Function of Human Consciousness* (1904) James Rowland Angell
- *Pragmatism: A New Name for Some Old Ways of Thinking* (1907) William James
- *Psychology: A Study of Mental Activity* (1925) Harvey A. Carr

outlined a kind of psychology that was very different from that of the time. Like the structuralists, he used introspection as his main method of examining how his mind worked, but unlike them, he viewed the workings of his mind as being adaptive and believed that they served a particular purpose.

James believed the individual had certain needs, and that the environment could provide certain solutions. The role of the mind was to mediate between the two. He thought that his mind worked in the way it did because it helped him adjust to the world around him. This belief that consciousness had a purpose immediately set him apart from structuralism. He also believed that to understand its use and purpose, one had to view consciousness as a whole, rather than breaking it down into its parts as the structuralists had done. As an analogy, imagine trying to grasp the concept of a watch. Understanding that it is made up of gears and springs does little to help you understand that its purpose is to tell time. To understand the purpose of the watch, you must observe what it does and its relationship with the environment.

James differed from the structuralists in his firm belief that the mind and body interacted. According to him, sometimes the mind influenced the body, and sometimes the body influenced the mind. James devoted a great deal of his book to physiology (the physical functions of the human body) and its effect on mental processes, and he categorized certain types of activity as the results of different kinds of interaction between the mind and body. For example, he thought that habits

> *"…but there is a function in experience which thoughts perform, and for the performance of which this quality of being is invoked. That function is knowing."*
> — **William James, 1904**

and instincts were a product of the brain and perceptual system, with only limited input from the mind. James thought this was adaptive because the mind was then free to do other work. Consciousness, reason, and self, on the other hand, he thought to be primarily a result of mental activity (the mind organizing behavior). In both cases, however, James showed that the mental and the physical affected each

PRINCIPLES OF PSYCHOLOGY

FOCUS ON

Begun in 1880, James' *Principles of Psychology* was intended as a psychology textbook; but 10 years later, when it was finally published, it had grown into a vast work in two volumes (an abridged textbook version was published in 1892). James presented several ideas in *Principles* that stood out as being especially influential. He identified consciousness as a process (he called it "the stream of consciousness") rather than a static system. James also examined the role of habit and instinct in human behavior. He believed that they allowed the mind to work at something else while the body was occupied with a task. James identified reasoning as a means by which the human organism enhanced its survival, and he developed an influential theory of emotion, suggesting that feelings caused behavior, which was then followed by

mental awareness of the emotion. James also identified and outlined the notion of the self, which was to become an important topic in psychology decades later. The main achievement of James' work, however, was to link the study of the mind with biology and scientific practice, and to link thinking and knowledge with the will to live.

James' book had an immediate effect on the growing field of psychology, especially in the United States. His was the first major work of psychology to appear in the United States, and the condensed version of the book served as the main textbook for generations of students studying psychology; indeed, it is still in print. Most importantly, a generation of researchers took careful notice of his work and were greatly influenced by it, earning James the honor of being called the father of psychology.

arc" was used to describe an organism's response to the world. Structuralists had attempted to explain the concept by separating sensation, perception, and consciousness. Dewey pointed out that the reflex arc could not be understood properly unless it was viewed as a whole event rather than just the parts. He used the example of a child viewing a flame, touching it, and burning her fingers. The child would reflexively withdraw her fingers, but thereafter would not touch flame, remembering how she had been burned in the past. The sequence of events had changed the child's perception of the flame from being attractive to being dangerous. Viewed in this way, the reflex arc serves a particular purpose: to help us avoid danger and injury. It demonstrates that organisms do not just passively receive information from the world, but actively manipulate their environment. Learning is involved from the very start.

Dewey later became interested in the psychology of education. He was one of the originators of student-centered rather than subject-based learning. It focused on the abilities and preferences of the student, and the teacher acted as a guide rather than a taskmaster.

other. In doing so, he gave functionalism a new method and focus for study—behavior. While structuralists focused on inner mental processes and did not think behavior was relevant to psychology, an interaction between mind and body made behavior very important indeed.

James also thought that the methods used to study psychology should be expanded and developed. While he believed that introspection was a useful method for studying consciousness, for example, he did not believe that a person had to be carefully trained to use it. It was enough to be perceptive and careful about reporting "facts." In this way introspection could be used more easily and flexibly.

James believed that experimentation and comparative studies (comparing people with animals) could also be used in psychology. Although experimentation in psychology had yet to be developed, James thought that it could be useful in understanding the mind and behavior. He also thought that studying animals, children, people of other cultures, and even mentally ill people could help develop psychology as a science.

The reflex arc
In 1896 John Dewey (1859–1952), a founding member of the psychology department at the University of Chicago, published a paper entitled "The Reflex Arc Concept in Psychology." The term "reflex

Regular commuters like these in Tokyo, Japan, repeat the same journey day after day. James believed that such habitual actions require only limited input from the mind, freeing it to concentrate on new tasks or thoughts.

James Rowland Angell
James Rowland Angell (1869–1949) studied under Dewey (at the University of Michigan) and James (at Harvard) but never received a Ph.D. Angell followed

John Dewey was one of the most widely known and influential teachers in the United States, and also wrote an enormous number of scholarly articles and books on psychology and philosophy. He is renowned for his contributions to pragmatism, functional psychology, and progressive education.

This baby's first reaction to a candle flame is attraction, and he will have to be prevented from reaching for it. But if he burns his fingers, the experience will permanently alter his perception of the flame. Psychologists such as Dewey and Angell believed that animals, including people, actively learn and adjust to their environment, rather than just passively receiving information.

Dewey to Chicago and established the department of psychology there as the center of functionalism. One of his most famous students was John B. Watson, who broke with functionalism and founded the field of behaviorism (*see* pp. 74–89), which was to have an enormous impact on psychology in the 20th century.

> *"Every mental act can...be studied from three aspects—its adaptive significance, its dependence upon previous experience, and its potential influence upon the future activity of the organism."*
> — *Harvey A. Carr, 1925*

Angell set out the differences between structural and functional psychology in a famous paper entitled "The Relation of Structural and Functional Psychology to Philosophy," which attacked the main ideas of structuralism, attempting to show that it was neither a useful nor an accurate way of understanding mental processes. Trying to understand the various components of mental activity without identifying their purpose was a pointless exercise, he said, because the parts could

not be understood without relation to the whole. Although these were not new ideas, Angell was attempting to define the main points of functionalism.

Angell's most famous work was *Psychology: An Introductory Study of the Structure and Function of Human Consciousness*. It covered a wide range of conscious experience, sensation, and perception, and also the physiology of the nervous system. Throughout the book Angell concentrated on functional explanations of various phenomena, always trying to show how they helped a person adapt to the environment. He also insisted on a close and interactive relationship between the mental and physical and was concerned with the way in which mental processes developed.

Harvey A. Carr

After studying under Angell at Chicago, Harvey A. Carr (1873–1954) took charge of the department when Angell became president of Yale University. Under Carr functionalism reached its peak of popularity and influence.

Carr's functionalism differed from that of Angell's in that he was more concerned with behavior. This reflected the trend of U.S. psychology toward the study of behavior, even though Carr himself continued to study mental processes. Like others, he realized that psychology could only develop as a science if its methods were considered to be properly scientific. As a result, functionalism relied more and more on experimentation as a way of collecting data, and introspection became less important. Experimentation was more objective than introspection: In carefully controlled experiments it was more likely that different researchers would find the same results, making the experiments more scientifically valid.

Carr published his most important work, *Psychology: A Study of Mental Activity*, in 1925. In it he surveyed the field of psychology, focusing mainly on human behavior and the ways in which behavior could be viewed as helping a person adapt to the environment. Each kind of mental activity, such as thinking, remembering, perceiving, and reasoning, was said to have a purpose, guiding a person's behavior. Carr believed that all behavior could be viewed as an adaptive act consisting of a stimulus, a perception of the stimulus, and a response that was appropriate to the stimulus.

The legacy of functionalism

Functionalism began to lose influence in the early 20th century, and by 1920 behaviorism had became the most popular form of academic psychology in the United States. In a way it was a result of functionalism, since functionalism had stressed the importance of behavior.

Because functionalism was more a method of psychology than a theory, over time it was absorbed into other systems. Its most obvious influence was ultimately in testing mental abilities, because psychologists thought they played an important role in people's capacity to succeed in school and at work. Most psychologists agree that it is important to understand the purpose of mental processes and that the mind and the body influence each other. Many functionalist methods are still used today.

MARY WHITON CALKINS

BIOGRAPHY

Mary Whiton Calkins was awarded two honorary degrees— although Harvard refused to give her one for her studies there.

Mary Whiton Calkins (1863–1930) was one of the first women to study psychology. She faced enormous challenges because of her sex but was able to rise above these difficulties to make a lasting contribution to the field.

Calkins began as a teacher of Greek at Wellesley College but soon became interested in psychology. She initially considered studying under Dewey (*see* p. 43) at the University of Michigan, but eventually decided to study with James (*see* p.41) at Harvard. At first, despite James' support, she was not allowed to attend lectures because she was a woman. This changed later, but she was never awarded a degree from Harvard. Despite this, she returned to Wellesley and established a psychological laboratory and a department of psychology there. In 1905 she was elected as the first female president of the American Psychological Association.

Calkins worked in a number of areas of psychology. She developed the paired-associates technique for studying memory, was an early pioneer in the study of the self as a psychological entity, and argued against the notion that men and women had significant psychological differences (an argument taken up recently by evolutionary psychologists).

Her main contribution to functionalism was her attempt to unite it with structuralism under the heading of self-psychology. Calkins believed that the purpose of mental processes could not be fully understand unless each of the parts of that process were identified. She further believed that both the structure and function of mental life could be best understood as serving the self, the individual at the center of the study of psychology.

CONNECTIONS

- Ancient Greek Thought: pp. 10–15
- Beginnings of Scientific Psychology: pp. 30–39
- Behaviorism: pp. 74–89
- Evolutionary Psychology: pp. 134–143
- Emotion and Motivation: Volume 2, pp. 86–109

Gestalt Psychology

———— *"...man does not perceive things as unrelated isolates..."* ————

Fritz Perls

Gestalt psychology was a reaction against earlier psychological approaches that had attempted to separate the functions of the mind. The German word *gestalt* means "form" or "whole," and Gestalt psychologists saw the mind as a whole, recognizing that people usually perceive unities rather than individual elements—a piece of music as a melody rather than a series of notes. In the 1950s Fritz Perls adapted Gestalt ideas to create a method of psychotherapy.

Gestalt psychology began in Germany in 1910. While traveling by train, Czech-born psychologist Max Wertheimer (1880–1943) saw flashing lights at a railroad crossing that resembled lights encircling a theater marquee and was seized by an idea. He got off the train in Frankfurt and bought a motion picture toy called a zoetrope (*see* right). In his hotel room he made his own picture strips, consisting not of identifiable objects but abstract lines, ranging from vertical to horizontal. By varying these elements, he was able to investigate the conditions that contribute to the illusion of motion pictures, in which stationary objects shown in rapid succession appear to move because the brain cannot perceive them as individual elements so sees them as one moving image. This effect is known as "apparent movement," and Wertheimer called it the phi phenomenon.

According to Wertheimer, the phi phenomenon disproved previous theories of how individual stimuli were perceived. He proposed that the brain perceived any stimulus as a meaningful "whole," rather than an assembly of separate data.

Founders of gestalt theory

Wertheimer studied the phi phenomenon with his two assistants, Wolfgang Köhler (1887–1967) and Kurt Koffka (1886–1941). They published their findings in 1912 in a paper entitled "Experimental Studies of the Perception of Movement."

Convinced that the segmented approach to the study of human behavior (taken by structuralists and other psychologists) was inadequate, these three became the central figures of the German Gestalt school. Separated by World War I (1914–1918), they were were reunited when Köhler was made director of the Psychological Institute at the University of Berlin, where Wertheimer was already a faculty member. Students at the institute were not required to attend lectures. Instead, they conducted research using other students as subjects and prepared articles for publication.

In 1920 Wertheimer and Köhler founded *Psychological Research*, a journal

This zoetrope was made in 1886. The figures inside it were based on a series of photographs showing a bird in flight. When they are rotated and viewed through the slits around the edge of the zoetrope, the succession of models appears to be a single, moving image.

Born in Prague in 1880, Max Wertheimer studied jurisprudence (the philosophy of law) before turning to psychology. He visited psychiatric hospitals in Prague, Frankfurt, and Vienna, and then began working on the ideas of Gestalt theory with Wolfgang Köhler and Kurt Koffka in Frankfurt.

background conversation was thought to be heard (sensed) but not perceived (listened to) because it was experienced outside of a person's attention. Earlier psychologists, particularly those of the structuralist school (*see* p. 38), had split up these phenomena into their individual components, such as feelings, images, and sensations. This view did not allow for the additional meaning given to phenomena when we perceive them as a whole.

Wertheimer claimed that an observer's nervous system organizes the stimulus experienced into a whole, or Gestalt, rather than making the effort to perceive many individual impressions. The brain looks for a shortcut, organizing stimuli into packages of information, just as we might put all our papers concerning one subject into a file or all the photos from one vacation in one album. Wertheimer,

that was to publish many of the central ideas of the Gestalt psychologists. In 1929 Wertheimer became a psychology professor at Frankfurt University, where he criticized traditional forms of logic for ignoring the way in which people group and reorganize the things they perceive when solving problems.

The least effort

According to perception theory at that time, our senses picked up information about the physical world as simple, often unnoticeable sensations. For example,

> *"There are contexts in which what is happening in the whole cannot be deduced from the characteristics of the separate pieces."*
> — *Max Wertheimer, 1924*

and later Köhler, believed that the brain's organization of perceived things into "wholes" was reflected in the makeup of the nervous system.

Modern neuropsychology (*see* pp. 90–95) has challenged most of the Gestalt ideas about how the brain is organized. Although we now know that nerve fibers are arranged into patterns that restrict their function, there is no evidence for the existence of the whole figure models that Wertheimer and his colleagues believed in. On the other hand, many of the questions posed by Gestalt psychologists about how we perceive phenomena are central to our understanding of modern theories of perception and the mind.

Wertheimer's concept of organization was called *Prägnanz* ("conciseness"). It stated that when things are considered as wholes, the amount of energy exerted in

KEY DATES

1912 Wertheimer publishes his first study of perception.
1927 Rudolf Arnheim visits the Bauhaus.
1933–1935 Leading figures of Gestalt psychology leave Germany for the United States to escape Nazism.
1947–1969 Fritz and Laura Perls develop Gestalt therapy in the United States.

thinking is minimized. His theory can be extended to thinking about people. For example, it is easier to think of a group of football players as a team rather than as individual players. This concept is seen most clearly if one tries to think about more than one sports team at a time: It is far easier for the mind to consider the players as two or three wholes (teams) than as many individual members.

Gestalt and social psychology

Another central idea of Gestalt theory was that of the figure against a background. For example, in a painting Gestalt theory maintains that the entire picture is important—the landscape and the figures —not simply one element, such as the human figure. Gestalt psychologists see

the individual as a figure against a background of social relationships with others. A person is not only part of her own life, she is also among other people. When a group of people work together, they are rarely a collection of independent personalities. Instead, the common enterprise becomes their shared concern, and each person works as a functioning part of the whole group.

According to Wertheimer, "Only under very special conditions does an 'I' stand out alone. Then the balance…may be upset and give way to a…new balance." His perception of how we relate to groups anticipates some of the findings of cross-cultural psychology (*see* pp. 152–161), which contrasts traditional western views of the individual's psychology with those

---

GESTALT LAWS OF PERCEPTION

In 1923 Max Wertheimer published a paper entitled "Theory of Form," which was nicknamed "the dot essay" because it was illustrated with abstract patterns of dots and lines. Wertheimer claimed that our inborn tendency to perceive elements as "belonging together" enhances certain forms. This enhancement occurs with elements that look alike (similarity grouping), are situated close together (proximity grouping), or have visual continuity (closure). This enhancement is shown in the three examples here of proximity, similarity, and closure.

Closure (left)
We perceive this figure as a square despite it being incomplete: The mind closes the gap.

Magicians exploit the effects of all these three phenomena, playing on our linking of similar things to secretly hide or reveal objects and using camouflage to fool our minds into grouping unlinked objects or surface areas. This grouping tendency is governed by certain laws outlined by Wertheimer:

(1) The appearance of parts is determined by wholes;
(2) Judgments about similarity and proximity will always be comparative;
(3) Compositions, such as paintings, purposely group certain elements together—by color or distance apart, for example.

A practical application is this book, which arranges elements (words, images) into groups (paragraphs and columns) using a grid. These laws of perception have been emphasized by being placed in a box, which you perceive as a unit separate from the rest of the page.

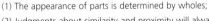

Proximity (left)
We perceive this figure as three groups of two lines or three stripes rather than as six separate lines.

Similarity (right)
We perceive these 20 separate dots as two columns of orange dots and two columns of yellow dots.

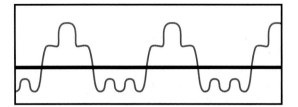 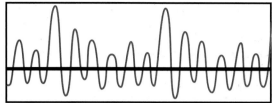

of other cultures in which the psychology of the whole group is taken into consideration. Such cultures take a much more "holistic" view of individuals compared with traditional psychology.

Gestalt in the United States

Nazi persecution in Germany eventually forced Wertheimer, Koffka, and Köhler to flee to the United States. There they published major elaborations of Gestalt theories over the next two decades, extending the Gestalt approach to other areas of perception, problem solving, learning, and thinking. Koffka performed

> *"There was a great wave of relief—as though we were escaping from a prison [of psychology as taught]."*
> — *Wolfgang Köhler, 1959*

original studies on perception and investigated how patterns of behavior develop in the early years. Köhler carried out important studies on chimpanzees, investigating how they learn and think, make tools, and, he claimed, show insight in planned actions. Due to his efforts Gestalt ideas were widely accepted into other schools of psychology.

Gestalt therapy

Gestalt therapy draws on the central ideas of Gestalt theory, such as the need for closure. It is a form of humanistic therapy and attempts to apply the laws of perception to a person's life experience. Humanistic therapy suggests that each individual must be understood within the context of his own life. Gestalt therapy emphasizes a whole or "holistic" view of

The diagrams above show sound waves produced by different instruments playing the same tune. According to Gestalt theory, if we hear one version of this tune, on hearing it again our memory will process the overall form, enabling us to recognize the melody even if it is played on another instrument.

French artist Georges Seurat (1859–1891) used Gestalt theory to exploit our grouping of like elements in his painting of the Eiffel Tower (1889). The image is made up of thousands of separate dots of color, but we perceive the structure as a whole.

the individual, focusing on the entire person and the client's sense of self-awareness. Just as a "gestalt" is a figure or pattern that can be distinguished against a field of perception or background, so Gestalt therapy encourages individuals to look at themselves (the figure) against the background of their own lives and experiences, considering the whole picture rather than simply thinking about their internal feelings. It is important in Gestalt

GESTALT AND THE BAUHAUS

Although none of the Gestalt psychologists were artists or designers, many of their ideas inspired the artists and designers of the Bauhaus: a major German school of art and design in the late 1920s and early 1930s that influenced design and architecture worldwide.

The Gestalt psychologist Karlfried von Dürckheim (1896–1988) lectured at the Bauhaus between 1930 and 1931 to an audience that included artists Paul Klee (1879–1940), Wassily Kandinsky (1866–1944), and Josef Albers (1888–1976). Klee had known about Max Wertheimer's research as early as 1925 and used some of the diagrams from Wertheimer's 1923 "dot essay" in his 1930s paintings. Albers reawoke interest in the idea of "simultaneous contrast": the phenomenon, known for centuries by artists, in which the same color seems to have a different brightness or intensity depending on its contrast with a background color. For example, a particular hue of red shown against a green background (high contrast) seems much brighter than the same hue shown against an orange background. This phenomenon supported the Gestalt idea that we perceive wholes rather than isolated parts—seeing only dynamic relationships between figures and their backgrounds rather than the figures alone. This concept was one of the central theories of Gestalt psychology.

Rudolf Arhheim (1904–1997) visited the Bauhaus in 1927. Later, he became the first professor of the psychology of art at Harvard University and published

When Gestalt psychologist Rudolf Arnheim visited the Bauhaus, he praised the clarity of its design.

13 books on Gestalt theory and art. His book *Art and Visual Perception: A Psychology of the Creative Eye* (1954) had a particularly strong influence on art and design.

Many artists embraced Gestalt theory because it seemed to provide scientific validation of age-old principles of composition and page layout. Gestalt theory became associated with the modernist belief that all art is essentially abstract design, and that design is at heart an abstract, formal activity. Meaning, or the subject being represented in an art form, became less important for modernism than the form or organization of the elements; in this it shared essential qualities with Gestalt theory.

A 1925 gathering in Paul Klee's studio in Weimar, Germany, of the artists known as the Bauhaus masters. They include Paul Klee (far right) and Wassily Kandinsky (second from left).

therapy for individuals to recognize who they are at the moment. Patients are often asked to recount unresolved or traumatic experiences and to say how they feel after recounting them. By acknowledging their feelings, they gain a better idea of the effect that experience has had on them and learn how to cope.

Fritz Perls (1893–1970) and his wife Laura (1905–1990) developed Gestalt therapy in the 1950s. Perls saw the task of psychotherapy as one of emphasizing the difference between figure (the patient) and ground (experience) in the areas, or gestalten (the plural of gestalt), that reflected the patient's needs.

According to Perls, a healthy person organizes experiences into well-differentiated gestalten so there is clear understanding of, and distinction between, a feeling and its context. The individual can then decide on an appropriate response. For example, someone whose body is dehydrated will will become aware of the gestalt of thirst and will get a drink. An angry person who is aware of the feeling similarly has a choice of responses: either to express the anger, to make others aware of it, or to

Gestalt therapy may be based on one-to-one discussion, as shown here, but can also involve group work in which individuals are encouraged to express to each other how they feel.

release it in some other way. A person who is unaware may suppress the feeling and so suffer frustration. On the other hand, a neurotic person continually interferes with the formation of gestalten, refusing to acknowledge how he feels at a particular time. He is unable to deal effectively with certain needs because he interrupts and avoids the formation of a relevant gestalt.

The legacy of gestalt

Today Gestalt theory's influence in the field of psychology is not that noticeable because many of its findings have been absorbed by more recent viewpoints, but in the history of psychology the Gestalt movement was an important corrective to earlier approaches. This is particularly the case in the area of visual perception, where Wertheimer's Laws of Perception are accepted as standard. Gestalt theories have also had a profound effect on "holistic" ideas of therapy.

CONNECTIONS

Psychoanalysis

——— *"If you give it your little finger it will soon have your whole hand."* ———

Sigmund Freud

Freud developed psychoanalysis more than 100 years ago, and it has had an enduring effect on psychology and on western culture. Some of the early ideas of psychoanalysis are not as popular or accepted as in the past, and few psychoanalysts still believe everything that Freud said was correct. But the evolving field of psychoanalysis still has a great influence on the way that modern psychologists think about the mind and behavior.

When we use the term psychoanalysis, we are really talking about two things. First, psychoanalysis has to do with a particular theory of human behavior. Psychoanalytic theories state that all human behavior is motivated (caused by something), but that motivations are often hidden from the individual—they are said to be unconscious. This idea of unconscious motivation is one of the main concepts that sets psychoanalysis apart from many other theories about human behavior.

Second, psychoanalysis refers to a kind of therapy or counseling that people might receive when they are distressed or troubled. Psychoanalytic therapy is derived from general psychoanalytic theories of behavior, and the therapist or counselor seeks to understand what kinds of unconscious forces might be making the person distressed or unhappy. What prompts a boy who hits or tries to harm his new baby brother, for example, or a woman who finds she is unable to make a commitment in close relationships?

Major points of theory

Several individuals stand out as major figures in early psychoanalysis, but the most important of them was its originator, Sigmund Freud (1856–1939). Freud was a physician who frequently treated patients with strange and inexplicable disorders that seemed not to have been caused by any underlying illness

or injury: Such conditions were commonly termed forms of hysteria. Freud became convinced that while there was nothing physically wrong with these patients, their suffering was still real and was probably caused by some hidden psychological problem. He began to question his patients about emotional and personal experiences, trying to determine the cause of their problems. Using this approach, he developed his technique of psychoanalysis, and over time he formulated various ideas about human behavior, which became known as psychoanalytic theory.

Psychoanalytic theory is a complex system for understanding human behavior, but is more easily understood by concentrating on three main principles. The first of these principles is that unconscious forces motivate most human behavior. This means that people are generally unaware of the reasons why they act the way they do. Even though people may think they know the reasons for their behavior, a psychoanalytic psychologist would say they are mistaken.

The second important principle is that past experience shapes the way a person behaves in the present. In psychoanalysis what happened in the past (particularly during childhood) is extremely important in determining how a person will react to events in the present and future.

The third important principle is that psychoanalysis provides a way to help

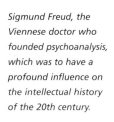

Sigmund Freud, the Viennese doctor who founded psychoanalysis, which was to have a profound influence on the intellectual history of the 20th century.

KEY WORKS

- Freud's 1894 paper "The Psychoneuroses of Defense" first outlined his notion of the defense mechanisms.
- *The Interpretation of Dreams* (1900) outlined the importance of analyzing the meaning of dreams to reveal suppressed desires.
- Other famous works by Freud include *The Psychopathology of Everyday Life* (1901), *Three Essays on the Theory of Sexuality* (1905), *Totem and Taboo* (1913), *Beyond the Pleasure Principle* (1920), and *Civilization and Its Discontents* (1930).
- Two books by Freud contain the basic tenets of his theory in some detail: *Introductory Lectures on Psychoanalysis* (1917) and *New Introductory Lectures on Psychoanalysis* (1933).

people become less unhappy and more comfortable with their lives. Through psychoanalytic therapy it is possible to enable people to cope with distress and trouble by helping them understand the unconscious forces that motivate them and the influences of their earlier experiences in life.

Origins of Freud's theories

Sigmund Freud was born on May 6, 1856, in the country now called the Czech Republic. He lived most of his life in Vienna, Austria; but being Jewish, he was eventually forced to flee Vienna for England to escape Nazi persecution. He died in London on September 23, 1939.

While he was still in medical school, Freud's interest in hysteria led him to study in France under the physician Jean-Martin Charcot (1825–1893), who used hypnosis to treat hysteria. (Freud later rejected the use of hypnosis as a form of treatment, but he remained interested in the study of hysteria.) When Freud returned to Vienna, he began working with a physician named Josef Breuer (1842–1925), who had been helping hysterics and had achieved some success in treating them by using a talking cure: discussing with patients the possibly overlooked reasons for their problems.

TENETS OF FREUDIAN THEORY

Freud and Breuer shared a fascination with delving into the private lives of patients. Freud believed that not only

could he begin to understand what might be troubling his patients, but also that he could find out what caused other people to behave as they did. An underlying principle of Freud's theory was that the main motivating force behind human behavior is an unconscious drive for sexuality. He suggested that all human beings, even children, have strong sexual impulses, and that these impulses motivate not just sexual behavior but all behavior. This is a major source of difficulty for the individual because sexual behavior is not socially acceptable (certainly not in children and only in certain circumstances in adults). What results from the combination of this motivating force and the realities of social life, said Freud, is conflict. The outcome of this conflict determines people's behavior and personalities in later life.

As one might imagine, the sexual aspect of Freud's theory was particularly shocking at the time in which he lived because sex and sexuality were topics that were not to be discussed. It is still widely criticized today, mainly due to Freud's insistence that children have sexual motivations (although they are unconscious).

According to Freud, the two other important motivating forces of human behavior

The general hospital in Vienna, Austria, where Sigmund Freud enrolled as a medical student in 1882.

are *eros*, the desire to procreate, and *thanatos*, the death force or desire to return to the oblivion of prebirth. Freud added *thanatos* after World War I (1914 –1918), when he revised his theory to include the tension between life and death, with the death instinct being displaced by aggression and replaced by the desire for self-preservation.

The second major principle of Freudian theory is that mental life is dynamic, driven by energy between the body and mind. Freud believed that the personality or psyche resides in three distinct levels of

> *"I count him braver who conquers his desires than him who conquers his enemies; for the hardest victory is the victory over the self."*
> — *Aristotle*

consciousness. Part of the personality is conscious and is concerned with thoughts and feelings—the things people generally experience when awake. A second part of personality is the preconscious, consisting mainly of memories and thoughts that, while not conscious at the moment, can become conscious. Imagine, for example, the answer to the question "What did you have for breakfast today?" It was not in your conscious mind until you read this question, but was available for recall from your preconscious mind. The third—and to Freud the most important—part of the personality is the unconscious, in which lie wishes, desires, and motivations of which people cannot become aware.

Id, ego, and superego

Freud also believed that the personality consists of different structures that manage the motivational force; he named them the id, the ego, and the superego. *Id* is Latin for "it," *ego* means "I," and so *superego* is the "over I." Freud located the source of motivation in the id, which is in the unconscious. In the id are impulses, motivations, and desires.

Freud stated that the id works according to the "pleasure principle"; its main task is to satisfy impulses and desires by discharging the energy behind them, resulting in pleasure. The ego is the part of the personality that tries to plan ways in which the id can release its energy and satisfy its impulses, and as such is mainly conscious. The ego is rational and operates according to what Freud termed the "reality principle," which states that desires and impulses can be fulfilled, but only in certain ways. The ego is what keeps the individual from doing whatever he or she (or rather the id) pleases at any given time. The superego is a structure that operates to constrain the ego from allowing the id to satisfy impulses. It is both conscious and unconscious, and can be compared to a person's conscience. Even if the ego can think of ways to satisfy the id without getting the person into too much trouble, the superego ensures that the person's behavior conforms to what society expects of him or her.

Freud theorized that human personality develops from these unconscious conflicts and their outcomes. From the moment of

Is this child teething? According to Freudian theory, young children put objects in their mouths in an attempt to rediscover the oral gratification they received as infants while feeding at their mothers' breasts.

birth the id's desire for pleasure is curbed by rules imposed by parents and society. Children's sense of bodily pleasure shifts as they grow from infancy to adulthood through five stages of psychosexual developmental: oral, anal, phallic, latency, and genital. Each stage involves a conflict between the desire for pleasure and the need to live by the rules of the real world. When conflicts are resolved, development is healthy; if they remain unresolved, the person may develop disorders later in life.

The oral and anal stages

According to Freud, during the first or oral stage (infancy) the person's focus for pleasure (sexuality) is through the mouth and the act of sucking and taking in nourishment. The conflict at this stage arises from the process of weaning (that is, moving from the breast or bottle to solid food). Failure to resolve the conflict at this stage can result either in a great dependency on others or in an aggressive and sarcastic personality.

In the second or anal stage (just past infancy) the passing of feces becomes the focus of pleasure. The conflict at this stage arises from being toilet trained and the way in which children learn to control their bowel movements. Failure to resolve this conflict can result in excessively fussy (anal retentive) or slovenly (anal expulsive) behavior in later life.

The phallic stage

During the third, phallic stage (early childhood) the phallus is the object that provides pleasure, so the genital area becomes the focus of attention. This is accompanied by feelings of attraction to the opposite sex. According to Freud, phallic pleasure is immature pleasure; and since children usually spend most of their time around their parents, he suggested that the natural object for a young child's affection is the opposite-sex parent (*see* box p. 57). He referred to this as the Oedipal conflict, based on the character of Oedipus, who inadvertently killed his father and then married his mother in the

ancient Greek tragedy by Sophocles (fifth century B.C.). A successful resolution of this conflict ends in the child identifying with the same-sex parent and no longer wishing to possess the opposite-sex parent. Failure to resolve this conflict results in sexual problems in later life.

Latency and genital stages

From about the ages of 6 to 12, said Freud, unconscious conflicts subside as children make conscious social adjustments. This is called the latency period because unconscious developmental conflicts are latent or hidden. The final, genital, stage occurs during adolescence, when children begin to have sexual feelings toward others closer in age. During this stage children struggle toward "sensible love," and conflict arises as they move away from the parents toward friendships with others. Freud believed that successful resolution of this conflict was important to develop healthy adult relationships.

Defense mechanisms

Defense mechanisms formed another important part of Freud's theories. As we have seen, the task of the ego is to plan

The main character in Shakespeare's Hamlet *is full of sexually motivated anger toward his mother and is thus a popular subject of Freudian analysis. This photograph is from a 1995 production starring Ralph Fiennes and Francesca Annis.*

ways in which the id can fulfill its desires. Yet the ego is always vulnerable to the id, since the desires and motivations within the id are powerful and extremely difficult to control, and may somehow escape. Also, the ego has to contend with the control of the superego, which can punish the ego for allowing the id to have its way. The defense mechanisms develop as a means for the ego to protect itself from the id and also from the superego. Some of these mechanisms prevent the id impulses from being fulfilled; others are designed to fulfill them in relatively harmless ways. Freud believed that these defense mechanisms develop as a person matures and passes through the various psychosexual stages.

Repression

The primary defense mechanism described by Freud is repression: an energy force that serves to keep the impulses in the id from escaping. It may be likened to putting a lid on a boiling pot of water. Repression requires effort and energy, however, and does not always work. It is not in operation, for example, when a person is sleeping. (Freud believed therefore that dreams contain material

> "If you hate a person, you hate something in him that is a part of yourself. What isn't part of ourselves doesn't disturb us."
> — Hermann Hesse, 1919

derived from the unconscious.) It also fails sometimes when a person is awake and preoccupied. Freud said that these failures occur as "slips of the tongue" (parapraxes) when a person means to say one thing and accidentally says something else, thus revealing an unconscious motivation.

Other defense mechanisms include projection: the tendency to observe traits or patterns of behavior in others that correspond to people's own unconscious impulses (for example, people who view

ACCESSING THE UNCONSCIOUS

CASE STUDY

Sigmund Freud used various techniques to gain access to unconscious material. One was free association, in which the patient was encouraged to say whatever came to mind freely and without censorship. He then searched for themes and clues to the patient's disorder.

Another therapeutic technique was dream analysis. Freud asked patients to write down and describe their dreams in detail, believing that in dreams the person's unconscious wishes and desires were revealed. In most cases these wishes and desires were not revealed directly, but were suggested through metaphors and imagery; what the dream appeared to say was not necessarily its literal meaning. For example, a dream about loose teeth or hair falling out was interpreted as reflecting a fear of castration, one of the main motivating forces in the Oedipal conflict. The importance of dreams was to indicate the nature of the unconscious: confusing and intense, but also puzzling and riddled with puns.

In 1906 Carl Jung (see box p. 60) used word association as a techique: He would say a word, and the patient would respond with the first word that came to mind. Since this was done quickly and without deliberation, Jung believed it tricked the ego into expressing some unconscious wish or thought.

others as being obsessed with sex will really be unconsciously obsessed with sex themselves). Displacement allows people to fulfill their id impulses but changes the object (for example, a person who is angry at his or her boss might instead kick over the wastebasket). Reaction formation is a defense mechanism that takes an unacceptable impulse and turns it into its extreme opposite (for example, hate into overprotective love), while sublimation turns an unacceptable impulse into another, socially acceptable one. Freud's goal was for patients to gain insight into their conditions. This insight would then alleviate the patients' symptoms.

Psychoanalysis as treatment

Freud based his theories of behavior on his assessments of various patients. He believed that patients displayed hysteria because they were unable to properly resolve conflicts at some stage of their development. To treat these patients, Freud needed to be able to see what resided in their unconscious. The patients, of course, had no idea what resided there, so Freud used a number of means to try and extract the information. Thus psychoanalytic therapy as developed and practiced by Freud was a time-consuming process: Most patients' analyses took several years to complete.

Psychoanalytic therapy is concerned primarily with talking. Freud believed that therapists had to get to know patients really well to understand the events that might have shaped their experiences. Consequently therapists and patients talk at length about the patients' past histories and lives, going over many important but seemingly irrelevant experiences and memories. They often seem trivial to the patients, but the fact that they remember them means these events may be connected to important unconscious motivations.

Freud developed his theories over many years. For example, his ideas about the unconscious, preconscious, and conscious mind were formed long before his ideas about the id, the ego, and the superego. Similarly, while he advanced a theory of childhood sexuality at an early stage of his career, his ideas on the development of personality took shape at a later point.

THEORISTS WHO FOLLOWED FREUD
Sigmund Freud had many followers. Some of them remained loyal to him during their entire lives, while others criticized his work and proposed their own theories. Leading figures in psychoanalysis included two of Freud's associates, Alfred Adler (*see* box p. 58) and Carl Jung (*see* box p. 60), and also Melanie Klein (1882–1960). Also prominent were Freud's daughter Anna (1895–1982) and Erik Erikson (1902–1994), who both worked to develop

The consulting room in London, England, where Freud analyzed the psychological motivations of his patients. They relaxed on the couch with Freud behind them.

ANNA O. AND LITTLE HANS

Two of Freud's most famous case studies were those of Anna O. and Little Hans. Anna O. was really Josef Breuer's patient, but Freud took Breuer's notes on the case and reexamined them in light of the theories he was trying to develop for himself.

Anna was a teenager who began to develop symptoms of hysteria following the terminal illness of her father. These included nervous tics and coughing, partial paralysis of her right hand and foot, and severe difficulty in speaking and attending to others. Eventually her condition became so bad that she was unable to get out of bed. Breuer spent a great deal of time treating Anna using the "talking cure," and she eventually improved and

ended up living a relatively normal adult life. Freud used the case to support his notion of childhood sexuality (disagreeing with Breuer's view).

The case of Little Hans was instrumental in Freud's formulation of the theory of Oedipal conflict (*see* p. 55). Little Hans had developed an intense phobia (irrational fear) of horses. He became so afraid that they would come up and bite him that he eventually refused to leave the family home. According to Freud, the boy was really antagonistic toward his father, whom he regarded as a rival for his mother's affections. However, Little Hans felt guilty about the sexual implications of these feelings and transferred them into a fear of horses.

ALFRED ADLER

Alfred Adler (1870–1937) spent most of his life in Vienna, Austria. Like Carl Jung, Adler was a physician who initially worked closely with Freud but developed his own views that were quite different from Freud's. This resulted in an end to their professional relationship and personal friendship. The sexual basis of Freud's theory of motivation was one main reason for this difference in opinion, but another was the fact that Adler was much more concerned with the effect of the social environment on the individual.

Adler's theory concentrated on the notion of goals and striving. He believed that all behavior is motivated by people trying to get or achieve something specific, rather than by some internal force. Adler believed that these goals and strivings are the main determinant of personality.

One important goal is a striving for superiority. All individuals strive to achieve as much as they can in life, and they will often try to do better than other people. Under the surface most individuals feel as though they are worth little, and so they strive for superiority to compensate for their feelings of incompetence and inferiority.

Another important aspect of Adler's theory was his exploration of the role of the family. Adler believed different styles of parenting, including both pampering and rejection, could have negative influences on children's development. He also thought that birth order was an important determinant of personality. Thus being an only child, first-born, last-born, or a middle child could all affect a person's later life roles, relationships, and behaviors.

psychoanalysis after Freud's death. Not only was Anna Freud a practicing psychoanalyst and the caretaker of her father's legacy, but she made important contributions to the science of psychoanalysis, developing her father's ideas about the ego and the defense mechanisms, and devising a system of child psychoanalysis (*see* box p. 62).

Erik Erikson also made numerous important contributions to the development of psychoanalysis. He explored the functioning of the ego in more detail and, using the child's social interaction as a base, developed his own theory of personality development and change. In a sense Erikson cannot strictly

be described as a psychoanalyst because his theories and ideas tended to stray from those of Freud and later psychoanalysts. Nevertheless, his work was firmly rooted in the traditions of psychoanalysis and has had a strong influence on subsequent psychological theory and practice.

Melanie Klein's theory

Melanie Klein was one of Freud's most important early followers, who later developed her own ideas. Klein did not meet Freud until 1918, when she heard him speak at a conference in Budapest, Hungary. She was very impressed and decided to train as a child psychoanalyst, becoming a lifelong defender of the psychoanalytic treatment of children. From the 1930s onward Klein formulated her own views, which gave rise to the object relations theory of psychoanalysis.

Klein adopted Freud's notion of the unconscious drive (instinct), but she disagreed with his claim that the object of the drive is exchangeable. Freud believed that the drive primarily seeks satisfaction, which does not depend on the object on

> *"The projection of good feelings and good parts of the self into the mother is essential for the infant's ability to develop good object-relations and to integrate his ego."*
> — *Melanie Klein, 1957*

which the drive is fixed. For example, food is not a necessary object for the satisfaction of the oral drive—cigars are equally good (and Freud himself was a heavy smoker). To Klein, however, a particular drive is always connected with a particular object. The drive cannot be separated from its appropriate object of satisfaction. The oral drive, for instance, is always related to food intake. Yet because the mind of the young child is immature, an infant's object of satisfaction will always be partial, as opposed to complete.

For example, when infants seek oral satisfaction (through the oral drive), they will not relate to the mother as a whole, but only to the partial object of her breast (or the bottle). Moreover, said Klein, the partial object is always inherently split in the mind of a child. When children experience the breast as an object of satisfaction, the breast is perceived as good. But if the breast is not there when a child wants food, the infant will perceive the partial object as bad.

Other psychologists joined with Klein in developing the object relations theory, which saw an individual's relations with people, parts of people, and symbolic representations of one or the other as central to life. These relations affect the degree of attachment to others and also the degree of attachment to the self.

Ego psychologists

Freud's daughter Anna (1895–1982) was faithful to her father's basic ideas, but she was particularly interested in the role of the ego rather than the id. This focus on the ego began a movement called ego psychology, which was taken up by two of the many psychoanalysts who came to the United States from Europe to escape Nazi persecution before and during World War II (1939–1945)—Heinz Hartmann (1894–1970) and Ernst Kris (1900–1957).

Hartmann and Kris believed that Freud's most important discovery about personality was the distinction between the id, the ego, and the superego (*see* p. 56). Like Anna Freud, they argued that the ego was more important than the id and the superego. They thought that the ego contained a "conflict-free sphere," and that it was not just an arbiter between the id and the superego, but used strategy to control them, like a business executive managing conflicts.

Ego psychology

According to the ego psychologists, patients experience mental problems because they have a weak ego, or because their ego is unable to deal with the id and the superego. Psychoanalysts can help patients solve their problems by making their egos more powerful and by making sure that they can adapt themselves to their environment. Psychoanalytic therapists achieve this by offering themselves as an example of someone with a strong, well-adapted ego. Ego psychologists believe that psychoanalysts can offer their own strong personalities as a substitute for the weak personalities of their patients.

Criticisms of ego psychology

Many psychoanalysts in Britain, such as Edward Glover (1888–1972), criticized ego psychology because they felt a patient could become entirely dominated by the psychoanalyst's personality. However, some principles of ego psychology, especially the role of adaptation, influenced the psychoanalytic theory of Margaret Mahler (1897–1985) on early child development. Her theory was based on the nature of the changing relationship between mother and child (*see* box p. 61).

This photograph of Melanie Klein was taken in 1957. She was one of the first psychoanalysts to apply Freud's theories to children and to use play techniques as a form of therapy.

During the early 1950s French psychiatrist and psychoanalyst Jacques Lacan (1901–1981) took issue with U.S. ego psychology. Lacan believed that it no longer had anything to do with psychoanalysis. He argued that ego psychologists had forgotten that psychoanalysis was about analyzing and not about educating.

Lacan feared that Freudianism would die at the hands of the ego psychologists and claimed that a return to Freud's texts was necessary. He criticized the notions of adaptation and adjustment that the ego psychologists promoted and claimed that they were not based on Freud's ideas.

The importance of speech

Lacan emphasized the role of speech in psychoanalysis. In psychoanalytic therapy a patient is asked to say everything that comes to mind, and from time to time the psychoanalyst interrupts the patient to make a spoken intervention. This is the only thing that happens, and it is what patients benefit from.

Relying on this simple observation, Lacan tried to develop Freud's work by combining it with other theories, such as

> *"Certainly the psychoanalyst directs the treatment. The first principle of this treatment...is that he must not direct the patient."*
> — *Jaques Lacan, 1958*

those of language and anthropology. Although Lacan remained loyal to Freud, he also introduced many new concepts in psychoanalysis, some of which are not easy to grasp. For example, he talked about symbolic castration. Freud had not used this term, but Lacan was convinced

CARL GUSTAV JUNG

BIOGRAPHY

"Nobody, as long as he moves about among the chaotic currents of life, is without trouble"—Jung

Carl Gustav Jung (1875–1961) lived most of his life in Switzerland. He was trained in psychiatry and had a great interest in mental disorders. He became interested in Freud's theories after reading *The Interpretation of Dreams* and began corresponding with Freud, later going to Vienna to study with him for five years.

Jung ultimately broke with Freud because he did not believe, as Freud did, that sexuality was the main motivation for human behavior. Furthermore, Jung disagreed with Freud about the best way to understand behavior. Freud believed that one must look into the past to understand present behavior, but Jung believed that one must understand the individual's desires for the future. Jung's theories developed over a period of years and ultimately differed dramatically from Freud's. Jung had been interested in culture, literature, religion, and spirituality, and he believed that these elements were important determinants of behavior, perhaps just as important as parental influence.

One of the main features of Jung's theory was the collective unconscious. Jung believed that individuals had two kinds of unconscious mind, a personal one that contained their own memories and a collective one that contained material that was common to all people. Material in the collective unconscious was organized around certain kinds of ideas that were common to people throughout history and across cultures. Jung called these ideas archetypes, and he identified several of them. Ideas about god and the self were also special, more powerful archetypes. He drew on anthropology, literature (especially myths, legends, and fairy tales), alchemy, and theology to develop these theories.

One of the most influential of the early psychoanalysts, Carl Gustav Jung coined many terms that are now in widespread usage, including "extrovert" and "introvert."

PSYCHOANALYTIC DEVELOPMENTAL PSYCHOLOGY

Margaret Mahler (1897–1985) was one of the first to integrate psychoanalysis and developmental psychology. During the 1930s she worked as a psychoanalyst with children in Vienna. Shortly before World War II (1939–1945) she moved to New York City, where she worked as a consultant to the Children's Service of the New York State Psychiatric Institute. In the United States she devoted most of her career to the study of young children with severe mental problems. Key terms in Mahler's theory were symbiosis and separation-individuation. The term symbiosis refers to the normal relationship between the mother and the young child. According to Mahler, this relationship is a fusion, or dual union. Child and mother are merged with each other and continuously support each other. However, the child is only able to grow up as a socially competent, well-adapted individual if this symbiosis is broken. Mahler defined this rupture of symbiosis as separation. The child's separation from the mother is the condition for "individuation" whereby the child develops a first awareness of identity (a sense of self). Mahler used these words, alongside others, to explain why some children have serious emotional and behavioral difficulties. When there is no symbiosis between mothers and infants, or when children fail to separate from their symbiotic relationship with the mother, they can suffer from severe developmental disturbances, such as autism and infantile psychosis. As a therapist, Mahler helped children by being a substitute mother or by modeling those ego functions (confidence and adaptation) that they had not yet developed.

that it was entirely in keeping with Freud's work. Symbolic castration refers to the enjoyment children have to relinquish when they became social beings. Every culture has norms and values; and when children start to function in a cultural context, they are no longer able to see all their wishes gratified. Lacan stated that children inevitably lose (symbolically) a piece of themselves when they start to comply with the cultural regulations and rules. Lacan called this process symbolic castration, and he designated the lost piece as *jouissance*, which is the French word for enjoyment. Another of Lacan's most popular ideas was the mirror stage (*see* box p. 63).

Lacanian interpretation

Due to the emphasis Lacan placed on the importance of language within the mind Lacanian psychoanalysts pay a lot of attention to how one particular speech sound (signifier) can have various meanings (which differs from a slip of the tongue in the Freudian sense). For example, when a patient talks about "youth in Asia," a Lacanian analyst could point out that "youth in Asia" sounds like "euthanasia." So what was the patient really thinking? When she was talking about the "youth in Asia," she was perhaps unconsciously thinking about death or even about these children being better off dead. A Lacanian psychoanalyst would always try to point out to the patient that an utterance can have many different meanings. Lacanian psychoanalysis is popular as a clinical practice in France, Spain, Italy, and parts of South America. In the United States and the UK Lacan's theory is often used in literature, film studies, and philosophy.

Self-psychology

The tradition of self-psychology within contemporary psychoanalysis originated in the work of Heinz Kohut (1913–1981). Born and raised in Vienna, Kohut obtained a medical degree from his hometown university in 1938. He settled in Chicago in the early 1940s, where he continued his training as a neurologist and psychiatrist. He also became a renowned psychoanalyst. In 1964 he was elected president of the American Psycho-analytic Association, and between 1965 and 1973 he was the vice-president of the International Psychoanalytic Association. Kohut did not agree with the ideas of the ego psychologists. Like Lacan, he was convinced that ego psychology was too rigid and did not see psychoanalysis as a technique for improving people's adjustment to the environment. Like the

> [Ego psychology was but] *"an armchair exercise directed toward the theoretical extension of ego adaptation."*
> — *Edward Glover, 1961*

object relations theorists, Kohut tried to develop a theory of psychoanalysis that was based more on human relationships. But unlike many of his contemporaries,

he did not use the word "object" as a term for describing people and things in the environment. Rather, he used it to describe how people thought about the people and things in the environment. Kohut therefore talked about the "selfobject," that is to say, an object as experienced by and within the self. For example, it is more important to know how people think about their parents than who those parents really are.

Kohut's theory of narcissism

Kohut described the normal stages of development, and various forms of pathology, with reference to this selfobject. He argued that normal children develop a nuclear, or core, self as a result of good,

---

THE METHODOLOGY OF CHILD PSYCHOANALYSIS

CASE STUDY

Melanie Klein was one of the first psychoanalysts to apply Freud's ideas to children. The first children she analyzed were her own, but to preserve confidentiality, she disguised their identities in her papers. During the 1920s Klein was often involved in personal and theoretical conflicts with Freud's daughter Anna, who was also a child psychoanalyst. Anna Freud believed that the psychoanalytic treatment of children should always be combined with a form of education (she had originally trained as a schoolteacher). Melanie Klein was convinced that a child psychoanalyst should only concentrate on the nature and development of the child's unconscious fantasies.

In 1926 Klein moved from Germany to London, where she lived until her death. There she devoted most of her time to the psychoanalytic treatment of children suffering from severe mental problems. This experience led her to further develop her own theories. She put great emphasis on the fantasy world of young children and did not hesitate to ask them daring questions, for example, their thoughts about death and sexuality. She believed young children often experience feelings of extreme anger and anxiety. Fantasies are a way of coming to terms with these feelings. Klein was one of the first psychoanalysts to use play techniques in her work with children, believing that it revealed their psychological impulses.

Little Red Riding Hood meeting the wolf in the woods, drawn by Walter Crane. Klein believed that, like fairy tales, fantasies provide a way for children to come to terms with anxiety or extreme anger.

responsive relationships with their environment. This nuclear self comprises two aspects: a grandiose (narcissistic) self that makes children feel they are perfect and brilliant, and an idealized image of the parents that makes children feel that others are perfect and brilliant. Kohut believed that mental problems could be explained in terms of conflicts within the self. While Freud had employed the Oedipus complex as an explanation for psychic conflicts, Kohut referred to the Greek myth of the youth Narcissus, who had a fatal attraction to his own reflection (*see* picture p. 64). Because the self is a subjective experience (private awareness), Kohut did not agree with the traditional image of the psychoanalyst as a distant figure. Rather, the analyst had to be warm, sensitive, and empathic (identify with the patient). These revolutionary new ideas were unacceptable to the orthodox psychoanalytic establishment during the 1970s, yet his theory remains popular in the United States, especially at the Chicago Psychoanalytic Institute.

Relational psychoanalysis

One of the most recent developments in psychoanalysis was the work of Stephen A. Mitchell (1946–2000) at the William Alanson White Institute of Psychiatry, Psychoanalysis, and Psychology in New York and also at New York University. Mitchell started from the observation that there are many different theories in contemporary psychoanalysis. He then argued that these theories could be classified under one of two headings: They are either in favor of Freud's model of the drive (instinct), or they are in favor of a model that emphasizes relationships between subjects.

Mitchell's work is often described as the integrated relational model. Like the object relations theorists, Mitchell said that Freud's model of the drive is based too much on the individual's own concerns. This means it does not take into account the fact that people are involved in relationships with other people.

THE MIRROR STAGE

FOCUS ON

Lacan argued that children develop their identity (their ego, or sense of self) when they are capable of recognizing that the image they see in a mirror is their own reflection. This happens some time between the age of 6 and 18 months. It is not a natural ability; an adult has to explain it to them. Thus, in Lacan's theory language is essential for the development of identity.

Many developmental psychologists have investigated when and how children acquire an awareness of themselves. In a classic experiment young children are put in front of a mirror so they

At 18 months old this child can recognize herself in the mirror. She will point to a red spot on her own nose rather than to the spot on her image in the mirror.

can observe themselves. Then somebody puts a red spot on each child's nose without him or her noticing it, and they are put in front of the mirror again. Will the children see the difference, and what will they do on seeing the spots? Will the children reach for the mirror or reach for their own noses? These and other experiments have largely proved Lacan's point that children first learn to recognize themselves in the mirror and then learn to see the difference between the mirror images and themselves, and that this usually happens at about 18 months old. However, recent research shows that dolphins and chimps make similar responses, which suggests language may not be essential.

Mitchell realized that psychoanalysts who favored a relationships emphasis never agreed with each other, so he developed this new model to integrate the various psychoanalytic theories of relationships.

The relational matrix

One of the most important notions in Mitchell's theory was the relational matrix. It refers to a typically human pattern of interaction comprising the self, the object (a thing or another person), and the possible ties between the self and the object. Mitchell used the notion of the

Echo and Narcissus, painted by John William Waterhouse in 1903. According to the myth, Narcissus fell in love with his own reflection in a pool of water. The Viennese psychiatrist Kohut used this story from ancient Greece to illustrate his theory that children develop a grandiose, or narcissistic, self.

relational matrix to interpret many traditional psychoanalytic topics in a new way. For example, he claimed that sexuality should not be understood as something that just happens in the individual, but as something that becomes meaningful in a relationship.

Mitchell also believed that object relations theory and self psychology could benefit from each other. In his clinical work he tried to combine these two perspectives. He viewed mental problems as a combination of poor relationships and unhealthy narcissism. The therapist, said Mitchell, should focus on the patients' relational needs and help them in creating more stable and enriching relations with other people. Mitchell was still working on his theories when he died suddenly in December 2000, but his pupils are developing his work.

Other psychoanalytic theories

Today there are many more types of psychoanalysis than the ones described above. For example, interpersonal psychoanalysis as introduced by Harry Stack Sullivan (1892–1949), humanistic psychoanalysis as developed by Erich Fromm (1900–1980), and hermeneutic psychoanalysis promoted by Roy Schafer. The work of Jung and Adler is still popular in many parts of the world, where people may refer to analytical psychology (Jung) and individual psychology (Adler) instead of psychoanalysis.

All these psychologists have different ideas about how the mind works and how to practice psychoanalytic psychotherapy, and thus tend to disagree strongly with each other. However, although they may criticize Freud, his theories and ideas continue to inspire them.

Psychoanalysis today

Psychoanalytic theory is controversial, and the main focus of this controversy concerns the notion of childhood sexuality and the events that occur during the development of the personality. Freud's descriptions of the Oedipus complex have been attacked for numerous reasons, primarily because they do not adequately address the experience of

KEY DATES

1891 Sigmund Freud publishes his first psychological paper.

1894 Freud publishes "The Psychoneuroses of Defense," which begins to outline his theory about childhood experiences.

1895 Case of Anna O. published.

1900 Freud publishes *The Interpretation of Dreams*, in which he outlines dream analysis and other details of his theories.

1902 Alfred Adler becomes a psychiatrist and begins working with other Viennese psychoanalysts studying personality.

1907 Carl Jung begins studying with Freud and Adler in Vienna.

1909 Case of Little Hans published.

1911 Adler resigns from the Vienna Psychoanalytic Society.

1913 Jung severs all personal and professional relations with Freud.

1920 Anna Freud leaves teaching and begins her career as a psychoanalyst.

1927 Erik Erikson begins training as a psychoanalyst under Anna Freud.

1927 Melanie Klein presents her views on child psychoanalysis.

1935 Anna Freud publishes *The Ego and the Mechanisms of Defense*.

1939 Heinz Hartmann starts the trend for ego psychology.

1947 Anna Freud and Dorothy Burlingham establish a training center for child psychoanalysts in London, England.

1950 Erik Erikson publishes his theories in *Childhood and Society*.

1953 Jacques Lacan delivers his first public seminar in Paris.

1971 Heinz Kohut develops the technique of self-psychology.

1980s Stephen Mitchell develops relational psychoanalysis.

young women during development. Most of Freud's writings were concerned with the experience of young men, and much of his theorizing about young women was either incomplete or frustratingly vague.

A further criticism of psychoanalysis is that it is not rigorously scientifically based. Although Freud believed that he was a mere observer and was reporting accurately on his observations, he did not follow traditional scientific methods in his work. He did not generate hypotheses and test them independently, and most of his clients were middle-class women. Neither did he test people on any standardized instrument or scale. He based his ideas on conversations that he had with patients, which might have been enlightening, but were not systematic or scientific. Thus some critics would argue that all of Freud's theories are in doubt. Despite these criticisms, Freud's work continues to attract interest, and many psychologists still practice in the manner that he advocated, although many do not.

Freud's influence is also felt in research. Numerous researchers are currently working on studies examining defense mechanisms, for example, and the evidence suggests that these devices do exist, even though they may differ in important ways from Freud's original descriptions. Freud also has an enduring place in popular culture: The notion of the psychiatrist with his notebook and couch originate with Freudian practice, for example. Freud's ideas regarding the importance of childhood experiences and the meaningfulness of dreams have also become popularly accepted notions.

CONNECTIONS

Phenomenology and Humanism

"Man is...a self-governing mover...center of his own life."

Abraham Maslow

Phenomenology was originally a philosophical perspective that emphasized the importance of an individual's subjective experience of reality. Later this idea was incorporated in humanistic psychology, which emerged in the 1940s as a reaction to both psychoanalysis and behaviorism. Humanistic psychology emphasized people's potential for personal growth and stressed the influence of conscious, as opposed to subconscious, experience on human behavior.

Austrian academic Edmund Husserl (1859–1938) first described the approach he termed phenomenology in 1913: a term that came from the Greek words *phenomenon*, meaning appearance, and *logos*, meaning study. He said it was important to study how people perceived and experienced events, placing emphasis on each individual's interpretation of a situation, rather than on objective reality. His ideas had a great effect on French philosopher Maurice Merleau-Ponty (1908-1961), who went on to develop his own phenomenological theory, influenced by his interest in political processes. Merleau-Ponty's major work on the subject was *Phenomenology of Perception* (1945), in which he stated that perception was not a general process but one unique to each perceiver.

Phenomenologists believe conscious life experiences, whether positive or negative, cause people to form models, or images of themselves. Behavior adds to and potentially reinforces these models (self-concepts). So if a man views himself

According to humanist psychologists, if people want to achieve their full potential in life, it is important that they give rein to their creativity through self-expression.

as an intellectual, he will act in ways that support his belief by using technical words or strongly conveying his opinions, even if intelligence tests indicate that he has an average IQ. Likewise, if a woman thinks she is fat and unattractive, she will develop an unfavorable self-image, even if others try to reassure her about her appearance.

HUMANISM

In the 1940s the work of U.S. psychologist Charlotte Bühler (1893–1974) became influential. Writing about experiments she had conducted in the 1920s, she remarked: "...what I observed were persons, and not reflexes." Thus, in a sense, her studies were precursors to humanistic psychology's interest in the person-as-a-whole. Bühler identified four basic tendencies: to strive for personal satisfaction in sex and love; to adapt and limit oneself for the purpose of fitting in, belonging, and gaining security; to strive for self-expression and creative accomplishments; to work toward upholding order and integrating with society.

This photograph of Abraham Maslow was taken shortly before he became head of the psychology department at Brandeis University, Massachusetts, in 1951. He was renowned for his work on the hierarchy of needs (see p. 68).

> *"Man can become good (probably) and better and better, under a hierarchy of better and better conditions."*
> *— Abraham Maslow, 1972*

The term humanism usually refers to a philosophy that is optimistic about human possibilities. Humanistic psychologists took this approach to understanding behavior, incorporating the philosophy of phenomenology and opposing reductionism (which broke behavior down into parts and assumed it was the result of conditioning or physiological drives). Gestalt psychologists (see pp. 46–51) had already studied people's perceptions, or things as they "appeared," suggesting that people never sensed the environment as it was, but only as it made "sense" to the brain. Humanistic psychologists took this concept even further, suggesting that it was people's interpretations of perceived situations that influenced their actions. Thus to truly understand human behavior, researchers needed to consider not the behavior, but entire people, their social networks, and the emotional and spiritual meanings they sought in their lives.

Psychologist Abraham Maslow (1908–1970) and psychotherapist Carl Rogers (1902–1987) built on these ideas to develop the key concepts of humanistic psychology, becoming major figures in the movement. Their approach offered psychologists a new perspective on the understanding of human behavior and continued to grow in popularity and influence throughout the 1970s and 1980s.

Abraham Maslow

Abraham Maslow studied at the University of Wisconsin, and his ideas contrasted with both behaviorist and psychoanalytic approaches, which placed little emphasis on conscious experience. Maslow believed that human motivation results from a

MASLOW'S HIERARCHY OF NEEDS

Maslow's hierarchy of needs is usually represented as a pyramid. The base of the pyramid shows the physical necessities of life; the top depicts self-actualization, or the achievement of complete psychological health or potential. Maslow emphasized that lower needs on the hierarchy must be met and maintained before the higher needs can be achieved. For example, immediate hunger must be satisfied before longer-term efforts to maintain a food source can be established (such as growing food crops independently). Likewise, an individual needs to be loved and accepted (social needs) to feel worthwhile and gain self-confidence (esteem needs). Movement up the pyramid is called progression, while movement down the pyramid is called regression.

1 Physiological Needs

Necessities for survival, including the need for oxygen, food, water, warmth/coolness, and shelter. These needs must be satisfied before people can successfully shift their attention to personal safety.

2 Safety Needs

Necessities for long-term stability and survival, including the need to be secure from environmental dangers (either physical or emotional). For example, protection from violence or health hazards. People always try to stabilize their physical and emotional environments before moving farther up the hierarchy.

3 Social Needs

People need to gain a sense of belonging through acceptance, companionship, and love. These needs have to be achieved to prevent isolation or exclusion from social groups. At this level love is based on need more than on giving.

4 Esteem Needs

As needs of hunger, safety, and belonging are achieved, people begin to strive for personal growth. They are motivated by a need for respect and acknowledgment from their social group, which enables them to develop a sense of self-confidence, achievement, and satisfaction. Failure to meet these needs often results in people developing harmful negative beliefs, such as feeling worthless or helpless.

5 Cognitive Needs

People's cognitive needs include the pursuit of knowledge and understanding. They can be gained when people have a consistent, stable environment and a level of acceptance and acknowledgement from their social group.

6. Esthetic Needs

As people approach self-actualization, their needs focus on order and beauty within their environment.

7. Self-actualization

Self-actualization represents the peak of Maslow's hierarchy. According to Maslow, self-actualized individuals have reached their potential and achieved a level of independence. They have accepted themselves, have established solid and trusting friendships, and have gained confidence with their roles in life. They also demonstrate an ongoing desire for personal growth and exploration.

Maslow's hierarchy of needs represents an increased desire to understand human behavior and an acknowledgment that people are active participants in their own lives. The ability of individuals to work consciously toward the enhancement of their skills and potential is a key principle of humanistic psychology—and these principles were further developed by another influential humanistic psychologist, Carl Rogers (see right).

7 SELF-ACTUALIZATION NEEDS: *to find self-fulfillment and realize one's potential*

6 ESTHETIC NEEDS: *symmetry, order, and beauty*

5 COGNITIVE NEEDS: *to know, understand, and explore*

4. ESTEEM NEEDS: *to achieve, be competent, and gain approval and recognition*

3. BELONGINGNESS AND LOVE NEEDS: *to affiliate with others, be accepted, and belong*

2. SAFETY NEEDS: *to feel secure and safe, out of danger*

1. PHYSIOLOGICAL NEEDS: *hunger, thirst, and so forth*

Maslow's hierarchy of needs

Generally, the lower needs, such as hunger, must be at least partly satisfied before an individual will feel strongly motivated by needs higher up the hierarchy. There are some exceptions, however. For example, some artists will starve rather than give up their art.

series of key drives and insisted that the individual is conscious of these drives. He suggested that people have a core set of needs that motivate and influence their behavior and that they have a need to reach their full potential. This approach is often referred to as Maslow's hierarchy of needs (*see* box left).

Carl Rogers

Carl Rogers also helped found humanistic psychology and is often associated with the notion of self-psychology, which states that a person's concept of him- or herself helps determine his or her perception of experiences. Rogers' approach followed Maslow's theory of self-actualization, and he emphasized that people have conscious desires and a motivation to fulfill their potential. He was influential in developing a new style of therapy called person- or

Carl Rogers at the World Symposium on Humanity held in Los Angeles in 1979. He was a graduate of the University of Chicago and one of the founders of humanistic psychology.

> *"Man has an instinctoid [instinctive] higher nature. It's possible to grow this or stunt it. Society can do either."*
> — *Abraham Maslow, 1972*

client-centered therapy, which promoted personal growth and the attainment of self-actualization. According to Rogers, this helped people achieve personal growth in a therapeutic environment that was nonjudgmental and accepting of their choices. In contrast with traditional psychologists' views that people seeking a therapist's assistance were patients, Rogers considered them clients.

Self-concept

Roger's style of therapy developed from his theories about the development of personality and the self-concept, and from his many clinical interactions with clients during therapy sessions. His experience working with these clients enabled him to construct his theories about human potential, in which he placed importance on the individual's personal experience

and proposed that personality could be considered as one central idea of "self." In contrast to either psychoanalytic or behaviorist approaches to personality, Rogers viewed the self-concept as a conscious experience. He proposed that people are aware of their view of self, behaving in ways that are in line with this concept. He also believed that individuals have the potential to achieve change, whether it be a shift away from psychological distress or a realization of their true abilities.

In line with earlier phenomenological theory, Rogers suggested that as people

KEY DATES

1913 Edmund Husserl outlines the phenomenological approach.
1920s Charlotte Bühler identifies four basic human tendencies.
1942 Carl Rogers publishes *Counseling and Psychotherapy*.
1945 Merleau-Ponty publishes *Phenomenology of Perception*
1951 Abraham Maslow becomes head of the psychology department at Brandeis University, Massachusetts.
1957 Albert Ellis opens his Institute for Rational Living, where he teaches REBT principles to other therapists.
1959 Rollo May, Arnest Angel, and Henri Ellensberger, introduce existentialist psychology to the United States.
1963 Carl Rogers helps found the Center for Studies of the Person.
1969 Rollo May publishes *Love and Will*.

experience life, their perceptions of reality either confirm or contradict their self-concept. Rogers proposed that the development of self begins from children's interactions with their parents and their immediate social group. The development of a healthy self-concept is the result of a stable and nurturing environment that recognizes children's need for acceptance and love. This is equivalent to the first three to four levels of Maslow's hierarchy of needs.

> "If I can provide a certain type of relationship, the other person will discover within himself the capacity to use that relationship for growth…"
> — Carl Rogers, 1961

Rogers also said that human needs can be met either conditionally or unconditionally. Conditional love refers to an environment where children are only given the love and acceptance they desire if they meet expectations. For example, children might have to attain certain grades in school before being praised, and acceptance is withheld if they fail to achieve the level expected of them. Unconditional love and acceptance refer to an environment that nurtures children's development regardless of attainment. Unconditional positive regard for a child also acknowledges that bad behavior does occur but that it does not make the child bad or unlovable.

Congruence and incongruence

According to Rogers, a self-concept that is supported by reality is congruent, meaning that both the individual's inner perceptions and outer experiences are consistent. He also proposed that an environment in which the individual experiences unconditional, positive regard assists in the promotion of self-worth. For example, if a child gains acceptance through trying hard at school and

participating in life, Rogers believed that this positive experience enables the child to learn to value him- or herself.

As a person's self-concept develops and remains congruent, a self-fulfilling prophecy can develop. This means that individuals begin to behave in ways that match their perceived sense of self. For example, if a woman views herself as responsible and sensible, she will act in ways that confirm these beliefs. And if she encounters or experiences information that contrasts with her self-concept, she will dismiss or avoid it.

On the other hand, if an individual's self-concept differs from reality, this creates incongruence. For example, if a boy works hard in school but is criticized unfairly by his parents as "lazy," his two experiences are incongruent, and he may develop a self-concept of unworthiness that does not match reality.

This child is being scolded for painting the furniture. According to Rogers, children who still feel loved despite naughty behavior will be happier and more secure than children who feel that love is conditional on their good behavior.

CLIENT-CENTERED PSYCHOTHERAPY

Carl Rogers believed that when people struggled with inner conflict, they could bring about positive change. The role of the therapist was to provide an environment that fostered self-development, helping clients discover solutions to their problems. He emphasized that clients were experts in their own development, and that the role of the therapist was as a listener who valued and trusted their experiences. Therapists achieve this by being warm and accepting of their clients and the problems they raise.

The three main features of client-centered therapy are genuineness, unconditional positive regard, and empathy. Rogers emphasized that the relationship between the client and the therapist had to be genuine, or based on honesty. Thus therapists had to be open to their clients'

reactions and experiences in therapy sessions. This helped create an environment that was safe and comfortable for their clients, enabling them to express themselves freely to another, nonjudgmental person.

Rogers also proposed that unconditional positive regard ensured that people developed to their highest potential. This regard needed to come from individuals themselves (congruence) and from their worlds (acceptance and love from parents without conditions). Rogers said this resulted in complete psychological harmony, in which people experienced life freely, independently, and creatively. Even if a person grew up in a conditional environment and developed inner conflict and incongruence, Rogers maintained that positive change was still possible by fostering an environment of unconditional positive regard in therapy sessions, enabling the individual to develop self-worth and congruence.

Empathy refers to an understanding of another person's emotional experiences or feelings. It differs from the concept of sympathy, which is an ability to feel pity for other people without a true understanding of their experiences. According to Rogers, to reflect or feed back on a client's experiences, therapists had to provide an accurate level of empathy for their clients. Again, this helped create an environment in which the client felt heard, and their experiences were valued and respected.

Rogers believed that a child who grew up in an environment of unconditional family love would generally be in harmony with herself and with others.

The wider the gap between the self and reality, the greater the possibility of confusion or problematic behaviors. If the gap between self-concept and reality is too wide, it can result in psychological illness. Well-adjusted people, in contrast, have a self-concept that is consistent with their thoughts, experiences, and behavior.

According to Rogers, people function more effectively if they are brought up with unconditional love. If parents only offer conditional love, children may grow up to believe that they need to be perfect to gain acceptance and love from others. This might lead them to set unrealistic expectations for work, social, or personal pursuits. They may never feel truly satisfied with their performance and may be highly critical of their abilities.

Humanistic therapy

Psychologists who adopt a humanistic approach emphasize that people are capable of striving to achieve their full potential. Thus the therapist uses methods that enhance this potential. Therapy consists of individual sessions that focus on clients' potential for personal growth, creating an environment in which they are accepted unconditionally. First the therapist stresses the importance of each person learning to accept responsibility for his experiences and interactions. The therapeutic relationship is then used to generate a nurturing environment in which the individual can grow and develop healthy self-concepts.

Rogers suggested that people have aims to develop and enhance themselves, and that this enables them to consciously accept or reject social norms. He used the term self-actualizing in reference to this motivation to achieve independence. Psychotherapy that incorporates a humanistic approach can assist both emotionally distressed individuals and healthy individuals who are eager to explore their full potential.

Humanism and psychoanalysis

The humanist movement began partly as a reaction to psychoanalysis (*see* pp. 52–65), so there are some key differences between the two approaches. Psychoanalytic psychologists propose that human behavior can be explained in terms of unconscious desires or processes. They emphasize the unconscious, something of which the individual is unaware. However, this approach does not acknowledge the importance of conscious experiences for the individual. Humanistic psychologists propose that both the conscious and unconscious need to be considered when trying to understand human motivation and behavior. Rogers said that people are aware of their self-conflict, and it is this that influences their drives and behavior.

Another difference between humanistic and psychoanalytic psychologists lies in their basic perceptions of people.

KEY TERMS

HUMANISTIC THERAPY

Humanistic psychologists use various approaches:
- **Encounter** (developed by Carl Rogers): A group therapy in which members discuss emotional issues with honesty and receive feedback from the group.
- **Rational-emotive behavioral therapy** (developed by Albert Ellis): A form of psychotherapy that emphasizes rational problem-solving approaches to help the client overcome distressing or unhelpful emotions and behaviors.
- **Existential analysis** (developed by Rollo May): A psychotherapeutic approach in which therapists focus on the immediate situation they are sharing with clients to enhance the clients' awareness of their distress and potential for change.

Humanists believe that people have the potential to enhance themselves and take an optimistic view of human nature and behavior. Psychoanalysts view people as primarily engaged in a continual struggle between unconscious conflicts and desires.

Humanism and behaviorism

The humanist movement was also a reaction against behaviorism (*see* pp. 74–89), which had again led to the development of specific therapeutic techniques. Behaviorists do not take the conscious experience of the individual

Kenya's Noah Ngeny wins the men's 1,500m final at the 2000 Olympics in Sydney, Australia. He thus realized his full potential as a runner and received a gold medal. Rogers believed that many people could achieve similar success in their respective fields if they were not held back by emotional limitations, and that humanistic therapy could help realize this potential.

into account either, proposing instead that personality is shaped through learning. They consider it impossible to scientifically study conscious experiences or the individual's interpretation of these experiences and therefore do not consider them in studies of human behavior.

Humanistic psychologists and behaviorists also disagree on the subject of reductionism. Behaviorists propose that human behavior can be explained as a result of conditioning processes or physiological drives. Thus behavior can be understood by breaking it down into its basic elements: a reductionist approach that does not consider an individual's entire experience. In contrast, humanists propose that individuals act consciously and can choose good or bad behavior. Humanists also take a holistic approach to understanding an individual's motivation and drives, focusing on the whole or complete person rather than dissecting her behavior into parts.

Limitations

As with most psychological theories, humanistic psychology has received some criticism. Its main limitations are considered to be its poor testability, its unrealistic view of human nature, and the inadequate evidence available to support its claims. Humanistic approaches are often considered to have poor testability because the concepts they describe (for instance, self-actualization) are not easily defined or measured. This leads to difficulties in effectively evaluating these concepts, since no standard measure of what they are can be established. Self-actualization, for example, is different for each person, so no single standard of achievement can be applied to everyone.

KEY POINTS

- Humanism is the "third force" in psychology and developed as a reaction to the previous two dominant approaches of psychoanalysis and behaviorism.
- Its foundations lie in the phenomenological approach, which suggested that the way people interpret events is an important factor in understanding their behavior.
- Humanistic psychology emphasizes the importance of recognizing people's conscious experiences.
- Maslow's hierarchy of needs provided insights into human behavior, and Rogers' therapeutic interventions led to a greater understanding of the development of a self-concept.
- Rogers went on to develop client-centered psychotherapy, in which the therapist's genuineness, empathy, and unconditional, positive regard for clients helped people toward personal growth and development.
- The holistic approach of humanistic psychology has expanded the scope of treatments for psychological problems, extending therapy to psychologically healthy individuals who are striving for self-actualization.

Abraham Maslow proposed that self-actualized individuals are at the top of the hierarchy of needs, but the search for individuals who have reached this level of potential is considered difficult. Both Maslow and Rogers viewed behavior as primarily good, and their views are often criticized for being too optimistic and an unrealistic view of human nature.

Humanistic psychology has also been criticized because its effectiveness as a method of psychotherapy has not been established through research. Instead, therapists have noted its effectiveness by clinical observations: observations of the positive changes in clients' behavior and experience through using this approach. Clear scientific data on effectiveness has been difficult to produce, which means humanistic therapy does not meet scientific requirements.

CONNECTIONS

- Psychoanalysis: pp. 52–65
- Behaviorism: pp. 74–89
- Research Methods: pp. 162–163

- Emotion and Motivation: Volume 2, pp. 86–109
- Emotional Development: Volume 4, pp. 112–129
- Social Development: Volume 4, pp. 130–149
- Personality: Volume 5, pp. 94–117
- Talking Cures: Volume 6, pp. 92–117

Behaviorism

"I see no evidence for an inner world of mental life."

B. F. Skinner

Behaviorism arose partly as a backlash against introspection, insisting on measuring only things that could be directly observed in the physical world—a fundamental requirement of sciences such as chemistry and physics. It began as a methodology, but soon developed into a body of theory to explain much of human learning and behavior. Although some of the early behaviorist views are now considered extreme, their methods provided a backbone for modern psychology.

Before behaviorism psychologists had talked about both people's behavior and the contents of their minds. The behaviorists, however, argued that the mind could not be studied scientifically.

Science involves the observation of events that everyone can see. In physics, for example, people study the movement of objects. Everyone can see an object moving from one place to another and, given the right equipment, can agree on how long it took. Similarly, when

It has long been known that dogs salivate at the sight and smell of food; Ivan Pavlov showed that they could also be taught to salivate in response to other stimuli associated with a meal.

KEY POINTS

• Behaviorists believe that since no one can know what another person is thinking, psychologists can study only outwardly visible behavior.

• Behaviorist approaches, introduced early in the 20th century, replaced introspection and helped make psychology a rigorous and objective scientific discipline, rather than a branch of philosophy.

• Behaviorists theorized that all human behavior could be explained as a complex collection of highly conditioned reflexes.

• Behaviorism was widely used in education and psychotherapy.

• Today behaviorism is still important in psychology but no longer dominates. Many psychologists see early behaviorism as extreme.

observing humans and other animals, we can generally find ways to agree on whether or not they've made a certain physical movement. The behaviorists argued that psychology should only concern itself with the way in which events in the world caused changes in animal (including human) behavior.

Previously William James (see p. 41) and other psychologists had defined psychology as the study of consciousness. The only way they could observe the processes of the mind, however, was by examining their own thinking, a process

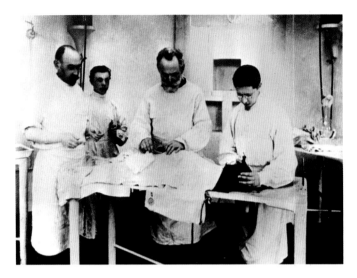

dogs began to salivate even before they were given food. The sight of the white coats of the lab attendants who brought food to the dogs was enough to trigger this response. To test this reaction formally, he rang a bell just before the food was presented. After a while he found that he could make the dogs salivate merely by ringing the bell without giving them any food. Pavlov called this behavior a "conditioned reflex," and it later became known as a "conditioned response." He also found that additional repetitions of the bell-food connection strengthened the effect, while many repetitions of the bell without food made the effect diminish and eventually go away, a process termed "extinction."

that Wundt called introspection. In the sciences, however, experiments must be repeatable. So if a scientist describes the procedure for an experiment, another scientist must be able to perform it and obtain the same results. The behaviorists believed that for psychology to be a true science, it could not depend on any one person's subjective impressions; any discussion of mind was meaningless because mental processes could not be reliably observed.

Russian physiologist and Nobel laureate Ivan Pavlov (second right) demonstrates his theory of conditioned reflex on a dog in a laboratory.

Ivan Pavlov

Behaviorism had its roots in several developments around the beginning of the 20th century. Among the most important of them were the conditioning experiments conducted by Ivan Pavlov (1849–1936). Pavlov studied the digestive process in dogs and was particularly interested in the production of saliva, which is an involuntary reflex action. The idea of a reflex—in which certain stimuli produce an automatic response—was well known. One of the most familiar examples in people is the jerk of the lower leg when a certain nerve at the kneecap is tapped. In animals the salivary reflex causes them to produce more saliva when food is placed in their mouths.

Pavlov devised a method of measuring this saliva flow, but soon noticed that his

E. L. Thorndike

Shortly after the turn of the 20th century E. L. Thorndike (1874–1949) also began to carry out experiments on learning. He was interested in finding out whether dogs and cats could learn by observation.

He placed the animals in cages called puzzle boxes that they could open from inside by pressing a lever, and he tried to teach them how to do so. He found that when an animal simply observed another

> *"A man's mind…is his connection system, adapting the responses of thought, feeling, and action that he makes to the situation that he meets."*
> *— E. L. Thorndike, 1943*

animal, or a person, pressing the lever to open the cage, no learning took place. Even when he guided the animal's paw onto the lever, the animal did not learn. But sooner or later the animal would step on the lever by accident, and after this happened many times, the animal eventually learned that stepping on the lever opened the cage and would do so immediately after it was put inside.

From this Thorndike deduced what he called the "Law of Effect," which stated

JOHN B. WATSON

John Broadus Watson grew up in South Carolina. His family was very religious, something against which he tended to rebel. He attended a small college in Greenville, South Carolina, and after graduation was supposed to enter Princeton Theological Seminary. However, he failed an important course, possibly deliberately, and was forced to spend another year in Greenville. During that time his mother died, and thus freed from parental pressure to study for the ministry, he studied psychology at the University of Chicago.

Watson was trained there in the introspective methods current in psychology, which he disliked, but he also met the German biologist Jacques Loeb (1859–1924), who was working on the conditioned reflex in humans, and neurologist H. H. Donaldson (1857–1938), who was studying the nervous system of the rat. Watson became an animal caretaker for Donaldson and went on to conduct his own research on rat learning.

After gaining his Ph.D. in a record three years, Watson continued to conduct research in Chicago until he was offered a professorship at Johns Hopkins University in Baltimore. He soon became chair of the department and used his influence to separate the psychology department from the philosophy department. His influential position also gave him the authority to spread the ideas of behaviorism, beginning with his famous 1913 lecture,

John B. Watson (1878–1958) moved from academe to advertising, where he used his behaviorist theories to influence consumer spending.

published in *Psychological Review* as "Psychology as the Behaviorist Views It." At first Watson's ideas were well received, and he was elected president of the American Psychological Association. He wrote two influential textbooks: *Behavior* (1914) and *Behaviorism* (1925).

After an interruption to serve in the army in World War I (1914–1918) Watson returned to Johns Hopkins, but because of a matrimonial scandal and a divorce he was forced to resign. He spent the rest of his working life in advertising (see box on facing page), but he continued to lecture and publish books and articles on psychological topics, including a book on child-rearing according to behaviorist principles entitled *Psychological Care of Infant and Child* (1928).

that a behavior that produces a positive result is likely to be repeated. Like Pavlov's conditioned reflex, this behavior seemed to be independent of conscious thought.

THE RISE OF BEHAVIORISM

Darwin's theory of natural selection (*see* p. 134) and an acceptance of the idea that people had evolved from lower animals led to a belief in a continuity between people and animals. Previously people were not considered to be animals—what made them different was their possession of "mind," which most philosophers regarded as equivalent to "soul" (*see* pp. 10–15). If there was indeed continuity between people and animals, then "mind" might also have to be taken into account in any attempt to explain animal behavior.

Early in the 20th century John B. Watson studied learning in rats, first as a student at the University of Chicago and later as a professor at Johns Hopkins University. The ideas of Darwinism,

> *"It can be just as thrilling to watch the growth of a sales curve of a new product as to watch the learning curve of animals or men."*
> — *John B. Watson, 1937*

coupled with the introspective approach to the study of the mind, demanded that he explain his results in terms of conscious thought by the animals, which he found unacceptable. Ironically, the idea that lower animals might possess what had come to be called "mind" led him to reject the idea that there was such a thing as this separate, unique feature.

Drawing on the works of Pavlov, Thorndike, and others, Watson concluded that for psychology to be a true science, it must study only an organism's observable behavior. We can, he said, observe only a stimulus (an event that takes place before an organism does something) and the response (the behavior that follows). Whatever occurs in between is a "black box" about which we can know nothing. The stimulus could be a signal, such as Pavlov's bell, or some internal event, such as the contractions of the stomach that signal hunger. In either case the response would have to be an observable action, such as salivation or getting up and

BEHAVIORISM AND ADVERTISING

After leaving academic life, John B. Watson went to work for the J. Walter Thompson advertising agency in New York City. There he attempted to use the principles of behaviorism to "predict and control human behavior."

Through his research with babies Watson decided that people are born with only three emotions: love, fear, and rage. In advertising he tried to associate these basic emotions with products. Accordingly, he decided that to be effective, advertisements should not simply state "buy this" or describe the qualities of the product, but should try to associate a product with positive or emotive images. An ad for automobile tires, for example, might show a picture of a baby both to arouse positive feelings and to instill fear of an auto accident. Ads for beer and soft drinks might feature young, attractive people having a good time, thus appealing to a general desire for pleasure.

Watson's attempts to apply the principles of conditioning to advertising were not entirely successful, but he also launched the idea of conducting consumer research. During his early training at J. Walter Thompson he was sent to work as a clerk at Macy's department store, New York, where he discovered that he knew little about what consumers really wanted. He therefore introduced consumer surveys. Their purpose was partly to learn what products people preferred, but mainly to establish what their wants and desires were in order to associate products with those basic feelings.

Most of the research ideas used in the modern advertising industry can be traced to Watson's influence. He is also credited with modifying the culture of large corporations to emphasize decision-making based on scientific research rather than instinct and preconception.

By hiring Russian tennis star Anna Kournikova to advertise its watches, Omega is trying to create an association in the minds of potential customers between its watches, female beauty, and sporting prowess.

walking to the refrigerator. Although several other psychologists had been moving toward a behaviorist approach, Watson was the first to popularize the idea in 1913, with a famous lecture that has come to be called "The Behaviorist Manifesto," later published in the journal *Psychological Review*.

Watson's principles
The basic principles of behavioristic psychology, as Watson proposed them, were as follows:
• Psychologists could measure only what happens outside the organism. Introspection and any concept of "mind" were irrelevant. (This led Watson to reject Freud's theories about the unconscious because the unconscious was a concept that could not be observed directly.)
• The purpose of psychological research is the prediction and control of behavior.
• There is no difference between people and animals, except a difference in degree (for example, level of intelligence).
• The behavior of people results entirely from physiological reactions and is not attributable to any nonphysical force.

Though he didn't say it directly, Watson also rejected the widely held idea that consciousness resided in the "soul."

The conditioned reflex
Watson saw the methodology of behaviorism as essential in making psychology a true science on a par with physics, chemistry, and other established disciplines. He went on to develop behaviorism as a theory, attempting to explain complex human behavior entirely in terms of the conditioned reflex.

He began by rejecting the idea that many common human activities are guided by "instinct." An instinct is a behavior that is hard-wired into the organism; present from birth, it does not need to be learned. Insects appear to operate entirely by instinct: As soon as they hatch, they are ready to hunt for prey. Higher animals seem to operate on a mix of hard-wired and learned behaviors.

ALBERT AND THE RAT

CASE STUDY

After observing infants in hospitals John B. Watson determined that children are born with only a few basic fears: of falling, loud sounds, pain, and of having their bodies restrained. All other fears, he said, were the result of conditioning, as objects or events in their lives became associated with the basic fears.

He first tested this idea on an 11-month-old boy known as Albert B., or "Little Albert," the son of a hospital nurse. Albert was first introduced to a white laboratory rat. He touched it, stroked it, and played with it completely without fear. Then, just as Albert reached for the rat, experimenters behind the boy struck an iron bar with a hammer. The noise frightened Albert, and after just a few repeats of the experience the rat became a conditioned stimulus that brought out the same fear response as the loud noise. Now presenting the rat alone would cause Albert to shy away and cry.

Behaviorists believe that the common human fear of rats is learned rather than natural.

Watson also planned to use Albert to test conditioning as a method for removing fears, but his mother decided to remove him from the hospital, so Watson conducted subsequent experiments in fear reduction on other children. He found that positive stimuli, such as food, could be used to condition children out of their fears. A child who was afraid of rats was given food while a rat in a cage was placed a long distance away. Each day the cage was moved closer at feeding time, until the child was eating with one hand and stroking the rat with the other.

A kitten, for example, knows how to groom itself even if it has been removed from its mother immediately after birth; but a kitten that has not been taught by its mother to hunt will usually not regard mice as prey because hunting is learned and not instinctive.

When Watson began his research, most other psychologists believed that people performed many everyday actions instinctively. William James had claimed that behaviors such as climbing, hunting, showing sympathy, playing, curiosity, modesty, shame, and parental love were all instinctive. After extensive observation of human infants Watson decided that only a few basic behaviors, such as grasping, sucking, and random movements of the limbs, were built into every infant. The complex behaviors James had mentioned grew out of conditioning, Watson claimed. An example was smiling: Infants smile in response to stroking and to internal pressure in the digestive system. "Quickly it [smiling] becomes conditioned," Watson wrote. "The sight of the mother calls it out, then vocal stimuli, finally pictures, then words, and then life situations either viewed, told, or read about."

Emotions, Watson said, also resulted from conditioning early in life. During experiments he found that newborn babies showed only a few emotional responses: They would exhibit fear when they heard a loud sound, felt pain, or experienced a loss of support; rage when their limbs were restrained; and pleasure when they were stroked or fed. All these responses, he thought, would have evolved as survival mechanisms. As life went on, other stimuli became associated with these experiences. For example, the mother's stroking and feeding would condition the child to "love" its female parent.

Similarly, no one was "instinctively" afraid of, say, spiders or bats. Such fears were conditioned early on by association with the simple inbuilt fears. Watson demonstrated this in a famous experiment with a boy and a rat (*see* box left).

Generation of emotion

When people experience emotion, it generally involves the association of physiological responses with thoughts and events. Fear and anger, for example, are accompanied by the release of adrenaline, which gives the organism more speed and strength for fight or flight.

Watson believed complex emotions grew through conditioning of reflexes. He suggested the example of the "shame" associated with sex and nudity. An infant will become flushed when stroked,

especially if the sex organs are touched. But when children touch themselves in these places, adults may yell at them and force them to stop. Eventually, Watson said, the flushing becomes conditioned to accompany references to, and even thoughts of, those parts of the body. More complex emotions resulted from

> *"John B. Watson was the most important figure in the history of psychological thought during the first half of the [20th] century."*
> — *Gustav Bergman, 1956*

more complex associations. Jealousy, for example, could result from the association first of love from a parent and then of rage if love was directed at another child.

Watson cautioned that he had not made enough observations to be sure of such explanations. He was sure, however, that all but the simplest emotions were results of conditioning physiological reactions to events in a person's environment.

Behaviorists believe that infants have only a few basic emotions and that all their other feelings are learned later in life.

Skills and conditioning

According to Watson, even the simplest physical skills were the result of early conditioning. A newborn is constantly bombarded by stimuli, both from the sights and sounds of the world around her and from internal events such as hunger and digestion. At the same time, the baby makes all sorts of random movements, and certain movements become conditioned to follow certain stimuli. Eventually, the movements that produce no reward fade away, through extinction of the conditioned response. So, Watson said, a baby seeing a bottle will first move at random, but will quickly become conditioned to perform a simple sequence of reaching, grasping, and pulling the bottle to his or her mouth.

As the child grows, increasingly complex behaviors are conditioned, building up from the simpler ones. A virtuoso playing a piece of music he or she knows well on the piano is executing a long series of conditioned responses in which each step (response) becomes the stimulus for the next. Eventually, stimuli from outside the organism are no longer needed, and the movements of muscles themselves serve as the conditioned

B. F. SKINNER

The son of a self-taught lawyer, Burrhus Frederic Skinner was born and raised in Susquehanna, Pennsylvania. Through high school and college he studied English, intending to become a professional writer. He also gained a reputation as a rebel and a practical joker.

After graduation Skinner returned home and spent a year writing fiction but without success. Then he happened to read an article on behaviorism by his favorite author, Bertrand Russell, and went on to read Watson's book *Behaviorism* along with articles on the work of Pavlov. He decided that behaviorism could explain many of the aspects of human behavior that he had been exploring in the characters he created as a writer, and subsequently

B. F. Skinner (1904–1990) wrote fiction as a young man; but after becoming interested in behaviorism, he decided to study psychology.

enrolled at Harvard as a graduate student in psychology. In 1936 he joined the faculty of the University of Minnesota and then, in 1945, the University of Indiana, where he was appointed to a chair in psychology. In 1948 he returned to Harvard, where he remained for the rest of his career.

Skinner believed conditioning could be used not only to explain human behavior but also to predict and control it. Returning to his roots as a writer, in 1948 he published a novel, *Walden Two*, about a utopian society in which conditioning was used to prevent and correct antisocial behavior. In his ideal world children were raised in community nurseries where they were conditioned to behave properly—as a result, they were "happy." In 1971 Skinner published *Beyond Freedom and Dignity*, a work of nonfiction in which he argued that the concept of freedom was often meaningless because a person's behavior was a result of lifelong conditioning. Therefore, he said, freedoms that interfered with the establishment of a planned society should be curtailed.

Skinner also introduced operant conditioning, a behaviorist version of E. L. Thorndike's Law of Effect (see p. 53). In operant conditioning there is no initial stimulus. Instead, a reward or satisfaction of some kind conditions the organism to perform a certain action. Conditioning begins not when a stimulus is presented to the organism, but when the organism performs an action. The operant (action) that is rewarded tends to be learned. To research this idea, Skinner developed an apparatus that he called an operant chamber, but others called the Skinner box, which was easier to use than any earlier device of its type.

stimulus to trigger the next movement. In playing piano, the sight of a note on the sheet music becomes conditioned to the movement of a finger onto a particular key. The muscular movement that plays any note is followed immediately by the sight of the next note on the page, and eventually the finger movement itself becomes a conditioned stimulus replacing the note on the page and triggering the next finger movement. Watson claimed that if he were given full control over a child from birth, he could soon train him to cultivate any chosen set of skills.

Language

Watson believed that even human language was just a series of conditioned muscular responses in the lungs, larynx, throat, tongue, and lips. Eventually, the patterns associated with one word become connected to those of another, and words flow in their proper order. Meanwhile, words and phrases are conditioned responses to objects in the environment. Babies say "mama" when they sees their mother, and eventually the connections become many and varied. "Mama" is

> *"I am trying to dangle a stimulus in front of you, a verbal stimulus which, if acted upon, will gradually change this universe."*
> — *John B. Watson, 1937*

associated with the mother herself, a photograph of mother, and finally, with the printed word "mother" in a book.

Thinking, Watson said, was simply an elaborate sequence of stimulus-response events in which the result of one connection acted as the stimulus for the next. Use of language was the result of conditioning that associated objects with words, while thought was just a flow of unspoken words. He suggested that words running through our minds might cause subvocalization—that is, electrical signals would be sent from the brain to the vocal

CASE STUDY

THE SKINNER BOX

A refinement of the puzzle box used by E. L. Thorndike (*see* p. 75), the Skinner box was a cage large enough to house an animal, such as a white rat. On one wall of the cage was a bar the animal could press, a chute through which a pellet of food could be delivered, and, usually, a source of water. The bar was connected both to a device that would deliver food according to a preprogrammed system and to a pen writing on a moving paper tape. Each press of the bar would register as a jump in the pen line, producing a graph of the animal's activity over time.

Experiments often began with a period of training for the animal. Operant conditioning depends on the subject randomly pressing the bar at the start of the experiment. But pressing a bar is not normal behavior for a rat, so the experimenter would begin by delivering food whenever it moved in the direction of the bar, then whenever it engaged in pawing behavior. As conditioning progressed, the graph would clearly show that the time between presses of the bar decreased. It would also show how a conditioned response became "extinguished" if food was not delivered after a press of the bar. Experiments with the box enabled Skinner to develop a large body of knowledge and eventually a theory about operant conditioning.

B. F. Skinner conducts an experiment on a rat using one of his operant boxes.

One of Skinner's pupils went on to train dogs to perform in Hollywood films. He devised a form of operant conditioning in which the animals were taught to associate a simple signal, such as a whistle, with a reward. The trainer blew the whistle and gave the animal food, repeating the process until the whistle became a reward in itself. The whistle was thus a conditioned stimulus. If the trainer wanted a dog to go to a bookshelf, pick out a particular book, and carry it to a table, he simply blew the whistle whenever the dog moved toward the bookshelf. Eventually, the dog would head straight for the bookshelf without prompting. Now the trainer blew the whistle whenever the dog moved in the direction of the particular book it was supposed to pick out. The process was continued until the dog has been conditioned to the entire sequence of events.

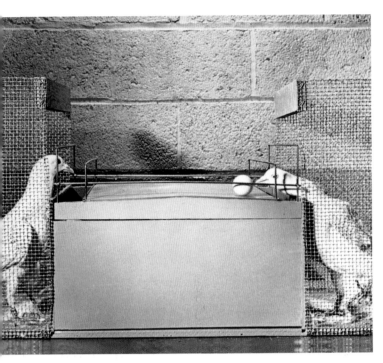

displayed. After absorbing the information, his students were shown a question written in such a way that they almost always got the right answer. The satisfaction of giving the correct answer, Skinner said, served as a reinforcement to help students remember the material. Mechanical teaching machines were quickly replaced by books designed to present short frames followed by questions on adjacent pages.

Effects on education

Unfortunately, the term "teaching machine" proved to be bad for public relations since real teachers worried that their jobs would be at risk, while most believed that the programmed instruction approach would be useful only for teaching simple tasks. Programmed instruction is seldom used in schools today, but is still common in business and industry, and its principles survive in computer-aided teaching.

Skinner wanted to follow Watson's proposal that psychology should be used to predict and control behavior, and he advocated a society in which

> "Behaviorism is treading on the hoof of somebody's sacred cow."
> — John B. Watson, 1930

cords, although the signals would be too weak to cause actual speech. Watson thus believed it might be possible to read people's thoughts by measuring the electrical activity in their vocal apparatus.

Established psychologists generally resisted the behaviorist approach, but younger psychologists took it up with great conviction. Behaviorism spread slowly at first, but by the 1930s had become the most common approach in psychology. There were various "flavors" of behaviorism: Some allowed for a redefined idea of "consciousness," but all stayed close to Watson's basic principles.

The teaching machine

The next major step forward in behaviorism resulted from the work of B. F. Skinner (*see* boxes pp. 80 & 81). Skinner is well-known for creating "programmed instruction," a method of teaching based on conditioning principles. He introduced programmed instruction in a "teaching machine": a box with a window called a "frame" in which a small amount of information was

Pigeons playing ping-pong: a task that might have been thought beyond them. This was one of the experiments devised by B. F. Skinner to demonstrate that animals could be conditioned to perform as long as the reward (in this case a grain of wheat) was a sufficiently attractive incentive to action.

conditioning was used to prevent and correct antisocial behavior. His ideas were widely applied to education, formalizing something teachers had always known: that behavior, if rewarded, is repeated. The elementary school teacher's gold star is a simple example of operant conditioning.

Before long, behaviorist methods were taught formally in teachers' colleges and incorporated into textbooks. Teachers were taught that students needed grades and other incentives to perform to their maximum potential and that material should be carefully sequenced to condition related ideas to each other. Undesired behavior in the classroom was also to be corrected by behaviorist techniques, such as reinforcing positive behavior and eliminating the stimuli that triggered negative behavior. Skinner did not advocate punishment, however, noting that pain and penalties might eliminate unwanted behavior but could not teach the correct action to replace them.

THE COGNITIVE CHALLENGE

For about three decades many psychologists agreed with Watson. They limited their studies to the relationship between events and behavior, and did not speculate about the mental processes causing these relationships. Consequently behaviorism grew more and more influential, dominating psychology in the 1940s and 1950s. In the mid-1950s, however, a new philosophy began to take hold. In 1956 a group of researchers, including Jerome Bruner, George Miller, and Herbert Simon, met at MIT. These cognitive psychologists (*see* pp. 104–117), as they later became known, revived interest in the mind. By the mid-1970s nearly all psychologists were again talking about how the mind worked. The behaviorists' views seemed irrelevant.

Controversial issues

Behaviorism was widely criticized on both emotional and logical grounds. For one thing, Watson, Skinner, and other behaviorists conducted most of their experiments on laboratory animals, and

KEY DATES

1903 Ivan Pavlov publishes the results of his experiments on dogs and introduces the concept of conditioning.

1925 John B. Watson publishes *Behaviorism*, stating that all behavior is based on conditioning and that psychology should be the scientific study of human behavior.

1938 B. F. Skinner publishes *The Behavior of Organisms*, the first of many publications on operant conditioning.

mid-1950s The emphasis shifts to cognitive psychology and the study of the mind rather than behavior.

1972 A mathematical equation for rat behavior, the Rescorla-Wagner rule, is devised.

1986 James McClelland and David Rumelhart create a computer program that can learn the past tense of verbs and makes mistakes similar to those that a child makes.

Eleanor, who is three years old, is pointing to the stickers on her motivational chart. Behaviorists focus on the relationship between events and behavior. Good behavior is rewarded, and bad behavior is ignored. The stickers may be a reward in themselves, or they may be exchanged for a treat such as candy.

critics said it was unacceptable to assume that the results they obtained applied automatically to the more complex nervous systems of people.

Like Watson, Skinner believed that language was built entirely of conditioned responses connecting words to objects

> *"Behaviorism is indeed a kind of flat-earth view of the mind."*
> *— Arthur Koestler, 1967*

and actions. Critics argued that individual differences in language learning meant there was also a genetic inherited component—that people learned language because they were prepared to form certain associations and not prepared for others. In other words, the organism itself was a part of the stimulus-response sequence, and thus not all behavior was determined simply by learning. But even the most hostile critics agreed that behaviorism was a useful theory when limited to certain areas of psychology.

BEHAVIORISM TODAY

Today, although most psychologists regard the behaviorism of Watson and Skinner as an extreme and overly simplistic explanation of behavior, they recognize that the theory opened a small window

THE FEAR OF PUBLIC SPEAKING

Most people feel a little nervous when asked to speak in public. Some people, however, are made so anxious by the prospect of talking to a crowd that they seek to avoid it at all costs. If their job requires public speaking, this can be a serious problem. Behavioral therapy can provide a fast and effective remedy to this situation. For the behavioral therapist anxiety is a response produced by certain objects or situations. A crowded classroom, for example, is a situation that, for some, produces the response of anxiety. One way of stopping this reaction is to train a new response to the situation. Psychiatrist Joseph Wolpe (born 1915) pioneered a technique called systematic desensitization that allowed the behavioral therapist to do just that. The technique helps the patient be less sensitive (desensitized) to frightening situations.

Systematic desensitization involves the therapist and client drawing up a list of anxiety-producing situations related to the problem under treatment. The client puts them in order, starting with the one that produces the least anxiety and ending with the most anxiety-producing situation. The client is then taught ways to relax such as controlled breathing and muscle relaxation. Once these techniques are mastered, the client is asked to relax while imagining the least anxiety-producing situation on the list. Should the client begin to feel anxious, he stops imagining the situation and uses the relaxation techniques again until ready to resume. This sequence is repeated many times, slowly working up the list to more stressful anxiety-producing situations. What the therapist is trying to do is train new relaxation responses to the situations that once produced anxiety. It is not possible to be both anxious and relaxed at the same time, so learning these new responses eliminates the earlier anxiety.

Research showed that five sessions using Wolpe's systematic desensitization methods could effectively treat the fear of public speaking. This behavioral treatment was also found to be more effective than five sessions with a traditional psychotherapist.

A confident public speaker, President Bill Clinton addresses a crowd of applauding students at Beijing University on the last day of his visit to the capital city of China in June 1998.

onto the human mind. Behaviorism's first major contribution to psychology was methodology—a way of doing science. The second was therapy—a way of treating psychological problems. The third was a philosophy—an idea about what psychology should and should not be. The first two contributions are still important in modern psychology; it is only the philosophy that is disputed.

Behavioral conditioning

The behaviorists' focus on the relationship between events and behavior led them to explore whether undesirable behaviors could be changed. Thus their contribution to therapy has been much longer-lasting than in other areas of psychology.

For instance, one of the goals of doctors in a psychiatric ward is to help the patients lead a normal life, and this often starts with basic tasks that address the patient's problems. In several cases these goals have been achieved by rewarding normal, healthy behaviors with tokens: small objects that have little value in themselves, but can be exchanged for rewards, such as going to the movies or receiving extra food. In token systems patients receive immediate rewards for appropriate behaviors that they would not receive for inappropriate behaviors. Rules are posted so that everyone knows how tokens are gained and how many tokens are needed for particular rewards.

Research showed that the introduction of a token economy had real, positive effects on the behavior of patients who had spent many years in hospital. The tokens were used to reward behavior such as dressing properly or socializing with other patients and were exchanged for privileges such as watching television. By the end of one experiment more than one in ten of the patients were well enough to leave. Without the token economy they would all have been expected to stay put. More sociable patients also improved the running of the ward.

Token economies have also been used effectively to improve behavior in both mainstream and special needs schools.

Behavior modification

More generally, behavioral methods have been shown to be effective in treating a wide range of problems, such as fear of spiders and anxiety about public speaking (*see* box left). The methods used to treat such phobias (irrational fears) usually depend on the principle of a conditioned reflex. Just as Watson banished a child's fear of a rat by gradually bringing the animal closer, the patient is gradually exposed to mild versions of the thing feared, often accompanied by pleasurable stimuli. People with agoraphobia (fear of going out in public) might begin by just sitting on the front porch. Later they might move to the end of the front walk, then to the corner, and so on, until they can tolerate crowded public places.

Other researchers developed a more extreme approach called "aversion therapy," which was particularly popular in the late 1960s and early 1970s. Based on Skinner's conditioning experiments with animals, this approach attempted to correct bad habits by associating them with unpleasant stimuli, such as loud sounds and unpleasant smells. In one example people who wanted to quit

A still from Stanley Kubrick's movie A Clockwork Orange (1971), a version of Anthony Burgess's novel of 1962. In this scene the protagonist, Alex, is injected with drugs and forced to watch violent imagery while listening to music. The drugs make him vomit, thus conditioning him against using violence and also against the music of Ludwig van Beethoven.

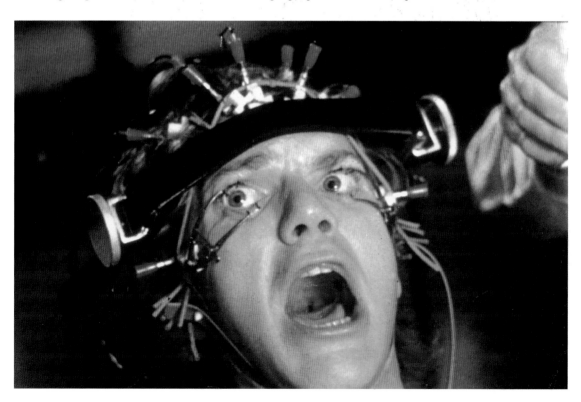

THE REMARKABLE MEMORY OF PIGEONS

Look at the two pictures in this box. Imagine someone showing them to you and saying, "In two years time I will show you these pictures again. If you pick the road sign, I will give you some money; but if you pick the house, you'll get nothing." Do you think you'd be able to remember which picture to choose two years later? And what if you had to learn not one pair but 160 pairs of pictures, all different, with no obvious theme or connection between them? How many would you get right after a gap of two years?

An experiment by William Vaughan and Sharon Greene showed that if you were a pigeon, the answer would be "nearly all of them." Vaughan and Greene collected two sets of 160 pictures each. The pictures in each set were chosen randomly and had no obvious themes or relations to each other. Let's call these sets of pictures set A and set B. Vaughan and Greene then trained pigeons to peck at pictures in set A, but to avoid pecking at pictures in set B. They did so by rewarding the pigeons for pecking at the pictures from set A by giving them some grain. The pigeons did not get grain for pecking at the pictures from set B.

Two years from now, if you choose this image from a huge selection, you will be given a cash reward. Do you think you could remember it?

You will not be rewarded for choosing this image. Out of 320 pictures a pigeon would remember not to choose this picture.

Learning which 160 of 320 random pictures to peck at was no easy task, and it took almost 200 sessions before the pigeons mastered it. But once they had, they remembered them even two years later, storing away the information. Even after the long delay the pigeons pecked almost exclusively at those pictures for which they had previously been rewarded.

smoking were administered with mild electric shocks (euphemistically described as "Faraday treatment") as they went through the motions of lighting a cigarette. A program based on this technique is still in use at Schick Shadel Hospital in Seattle, Washington, and

> *"Do we lose our humanity if we are deprived of the choice between good and evil?"*
> — *Stanley Kubrick, 1971*

claims a 95 percent success rate. Similar techniques have been applied to alcohol and drug addiction, obsessive-compulsive behavior and to "cure" homosexuality. The ultimate extreme was portrayed in the book and movie *A Clockwork Orange*, in which a delinquent called Alex is

conditioned to be incapable of violence and antisocial behavior using drugs that induce nausea (*see* photo p. 85).

Learning

The behaviorists were also well known for promoting particular ways of approaching psychology, particularly people like Ivan Pavlov (*see* p. 75) and B. F. Skinner (*see* pp. 80–82). These scientists did much to promote the use of carefully controlled experiments with rats and pigeons as a way of discovering more about ourselves. Today the methods they developed are used to investigate the complexity of the animal mind. Many animals have been shown to have remarkable memories (*see* box above), and we now know that they use these to learn more efficiently and to help them survive.

The behaviorists showed that animals such as rats can learn that two events go together, for example, that a certain behavior will result in a reward such as food or a punishment such as an electric shock. In 1968 research showed that if a rat has already learned that a flashing light predicts shock and a buzzer sounds at the same time as the light flashes, the rat will not waste time learning about the buzzer. The rat already knows that a shock is coming because the light is flashing.

Rats and other animals seem to be continually anticipating what will happen next. If their predictions are right, then they understand the world sufficiently and do not need to learn. If their predictions are wrong, however, more learning is required. Consequently, they pay more attention to the unexpected.

The surprise factor
In 1972 two U.S. psychologists, Bob Rescorla and Alan Wagner, made an important discovery. They first pointed out that in many situations the amount a rat learned was affected by how surprised it was: An unexpected stimulus meant that more conditioning occurred. They went on to say that the rat's behavior in such situations could be explained by a single mathematical equation. This equation became known as the Rescorla-Wagner rule. At the time, most psychologists were not particularly interested in this formula for learning. They thought that because it described rat behavior, it could not be applied to people.

> *"Everything important in psychology...can be investigated in essence through the...analysis... of rat behavior at a choice point in a maze."*
> — *Edward Tolman, 1938*

That began to change in the 1980s when James McClelland and David Rumelhart developed the delta rule, based on the Rescorla-Wagner rule. The delta rule applied the theory of conditioning in rats and enabled a computer to learn. In this way McClelland and Rumelhart showed that a computer could learn the past tense of verbs. For example, given the word "go," their program could tell you

---

 ## OUT OF SIGHT, OUT OF MIND?

FOCUS ON

If you were to travel to a neighboring town, you would no longer be able to see your house, but you would know that it was still there. For a long time many psychologists believed that infants could not grasp this fundamental concept. Unfortunately, the problem with trying to test theories about babies is that babies have difficulty interacting with people and objects in ways researchers can measure accurately. In the 1990s psychologists got around this by using the techniques developed by behaviorists to test rats and pigeons.

Virtually all animals, including people, habituate (get used to repeated events). For example, the first time a blue light flashes in a rat's cage, the rat will turn and look at it for a while. However, by the time the light has flashed perhaps 40 times, the rat ignores it. This gradual reduction in responding is called habituation. Habituation vanishes if something surprising happens: If a red light flashes, the blue-habituated rat will start to pay attention to the light again. This means the rat must be able to tell the difference between the red and blue lights.

Researchers have used the fact that surprise removes habituation to see whether babies find certain events surprising or not. For example, a baby will be repeatedly shown an event until she shows habituation. The event is then changed. If the baby starts looking again, she must be able to detect that change.

In one experiment two different changes were made. One of them involved an object that babies could no longer see stopping another object from moving. The babies did not find this event particularly surprising, which suggested they knew the first object still existed. The other event, thanks to some stage magic, appeared impossible unless the babies believed that the initial object did not exist. The babies were particularly surprised by this event.

that the past tense was "went"—and it could do this for more than 500 verbs. Not only that, but as the program first began to learn past tenses, it made the same kind of errors that children do. Many young children go through a phase in which they forget that the past tense of "go" is "went" and will use "goed" instead. Rumelhart and McClelland's computer program did exactly the same thing.

Today many psychologists use computers to mimic the human mind in order to understand it better. Crucial to these attempts is the Rescorla-Wagner model that explains conditioning and the relationship between conditioned and unconditioned stimulus.

Breaking the habit

Behaviorism has also helped psychologists and other scientists develop medical treatments for psychological problems. Many people get addicted to illegal and dangerous substances, such as cocaine. Once addicted, it is difficult to stop taking the drug without help. It is also easy to start taking it again, even if you have stopped for a long time. One reason seems to be that drug-taking becomes a habit.

Habits are learned behaviors that are automatically produced by familiar environments. Many habits are normal and useful, such as brushing your teeth in the morning. Others, such as nail-biting, are useless and can be irritating. Some habits, such as drinking alcohol or taking drugs, are physically addictive, difficult to stop without medical or professional help, and cause long-term health problems.

In 1999, in an article in *Nature*, Maria Pilla and colleagues described how they got rats addicted to cocaine. After they had done so, they set up a situation in which a light being turned on indicated that cocaine would soon be available. After a while the rats tried to get cocaine as soon as the light came on: The rats associated the light coming on with satisfying their addiction to cocaine.

Once the rats had acquired a cocaine habit, could they be cured of it? Using

what they knew about the effects of cocaine on the brain, the scientists developed a new medicine. The medicine itself did not seem to be addictive, and if rats were given it, they would not look for cocaine when the light came on. Obviously, there is still a long way to go, but experiments such as these offer hope for a solution to some difficult social problems. Such experiments would not have been possible without the procedures developed by the behaviorists.

> *"The better we understand how people learn...the better able we will be to help them learn appropriate behaviors and eliminate inappropriate ones."*
> — David Lieberman, 1990

The most significant contribution the behaviorists made to modern psychology is the one that is hardest to see. They insisted that psychology should be a science. Scientists perform carefully controlled experiments, and so should psychologists. Psychology, the behaviorists said, could not make progress simply through discussion and debate. It needed objectivity and hard facts.

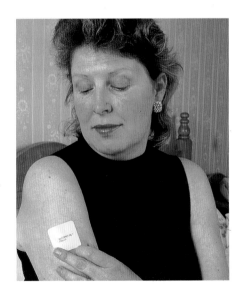

Some habits (or learned behaviors) are useful, but others, such as smoking, will damage your health. Once a person is physically addicted to nicotine, it is difficult to give up smoking without some sort of medical assistance such as wearing a nicotine patch, as this woman is, or chewing gum.

THE BEHAVIORIST LEGACY

Most modern psychologists would agree with the need for psychology to be an objective science. Look at many areas of psychology, and you will see how they have been revolutionized by the behaviorists' views.

In the late 19th century, for instance, early psychologists such as Wilhelm Wundt (*see* p. 32) had tried to understand the mind by training people to break down their conscious experience into its "raw" components. For example, Wundt would ask his students to describe what they saw out of a window in terms of patches of light of particular shapes and colors, not in terms of objects like trees.

Many modern psychologists believe that our conscious experience is composed of simple components, and we can see things like trees only because we combine these components into objects. However, the reasons modern psychologists would give for this belief are more scientific than Wundt's and would probably point to something like visual search experiments.

Seeing red

Visual search experiments are a bit like children's games. Look at the two pictures to the right of this page. Try to find the red T in each picture as quickly as you can. Game 1 is easy. The T seems to "pop out" at you. Game 2 is more difficult. Perhaps the reason for this is that you have to construct each object from its components of color and shape. You don't need to do that for the first picture. All you have to do is see a patch of red.

Before behaviorism most psychologists would not have analyzed these results any further. In contrast, modern psychologists demand some evidence. In 1980 a researcher called Anne Treisman provided it by showing people many pictures like those above. For each picture she asked them to find an object as quickly as they could and press a button as soon as they had. She measured the time between showing the picture and the button being pressed, and found that people took a lot longer to find objects in the second game, providing clear evidence that they found the second game harder than the first. The way forward for psychology is through objective experiments like these.

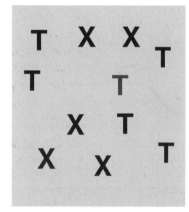
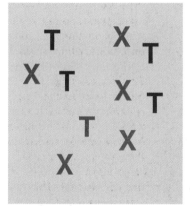

In which game is it easier to find the red T? Visual search experiments such as this provide psychologists with an objective test that can be duplicated by other researchers.

CONNECTIONS

- Nature and Nurture: pp. 22–29
- Cognitive Psychology: pp. 104–117
- Psycholinguistics: pp. 118–125
- Research Methods: pp. 162–163

- Perception: Volume 2, pp. 62–85
- Learning by Association: Volume 3, pp. 44–63
- Storing Information: Volume 3, pp. 88–113
- Infant Cognition: Volume 4, pp. 24–39
- Perceptual Development: Volume 4, pp. 40–57
- Physical Therapies: Volume 6, pp. 118–141

Neuropsychology

"...an exercise in carving cognition at the seams..."

R. McCarthy & E. Warrington

Neuropsychologists study the way in which the mental apparatus is organized in the brain— a field that only began to move from speculation to true science in the late 18th century, when researchers made the link between brain injury and loss of funtion. Since then scientists have made many discoveries about the biological basis of psychological activity, and technological advances have helped psychologists measure brain activity in normal individuals, too.

How do we know that the brain is the organ of mental life, apart from the fact that that is what we are taught in biology classes in school? Perhaps some other part of the body, such as the liver, is actually the organ that we use for thinking. Without formal instruction we might imagine ways in which we could figure this problem out for ourselves.

We know, for example, that four of our five external sense organs are located exclusively in the head, and even the

> *"What is Descartes' error?...*
> *The separation...of the mind from*
> *the structure and operation of a*
> *biological organism."*
> *— Antonio Damasio, 1994*

simplest understanding of any fish, bird, or mammal anatomy shows that the nerves from the sense organs travel toward the brain. Also, powerful blows to the head often cause a sudden loss of consciousness, dramatically disturbing our mental process and abilities. In contrast, similar blows elsewhere to the body merely cause intense physical pain, while we remain mentally alert.

Although the brain seems an obvious place to look for the biological basis of the mind, the importance of the heart as the organ of the mind (especially in emotion) was the topic of a long-standing debate

dating back to the philosophers of ancient Greece (*see* pp. 10–15). By the Middle Ages, however, much was being made of the series of interconnected chambers in the brain (which are called ventricles and are filled with cerebrospinal fluid). This model of the brain was called the ventricular localization theory and was expanded by the French philosopher René Descartes (1596–1650), who was most famous in psychology for claiming that the mind (soul) and body were separate (*see* p. 18). Descartes was interested in finding a structure that might act as the mediator between the body and the mind (or soul). He thought that the pineal gland in the brain seemed small and "nimble" enough to move around and

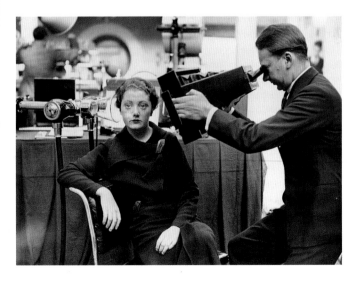

A woman has her head x-rayed at the London Medical Exhibition in 1934. The shock-proof equipment was designed for use in the doctor's office: It was simple to use and could be plugged into any electrical outlet designed for domestic lighting.

interact with the "animal spirits" contained within the nearby ventricles. The arguments about ventricles and glands did represent a reasonable (though entirely incorrect) initial hypothesis about brain function, but there was little suggestion of testing it. Neither was there any logical reason why the most anatomically visible parts of the brain should have been the regions carrying out interesting psychological processes.

The influence of phrenology

A famous attempt at understanding the relationship between brain and mind was suggested by Franz Gall (1758–1828), who argued that different regions of the outer surface of the brain might be specialized for various personality traits, such as

EXPLORING THE BRAIN

KEY DATES

Middle Ages (about 5th to 15th century) The ventricular localization theory is the popular model of the brain.

1790s German physiologist Franz Gall introduces phrenology, the idea that cognitive functions are organized independently from each other and localized within specific bumps on the head.

1861 Paul Broca reports the case of the man who can only say "tan." An autopsy reveals damage to the left frontal lobe of the brain.

1960s Roger Sperry's "split-brain" experiments demonstrate that the left-hand side of the brain controls language, and the right-hand side of the brain controls spatial awareness.

1970s Cognitive neuropsychology is introduced.

1980s Structural brain imaging becomes widely available.

1990s Functional brain scans become widely available.

PHINEAS GAGE

CASE STUDY

Phineas Gage worked on the railroads of North America in the 1840s and was one of the most famous patients in neuropsychology. He was supervising the tamping down of an explosive with a long rod as workers put a charge into a rock formation when the charge exploded too soon, propelling the tamping rod through Gage's skull and the frontal lobe of his brain. The rod shot through so rapidly that it is thought to have cauterized the tissue as it passed through, so only a relatively small area of the frontal lobe was damaged. Gage did not even lose consciousness and made a rapid physical recovery, but he underwent some distinctive psychological changes as a result of his injury. His physician, a Dr. Harlow, wrote up the case a few years after the incident occured.

Despite the relatively small extent of the brain injury Gage suffered, his personality altered radically, changing him as a person. Previously he had been the team foreman —a position of some responsibility. He was regarded as a reliable character and was valued by his employers. After the accident he became uninhibited and acted in socially inappropriate ways, making a series of bad decisions in his work and personal life. Toward the end of his life he worked as part of a traveling show, exhibiting himself and the rod that had passed through his brain.

We now know, from countless cases since Gage's, that damage to this part of the frontal lobes almost always

leads to this particular type of personality change. Research shows that patients like Gage are unable to use their emotional experiences about the world to make decisions about the right and wrong things to do. Thus they seem unable to consider whether they should trust a salesman in a store offering a computer for $1,000 or a shady character that they meet in a bar who offers one that's "as good as new" for $100. Consequently, patients with this type of deficit usually make a series of bad decisions, and after a few years their lives can be in ruins.

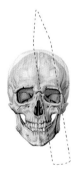

A diagram of Phineas Gage's skull and brain, showing the site of injury to his frontal lobe.

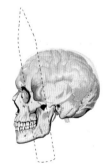

A side view showing the angle at which the tamping rod passed through Gage's brain.

"destructiveness" and "veneration" (worship or respect). His colleague Johann Spurzheim (1776–1832) expanded the argument, which came to be called phrenology (*see* p. 37).

The doctrine of phrenology suggested that scientists could gauge a person's personality by feeling the skull for bumps. These bumps were thought to develop in particular places because the underlying brain regions responsible for particular faculties made an impression on the skull. Gall is reputed to have developed his theory at the age of nine, after observing that a friend who had especially good verbal memory also had large, bulging eyes, suggesting a connection between inner abilities and external features.

THE STUDY OF DEFICIT

Jean-Baptiste Bouilland (1796–1881) made an important bridge between phrenology and a more scientific theory. A founder of the French Phrenological Society, he was also a respected scientist. Unlike Gall, however, he stressed the value of examining the brain itself (at autopsy)

The French neurologist Jean-Martin Charcot was a brilliant teacher who attracted students from all over the world. This painting, entitled Charcot at the Salpêtrière, *was completed in 1887.*

as evidence for inferring the importance of brain regions, rather than by merely investigating bumps on the skull.

Unlike Gall, instead of investigating people with an excessive overdevelopment of a mental faculty (such as having superb verbal abilities), Bouilland investigated those with a loss of a particular mental faculty. He noticed that people who had suffered a stroke (caused by a loss of blood supply to a portion of the brain), and who had experienced language problems as a result, tended to have endured their damage in the anterior (front) regions of the brain. While Gall viewed bumps as a sign of over-development, Bouilland's patients had suffered loss of function because of observable damage. This focus on function, rather than structure, was a significant advance in brain science.

Clinicoanatomical method

The method adopted by Bouilland was by no means unique to him and is commonly associated with Jean-Martin Charcot (1825–1893). In 1882 Charcot opened his world-famous neurological clinic at the Salpêtrière Hospital, Paris. His approach to finding the locations of neurological and nonneurological disorders was similar to that of Bouilland and was later called the "clinicoanatomical" method. The name derived from the fact that it involved comparing two separate classes of evidence: the clinical evidence of the patient's behavior and the anatomical evidence of the site of the patient's injury.

The best-known example of this sort of correlation comes from the work of surgeon Paul Broca (1824–1880). His 1861 report on the patient known as "Tan" is usually taken as the founding event of neuropsychology (*see* box p. 93). Broca concluded that the frontal lobe of the left hemisphere of the brain was specialized for language production, with other brain regions presumably specialized for other, yet to be discovered functions. Later, other researchers applied a similar logic to dozens of psychological functions in

the brain, producing diagrams of brain function that resembled a patchwork of regions of specialization.

A century of discovery

In the 140 years since Broca's discovery his basic approach has been applied to a wide range of psychological functions, and these findings form the core of neuropsychology. There have been several landmark discoveries. In the late 1800s scientists realized that the outer surface (cortex) of the left hemisphere is involved in several language functions, of which Broca had identified only one. Various aspects of language, such as production, repetition, and comprehension, all seem to have regions of specialization in the left hemisphere, and the investigation of language remains one of the central areas of research in neuropsychology today.

It was only about 100 years later that attention focused clearly on the functions of the right hemisphere. We now know

> *"The great regions of the mind correspond to the great regions of the brain."*
> — *Paul Broca, 1861*

that this hemisphere is involved in other areas of speech, such as rhythm and melody, and in a range of spatial and attentional functions. In the 1960s Roger Sperry conducted a series of experiments on epileptic patients (*see* box p. 94), who had all been treated by having their hemispheres surgically disconnected by cutting through the bundle of nerve fibers between them called the corpus callosum. Sperry's "split-brain" work showed that if he controlled the information that appeared in his subjects' field of vision—left or right—and then asked questions about it, they responded quite differently depending on which hemisphere was processing the information. With the corpus callosum severed, each hemisphere seemed in some ways to act like a separate

PAUL BROCA AND LEBORGNE

CASE STUDY

Surgeon Paul Broca first used the clinicoanatomical approach in 1861, in one of the most celebrated cases in neuropsychology—which is commonly taken to mark the beginning of scientific neuropsychology. Broca reported the case of one his patients who had great difficulty expressing speech—a problem so severe that he could produce only the word "tan." Thus the hospital staff named him, somewhat unkindly, after the only syllable he uttered (his real name was Leborgne). In spite of his difficulty expressing himself, Tan appeared to understand Broca and seemed to be of relatively normal intellect.

Perhaps fortuitously for science (though not for Tan), he died a few days after Broca examined him. At autopsy Tan's brain revealed a large area of damage to the frontal, temporal (side), and parietal (upper rear) lobes of the left hemisphere—although the most important areas of damage (those that seemed to have been there longest) were in the inferior (that is, lower) frontal lobe. In memory of this discovery the region of the frontal lobe that Broca identified is now called Broca's area.

brain. In 1981 Sperry was awarded the Nobel Prize for Physiology or Medicine on the basis of these dramatic findings.

Not all of the great findings in neuropsychology have been in the domains of language and hemispheric asymmetry; researchers have also come to understand a great deal about the way in which people recognize objects, remember things, and interact with the world.

Brenda Milner made one of the most famous finding of this type in Montreal, in the 1950s, when she identified the importance of the hippocampus (a structure in the forebrain, *see* Vol. 2, pp. 20–39) for memory. She was researching the effects of damage to this structure when she discovered that people with this type of injury could not learn some types of new knowledge. Thus it appeared that the hippocampus was crucial for storing new information and for consolidating new memories. Short-term memory is not affected by the removal of the hippocampus, suggesting it is an interim depository for long-term memory (*see* Vol. 4, pp. 78–93) that processes information before it is stored permanently in the cerebral cortex (*see* Vol. 2, pp. 20–39), or that it is a device for creating associations between events and memories.

Neuropsychologists have also carried out important work on patients with selective disorders of object recognition, such as the inability to recognize faces (prosopagnosia). Selective losses of categories of knowledge (for example, selective impairment of knowledge about animate objects) were first described in detail in the 1970s by Elizabeth Warrington in London, England. This type of work is also associated with Ennio DeRenzi and Andy Young in the 1980s.

Brain regions
Psychologists need to be cautious about how they interpret neuropsychological findings. Neuropsychologists might suggest that some areas in the brain are "centers" for face recognition, memory, or language, but making an intellectual leap like this requires several assumptions. One obvious problem is that we may be seeing an injury to just one part of a widespread network in the brain—one in which all of the parts perform the task of face memory, recognition, or language by their combined action. If a series of brain

regions participate in a given process, then damage to any of them will disrupt the person's ability to do that task (though probably in different ways). Rather than jumping to conclusions about "centers," researchers should seek to identify the many different brain regions linked to a given function and understand their individual contributions. Much of the important work in neuropsychology has been in understanding the way in which several brain regions contribute to forming a "functional system," a concept introduced by neuropsychologist Alexander Luria (1902–1977) in the 1960s.

THE LATEST DEVELOPMENTS
During the 1970s and 1980s it became increasingly clear to some cognitive psychologists that neurological patients offer an excellent method for testing various theories of cognitive function— and before long the hybrid discipline of cognitive neuropsychology emerged. This new field involves both cognitive psychologists and neuropsychologists, and developed initially in Europe (especially Britain and Italy), but has since had a dramatic effect worldwide.

Many cognitive psychologists were attracted by the opportunities offered by

H. M. AND AMNESIA

CASE STUDY

Several classic cases have been reported of dramatic and extremely severe amnesias. The best known is the case of H. M., who had an operation on the brain for the relief of epilepsy in 1953. He has been repeatedly tested for almost 50 years, so psychologists know more about him than perhaps any other patient in the world.

Though H. M. retains most of the details of his life before 1953, he suffered a severe loss of the ability to form new memories. Day after day he will do the same jigsaws and read the same magazines, and he cannot report any new events after a break of, say, half an hour. When he moved, he was unable to find his way to his new home. He can remember only a few personalities who became known after 1953 (some, such as Elvis

Presley, seem to be sufficiently well known and unusual to be slightly familiar to him). Thus he has a profound amnesia: a loss of the ability to encode new memories (especially personal, so-called episodic, knowledge).

H. M.'s memory for many kinds of material remains the same, however. He still knows what a dog is (semantic knowledge), for example, and he is capable of learning a new skill such as juggling (procedural knowledge). He also has a normal ability to retain information for very short periods (for example, to repeat sentences and digits). Consequently, he can hold an almost normal conversation as long as the contents of the discussion don't refer back beyond a few seconds. Shortly afterward, however, he will completely forget that the conversation has taken place.

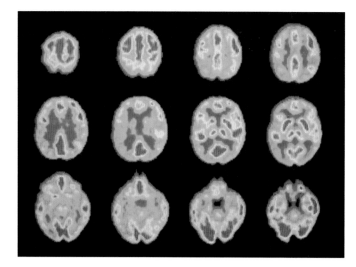

years the only available method was to wait until the patient died and then perform an autopsy, which had major disadvantages—especially since it could be years, or even decades, before the patient died. The solution to this problem has come with techniques that allow us to view, or "image," the brain in a living person (*see* pp. 96–103).

The new technology

Technological changes have enabled scientists to observe brain activity in neurologically healthy subjects and to visualize which areas of the brain are more active when a person is involved in a particular mental task. Although in many ways this is a different method from that of traditional neuropsychology, the basic clinicoanatomical principle is the same whether a person has a neurological disorder or not. If a person has a disorder, the researcher links the loss of function to an injury in the brain. If the subject is free from neurological disease, the researcher links brain function to a site of activation.

A final change in neuropsychology began in the 1990s, with an increasing interest in the long-neglected issue of emotion, much of it led by Antonio Damasio at the University of Iowa. The most exciting aspects of this work have been the startling demonstrations of the key role that emotions play in various aspects of cognition such as memory or language. This area of research has also enabled psychologists to investigate a range of "psychiatric" disorders, such as autism, depression, and schizophrenia, for which the neurological basis may lie in the realm of emotions—and discoveries about the basis of these disorders present a real possibility of finding new treatments.

studying psychological processes (such as language and thinking) with neurological patients. The appeal lay especially in the selective nature of the neuropsychological deficits suffered by patients and the fact that the disturbances were so dramatic. H. M.'s memory deficit, for example (*see* box p. 94), affects only one class of memory, and his memory is so poor that he can recall almost nothing after a few minutes. The evidence produced by this sort of investigation is typically far more striking than that produced in traditional cognitive psychology experiments, where effects are measured in reaction time differences of a few milliseconds.

In addition to the arrival of cognitive neuropsychology, other changes in the discipline have come about because of technological improvements. The clinico-anatomical method (*see* p. 92) has always required scientists to collect "anatomical" information from patients, but the techniques have changed greatly in the history of neuropsychology. In the early

Rapid developments in technology have enabled psychologists to observe brain activity in healthy subjects. These are the color-coded results of a PET scan made while the subject was involved in various mental tasks, showing the different sites of brain activation.

CONNECTIONS

- Brain-imaging Techniques: pp. 96–103
- Cognitive Psychology: pp. 104–117
- Biology of the Brain: Vol. 2, pp. 20–39

- The Mind: Vol. 2, pp. 40–61
- Emotion and Motivation: Vol. 2, pp. 86–109
- Attention and Information Processing: Vol. 3, pp. 24–43
- Storing Information: Vol. 3, pp. 88–113
- Language Processing: Vol. 3, pp. 114–135

Brain-imaging Techniques

"...seeing the brain think..."

Thales

Brain-imaging began in the 1920s, when Hans Berger first measured electric impulses from the human scalp. Since then new and improved techniques for seeing the brain at work have helped doctors study brain disease and psychologists pinpoint precise areas of activity.

Sixty years ago if you had told brain scientists that by the end of the 20th century they would be able to image the living human brain, they might have been doubtful. At that time they could ethically study only animal brains at work. Since then several ground-breaking techniques have been invented that image the workings of the human brain—and possibly the human mind. They have been crucial in our understanding of how the human brain processes movements

> *"Welcome to the human brain, the cathedral of complexity."*
> — P. Coveney & R. Highfield, 1995

and sensations, and how it learns and maintains cognitive capacities such as language, memory, and attention. Brain-imaging techniques have also helped psychologists understand what is happening in the brains of people with mental disorders (*see* Vol. 6, pp. 20–67), and such knowledge may eventually lead to ways of treating these people.

Techniques

There are several brain-imaging (also called neuroimaging or functional imaging) techniques that can be used to study the human brain. The earliest, called electroencephalography (EEG), measures electrical activity emitted from the brain's surface and was first used in the 1920s. A related technique developed in the 1970s—magnetoencephalography (MEG)

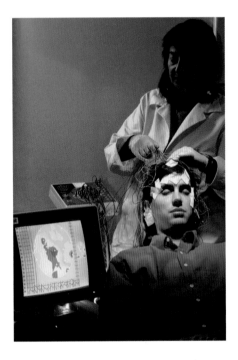

This researcher is carrying out an EEG scan: a technique pioneered by Hans Berger in the 1920s. By recording electric impulses at the scalp, she can then view a computer-generated image of her scan: The areas with the greatest levels of activity show up as red and orange.

—measures the magnetic fields generated by brain activity. More recent techniques such as positron emission tomography (PET), single photon emission computed tomography (SPECT), and functional magnetic resonance imaging (fMRI) measure the blood flow in the brain.

All of these techniques are noninvasive, which means they can be used to study the living human brain and to reveal abnormal brain patterns without surgery.

Electrical and magnetic fields

The human brain contains about 100 billion nerve cells called neurons (see p. 36), which connect to other nerve cells by means of long fibers (dendrites and axons). Like all cells in the body, neurons act like tiny batteries. There is a voltage difference (nearly one-tenth of a volt) between the inside and the outside of the cell, with the inside usually carrying a more negative charge. When a neuron is activated, positively charged sodium ions rush in through pores in the neuron's

> *"Impressions arriving at the brain make it enter into activity, just as food falling into the stomach excites it to more abundant secretion of gastric juice."*
> — *Pierre Cabanis, 1757–1808*

membrane, briefly reversing the voltage and causing the neuron to "fire" an impulse, or action potential.

The voltage changes inside active neurons produce tiny electrical fields that radiate through brain tissue, the skull, and the skin, and can be picked up through electrodes stuck to the surface of the scalp: This is an EEG recording. Magnetic fields accompanying the electrical fields also radiate through the skull, and they can be measured with sensitive magnetic field

detectors to produce an MEG recording. Both EEG and MEG measure activity from populations of neurons and require thousands of neurons to be active to detect a signal and produce an image.

Electroencephalography

Hans Berger was the first to measure electrical activity at the scalp (*see* box below). He used two large sheets of tin foil (which served as electrodes), placed them around his son's scalp, and recorded a rhythmic pattern of electrical activity arising from the boy's brain. This was the moment-by-moment electrical response of cells near the surface of the brain.

In the 1950s—using small electrodes instead of tin foil—hospitals began to routinely use EEG to detect abnormalities in brain function caused by head injuries, brain tumors, infections in the brain, epileptic seizures, and sleep disorders. More recently, further technological advances—such as the introduction of fine-grain electrodes, more powerful computers, and conducting gel—have increased the ability of EEG to measure brain activity, and researchers can now record activity from the entire head simultaneously on a millisecond timescale. Today EEG is widely used around the

---

HANS BERGER

BIOGRAPHY

Hans Berger (1873–1941) was born in Germany. After gaining his doctorate in 1897, he became an assistant in a psychiatric hospital where Oscar Vogt and Korbinian Brodmann were working. Vogt and Brodmann were well-known pioneers of brain research, and they encouraged Berger to join in their work on brain localization—identifying regions of the brain by function. Berger was also influenced by the work of Richard Caton, a British surgeon who was studying nerve impulses in animals, and began studying electrical activity in the human brain. He made the first EEG recording of the brain in 1924, using his son Klaus as the subject.

Over the next decade Berger made many discoveries from EEG recordings. He found that brain waves oscillate at about 10 cycles per second when the eyes are closed and a person is relaxed, and he named this pattern alpha waves. During a period of mental activity when the eyes are open, alpha waves are replaced by beta waves, which move faster. In the 1930s Berger found that alpha waves diminish during sleep, general anesthesia, and cocaine stimulation, and that their frequency decreases in patients with brain injury and increases in epileptic patients. Later, when he was able to use more sensitive equipment, Berger recorded EEGs from infants, discovering that brain waves begin to appear at about two months of age. This corresponds to the time when brain neurons become sheathed in myelin, a substance critical to neural activity. Berger is known as the father of EEG for his work.

world in neuropsychological research and to detect and diagnose abnormalities in brain function.

In a typical EEG experiment between 1 and 240 electrodes are stuck to a subject's scalp. The electrodes are made of a conductive metal, such as gold or tin, and are attached to the scalp in a coating of conductive gel (salt solution), which maximizes the amount of electrical activity picked up. They feed into a sensitive amplifier that records the electrical impulses from each electrode. A computer then transforms these measurements into a scalp-shaped, multicolored image that can be displayed on screen. Different colors on the image indicate the different levels of electrical activity (that is, neuronal firing) in the brain.

Event-related potentials (ERPs)

To investigate the areas of the brain activated by a particular psychological or sensory stimulus, psychologists often use EEG to record event-related potentials (*see* box p. 99). EEG provides a constant measure of electrical activity in the brain, while an event-related potential (ERP) is an electrical response that occurs at a fixed time relative to a particular stimulus, such as a tone, a word, or an image (the event). These changes in electrical activity may occur at the same time or immediately after a given event.

To understand the concept, imagine a simple stimulus such as a single tone. If you recorded the brain activity following the sounding of this tone, you would have recorded a brain-evoked, event-related potential. That is to say, you would have recorded the voltage fluctuations induced in the brain by the event (the tone). Such changes in activity are tiny, so to see any

In an EEG scan electrodes attached to the scalp detect brain activity by measuring electrical currents in the brain cells. This produces a continuing measure of activity over time, and the information is converted into images that can be displayed on a computer screen.

reliable effects, researchers must present the same stimulus many times and record the average response, or ERP.

Magnetoencephalography (MEG)

The electric currents produced by brain activity generate tiny magnetic fields. If subjects are studied in a magnetically shielded room, it is possible to measure these fields using sensitive detectors—a technique called MEG. This method only became possible with the development of the superconducting quantum interference device (SQUID), an ultrasensitive detector of magnetic flux introduced by James Zimmerman in the late 1960s. David Cohen carried out the first successful measurements of magnetic brain activity in 1968. He showed that the alpha rhythm, a spontaneous brain activity originally discovered using EEG (*see* box p. 97), could also be detected magnetically. Measurements made in this way are called magnetoencephalograms (MEGs). In the first MEG experiment in 1975 subjects were presented with visual stimuli while scientists measured the magnetic fields on their scalps. The experiment showed that there were magnetic responses at the back

KEY DATES

1920s Hans Berger records the first EEGs from his son's scalp.

1932 Charles Sherrington receives the Nobel Prize in Medicine for his work on animals' brains.

1950s Radioactive substances are used to create images of the brain: positron emission topography (PET).

1968 David Cohen successfully produces the first magnetic measurements of brain activity: magnetoencephalograms (MEGs).

1980s–1990s Major technological advances are made in brain-imaging techniques, enabling scientists to use MEG and fMRI for brain research.

of the brain, which is where the visual cortex lies (an area previously identified from animal research and from studying human patients with damage to that region). Since then MEG measurements have been used clinically to characterize the magnetic abnormalities accompanying a wide variety of brain diseases and to investigate the normal workings of the human brain (*see* box below right).

> *"How the brain behaves in health and disease may well be the most important question in our lifetime."*
> — *Richard Broadwell, 1995*

EEG versus MEG

There are several differences between EEG and MEG, the main one being the "orientation" of neuron activity they measure. The electric and magnetic fields arising from neurons in any one brain area radiate in different directions: The electric field radiates in all directions, while the magnetic field arising from the same activity comes off at right angles to the neurons. This means that MEG is more sensitive to neurons with a certain orientation (such as those that lie in the brain's folds, or sulci) and less sensitive to others (such as those on the surface). Another difference between EEG and MEG is the strength of the nerve signal they measure. Electrical activity is reduced as it passes through the brain tissue and skull, while magnetic fields are not. Therefore the signals measured by EEG are slightly weaker than the signals measured by MEG.

EEG and MEG both record brain activity on a millisecond timescale, an interval of measurement that no other brain-imaging tool can match. For this reason many discoveries involving the processing of sensory and cognitive processes have been reported using both EEG and MEG. Both methods have limits,

EXPERIMENT

A TYPICAL ERP EXPERIMENT

A classic example of an ERP experiment investigates how the brain responds to inappropriate stimuli. For example, you would expect the sentence "I like my coffee with cream and…" to end with the word "sugar." An inappropriate version of the sentence would contain an unexpected word such as "cement" instead of the predictable word "sugar." By presenting subjects with a series of sentences—some containing predictable words, and some unexpected ones—and recording the ERPs, researchers can contrast the electrical activity that occurs when subjects hear appropriate words with the activity that occurs when they hear inappropriate ones.

Marta Kutas and Steven Hillyard performed this experiment in the 1980s at the University of California in San Diego. They found that when subjects were presented with an unexpected word, there was additional activity in the brain. They called this event-related brain activity the N400 wave because it was a negative ERP (at the sides of the brain) that occurred 400 ms after the stimulus was presented. This suggested that the brain has a system that reacts to unexpected stimulation, helping people respond to errors or signals for attention.

EXPERIMENT

A TYPICAL MEG EXPERIMENT

Let's say a researcher wants to study the brain activity that occurs when a subject processes musical chords that do not harmonize. The subject would remove any metal objects that might interfere with the magnetic fields produced, sit or lie in the MEG scanner, and the researcher would play a series of musical chords while the MEG scanner recorded magnetic activity from the subject's brain. Some of the chords would be harmonious, and some would not, and the magnetic fields associated with each type of chord would later be distinguished using sophisticated statistical analysis.

Burkhard Maess and colleagues performed this experiment in 2001 at the Max Planck Institute for Cognitive Neuroscience in Leipzig, Germany. They found that when a subject heard inappropriate harmonic chords, there was an extra activation at the sides of the brain (a negative magnetic field) in the area that processes language in the left frontal cortex (Broca's area, *see* box p. 93) and its equivalent on the right. As in the experiment in the box above, this suggested that the brain is constantly predicting what will happen and looking out for unexpected information, such as chords that sound out of place in a melody.

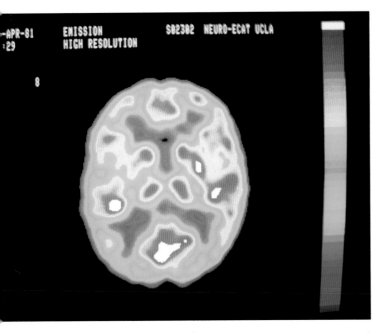

EMISSION
HIGH RESOLUTION
-APR-81
:29
S82382   NEURO-ECAT UCLA
8

Prize for Physiology or Medicine for his work. The main brain-imaging techniques that measure blood flow are positron emission tomography (PET), single photon emission computed tomography (SPECT), and functional magnetic resonance imaging (fMRI). The principle underlying all three is the tight coupling of neuron activity with glucose and oxygen metabolism.

Positron emission tomography (PET)

The history of positron emission tomography (PET) dates back to the early 1950s, when researchers at Harvard University discovered that it was possible to produce images of radioactive substances. PET measures the volume and location of blood flow in the body by tracking radioactively labeled chemicals (called "tracer chemicals") injected into the subject's bloodstream. These tracers emit positrons (minute particles with a positive charge), and a radiation detector camera surrounding the subject's head tracks where in the subject's brain the positrons are emitted.

however. First, EEG and MEG have a relatively low spatial resolution—they measure activity arising from several centimeters of brain tissue. Second, it is difficult to accurately localize the source of the electrical or magnetic activity arising from within the brain. Third, EEG and MEG measure activity mainly from the cortical regions: the areas of the brain that lie near the surface. It is much harder to measure neuron activity in the deep structures in the brain.

Measuring blood flow

The limitations of EEG and MEG can be overcome using other techniques that measure blood flow in the working brain. When a population of neurons becomes activated, these cells require an increased flow of blood to replenish their supply of oxygen and glucose, which they depend on for energy. A regular supply is crucial for normal brain function—in fact, the brain uses one-fifth of all the energy produced by the body. In the 1880s the British physiologist Sir Charles Sherrington was the first to suggest this link between brain metabolism and a local increase in blood flow. In 1932 he was awarded the Nobel

The color-coded results of a positron emission tomography (PET) scan—displayed as a 2-D "slice" through the brain—showing the volume and location of blood flow.

> *"Swiftly the brain becomes an enchanted loom, where millions of flashing shuttles weave a dissolving pattern, always a meaningful pattern though never an abiding one."*
> — *Sir Charles Sherrington, 1941*

PET studies normally involve inserting a small needle into a vein in the subject's arm. The needle is then attached to a driplike device that is used to introduce a radioactive tracer into the subject's bloodstream. Different compounds can be introduced, and they can show blood flow, oxygen and glucose metabolism, or the location and concentrations of drugs or naturally occurring brain chemicals (neurotransmitters) in the tissues of the working brain. High-powered computers then use the PET data to produce

CT SCANNING

Computed tomography (also called CT scanning) is another diagnostic technique that combines the technology of X-rays and computers. It produces static, cross-sectional images of the brain or body, revealing structure but not function. The term tomography comes from the Greek word *tomos,* meaning "slice," and *graphia,* which means "describing."

The technique was invented in 1972 by British engineer Godfrey Hounsfield and independently by South African born physicist Allan Cormack. It was originally used to image the brain. During a scan patients pass through a doughnut-shaped scanner containing an x-ray tube and a detector, which rotate around them. Lead shutters focus the X-rays on a tissue thickness of 1–10 mm. During each 360 degree rotation the detector takes numerous profiles, or snapshots, of the x-ray beam—usually about 1,000—which a computer combines to form a single 2-D image.

CT scans provide detailed images of the body's soft tissues and can be manipulated by an operator to provide the best view of the area. The 2-D slices can also be put together to create a 3-D image. Images are similar to those produced by MRI scans but provide less contrast between normal and abnormal tissue and between white and gray matter in the brain.

multicolored images that show where the blood flowed, which researchers use to study brain activity during different experimental tasks and conditions. The PET camera surrounding the subject's head is capable of producing 3-D images, but researchers often show the areas of activation as 2-D "slices" (*see* image p. 100) so that people can see exactly where in the brain the activation occurred.

PET is widely used in hospitals to detect abnormal blood flow in the brain, which can occur with epilepsy, brain tumors, and Alzheimer's dementia, and after a stroke. It is also used to detect tumors in other body organs. Psychologists also use PET to evaluate human brain function.

Single photon emission (SPECT)
Single photon emission computed tomography (SPECT) is an imaging technique similar to PET. Like PET, it uses radioactive tracers and a scanner to record data from which a computer constructs 3-D images of active brain regions. SPECT tracers are more limited than PET tracers in the kinds of activity they can monitor, however, and they are less powerful, which means that SPECT studies require longer test and retest periods than PET studies. SPECT has some advantages, however, because it requires fewer medical and technical staff and is much cheaper.

Magnetic resonance imaging (MRI)
Magnetic resonance imaging (MRI) uses a large magnetic field to produce high-quality, 3-D images of brain structure without the need for radioactive tracers. These days researchers use a large cylindrical magnet to create a magnetic field around the subject's head and then send radio waves through the magnetic field. Different structures and tissues in

This woman is undergoing a positron emission tomography (PET) scan, which is used to measure blood flow in the brain. The data are translated into a multicolored image showing areas of activation.

"Jedi" helmets used by Ian Young in 1984 to obtain MRI readings from a child's brain. The coils around the helmets acted as "aerials" that picked up the magnetic signals. Helmets such as these are no longer used in MRI today.

the brain, such as white matter, gray matter, cerebrospinal fluid, and bone, have different magnetic properties, and the radio waves make their component particles appear differently on the MRI image. A computer uses this information to construct an image. A single MRI scan produces many static 2-D "slices" of the brain, and by putting these slices together, a computer can produce a complete 3-D image of the brain, showing images of

> "New advances in neuroscience will yield increased understanding of how the brain functions and of more effective treatments to heal brain disorders and diseases."
> — Richard Broadwell, 1995

both surface and deep brain structures in great anatomical detail. MRI is often used in hospitals to detect minute changes in brain structure and to detect strokes, hemorrhages, and brain tumors.

In contrast to PET images, which show activity patterns over a period of time, MRI scans are a series of static images. In the 1980s and 1990s, however, techniques were developed that enabled scientists to use MRI to image the brain at work: a process known as functional MRI or fMRI. When neurons become active, they need an oxygenated supply of blood: The fMRI scanner can detect the oxygen

because it is magnetic. So, in the same way that PET measures the amount of blood flowing to particular regions in the brain, fMRI measures the amount of oxygenated blood sent to particular regions in the brain. This information is used to make "films" of changes in brain activity as people perform tasks or experience sensory stimuli (*see* box p. 103).

Comparison of PET and fMRI

There are several advantages of fMRI over PET. First, fMRI does not involve exposing subjects to ionizing radiation, so people of all ages, including children, can be scanned on numerous occasions without any harmful side effects. Second, fMRI has a much higher temporal resolution (the interval of time between measurements) than PET. PET usually takes 40 seconds or longer to image brain activity, while an fMRI scan can produce images every second. Thus fMRI can show us when brain regions become active and how long they remain active with greater precision than PET, assessing blood flow and brain function in seconds. Third, fMRI has a higher spatial resolution than PET, producing high-quality images that can distinguish structures less than 1mm

A doctor examining magnetic resonance images (MRI) of a person's head: The brain is clearly visible and is viewed from different angles. MRI scans show structures in the brain with a great deal of precision.

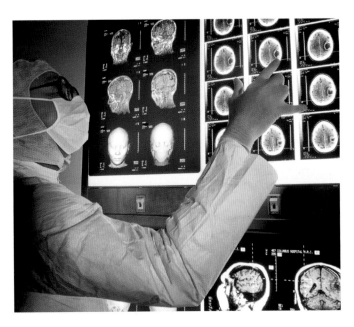

A TYPICAL fMRI EXPERIMENT

If you look at the image on the right, you will see either a young woman or an old lady; rarely will you see both at the same time. The question is, which parts of the brain are responsible for the switch between the two images?

Let's say a psychologist wants to use fMRI to test which areas of the brain interpret ambiguous figures like this one. After ensuring that the subject removes all metal objects and puts in earplugs before lying in the scanner (which is important for safety reasons), the researcher would show the subject several ambiguous figures while the scanner continuously scanned the brain. The subject would indicate the moment at which an image switched by pressing a button. By analyzing the timings of the button presses, the researcher could then find out where oxygenated blood flowed to in the subject's brain at the exact moment of the switch.

Andreas Kleinschmidt and his colleagues at University College, London, England, carried out this experiment in the late 1990s. They found that during the perceptual switch from one image to the other, transient activation occurred in the areas of the visual cortex that process

high-level aspects of a visual scene, such as whole objects (in contrast to lower-level areas, which process single aspects such as color, shape, or movement).

apart, while the latest PET scanners can only resolve images of structures within about 5mm of each other.

There are some disadvantages of fMRI. It is extremely loud, so the subject must wear earplugs, and it is more enclosed than the PET scanner, which can be a problem for claustrophobic people. Also, fMRI images can be contaminated by even a tiny head movement, which can disturb the scanner's magnetic field. This makes PET more suitable for studies of large movements or speaking. PET can also identify which brain receptors are being activated by neurotransmitters, drugs, and potential treatment chemicals, which is beyond the scope of fMRI.

Multimodal brain imaging

Each brain-imaging technique has its own advantages, and each provides different information about the brain's structure and functions. An advantage of EEG over PET and fMRI is speed—EEG can record complex patterns of neuronal activity occurring within fractions of a second of a stimulus being presented. But while EEG has a much higher temporal resolution, its biggest drawback is that it provides less spatial resolution (the size of the area that can be measured is less). Thus researchers are starting to combine the techniques of EEG and fMRI to combine the advantages of both and pinpoint more accurately where activity occurs in the brain.

CONNECTIONS

• Neuropsychology: pp. 90–95
• Cognitive Psychology: pp. 104–117

• Psycholinguistics, pp. 118–125
• Biology of the Brain: Volume 2, pp. 20–39
• Attention & Information Processing: Volume 3, pp. 24–43
• Mental Disorders: Volume 6, pp. 20–67

Cognitive Psychology

—— *"Cognition is the...acquisition, organization, and use of knowledge."* ——

Ulric Neiseer

Cognitive psychology emerged in the late 1950s as researchers developed theories based on the idea of the mind as an information-processing device. They believed that stimulation received by the senses was transformed into some kind of internal representation that the mind could interpret, store, and act on. Sometimes the definition was broadened to include studies of how computers worked, which psychologists then compared with their models of brain function.

Cognitive psychology is closely tied to the study of the physiology of the brain and nervous system, and to the study of artificial intelligence (AI) in computers. Sometimes experimental cognitive psychology, physiological psychology, and the study of artificial intelligence are combined under the heading of cognitive science.

Cognitive psychologists divide thinking into separate processes, such as attention, perception, memory storage, memory recall, decision-making, and problem solving. The lines between these areas are hard to draw, and the different areas often interact. For example, perception depends on memory recall to identify the thing being perceived, while problem solving draws on a perception of the problem and memories of previous solutions.

KEY POINTS

- Cognitive psychologists study thought processes, including perception, memory, problem solving, decision-making, and the use of language.
- Modern cognitive psychology arose partly because scientists noticed the similarity between the ways the mind and a computer process information.
- The cognitive revolution began partly a reaction against the behaviorists, who insisted that researchers could not study unobservable mental processes in a scientific manner.
- Experiments in cognitive psychology still measure outward behavior, however, examining the way subjects perform simple tasks to reveal the processes going on inside their minds.

The words cognitive and cognition come from the Latin *co* (intensive) and *gnoscere* (to know), and the study of thinking and knowing goes back to the very beginnings of psychology, when

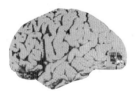

Left: Brain activity as sight lights up the occipital cortex at the back of the brain.

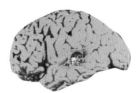

Left: Brain activity as hearing lights up the auditory area in the temporal cortex.

PET scans of the side of the cerebral cortex, with the front of the brain to the left.

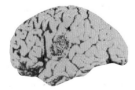

Left: Activity as speaking lights up the speech centers in the insula and motor cortex.

Left: Thinking about verbs and saying them activates speech, auditory, temporal, and parietal areas.

ancient Greek philosophers tried to explain thought processes (*see* pp. 10–15). Plato (about 428–348 B.C.) theorized about memory, saying it was like writing on wax tablets—although he had no understanding of how memories were really stored by the brain.

The modern science of psychology began with philosophers of the late 19th century who carefully analyzed their own thought processes. It became a science when Wilhelm Wundt (1832–1920) began to conduct systematic experiments on thought and conscious experiences using "introspection" as his method (*see* pp. 30–39). In the early 1920s the behaviorists (*see* pp. 74–89) rejected introspection, saying that researchers should deal only

> *"During the high tide of behaviorism experimental psychology focused on relatively simple cognitive performance.... The intelligence of rats and pigeons received as much attention as the intelligence of people."*
> — *H. Simon & C. Kaplan, 1989*

with what could be directly observed and measured in the form of stimuli and responses, or behavior. The behaviorists said "mind" was something no one could observe or measure, and they tried to explain all human and animal behavior as being built up from a collection of simple conditioned reflexes. For John B. Watson, the founder of behaviorism, thinking in words was merely an echo of physiological activity in the vocal apparatus, while he considered images and sounds to be echoes of bodily processes.

THE COGNITIVE REVOLUTION
Despite some resistance to these ideas, behaviorism dominated psychology until the late 1950s. Then, in the early 1960s there was a slow build up to what some people called the cognitive revolution.

The first factor that had contributed to this return to cognition was the rise of the Gestalt school of psychology (*see* pp. 46–51). Gestalt psychologists had showed through experiment that some perceptual patterns and structures possess more qualities as a whole than the sum of their individually considered parts, which seemed at variance with the behaviorist idea that perception was simply a collection of conditioned responses.

Another influence on cognitive research began with discoveries in neurosurgery during World War II (1939–1945), when many people suffered head injuries that destroyed parts of their brains. Doctors examining these patients found that injuries to specific parts of the brain resulted in the loss of specific abilities (*see* pp. 90–95). For example, damage to the frontal cortex could result in the loss of speech but leave understanding intact, while damage to the temporal lobes could result in the loss of long-term memory. These and similar discoveries suggested that various mental processes were carried out in separate parts of the brain, so the idea that every aspect of human behavior was built up from a series of conditioned reflexes became even more suspect.

Another development that occurred during the war was the emergence of the digital computer. Some researchers believed that if they could model thought processes on the way a computer worked,

KEY DATES

1948 An influential conference based on the workings of the nervous system provides a forum for the theories of Karl S. Lashley and John von Neumann.

1948 Norbert Weiner's book *Cybernetics* is published.

1956 A conference on information theory is held at M.I.T., and Noam Chomsky presents his paper "Three Models of Language."

1957 Herbert Simon and Allen Newell create the General Problem Solver, an intelligent computer.

1980s David Rumelhart and James McClelland develop parallel distributed processing models of cognition.

1982 David Marr publishes *Vision*, containing ideas developed by John Anderson.

1983 Jerry Fodor publishes *The Modality of Mind*.

it might also help them understand how the mind worked (*see* pp. 126–133).

Historians of science point to two events that finally launched the cognitive revolution. The first was a conference on the workings of the nervous system in 1948, at which Karl S. Lashley (1890–1958)—a psychologist associated with behaviorism—argued that behaviorism could not adequately explain many psychological phenomena.

Lashley used language as his main example. To speak a sentence, he said, a person has to begin with an intention and have an overall plan for what is to be said. Slips of the tongue such as "the blight of the fumble bee" for "the flight of the bumble bee" indicate that the brain has the entire sentence in mind before the speaker gives voice to it. The behaviorist view that one word served as the cue for

the next could not explain such things. Lashley then laid out a plan for many phenomena that psychologists should study that behaviorism had ignored.

Mathematician John von Neumann (1903–1957) also spoke at the same conference, suggesting parallels between the way that information is processed in a computer and in the human brain. He proposed that actions of both the brain and the computer are based on data received from the environment and processed in the light of internal rules.

The second event was a conference on information theory held in 1956 at the Massachusetts Institute of Technology, where many parallels were drawn between the brain and the computer. It was also at this conference that linguist Noam Chomsky (*see* pp. 118–122) presented a paper titled "Three Models of Language"

NORBERT WEINER AND CYBERNETICS

BIOGRAPHY

During World War II Norbert Weiner (1894–1964), a professor of mathematics at Massachusetts Institute of Technology, worked on mechanisms for the control and aiming of weapons. Most of these systems used feedback, meaning that they would try to aim at a particular target, would then receive information about how close they had come, and would reaim based on this information.

Weiner came to realize that people also use feedback systems. When you reach for a pencil, for example, your eyes supply information on the pencil's location, while your brain and nervous system send commands to your arm and hand to move to that position. As your hand moves toward the pencil, your eyes send back continuous reports, enabling your nervous system to make finer adjustments until you zero in on your intended target.

Weiner launched a new science that he called "cybernetics" to study the process of command and control in both people and machines. The word came from the Greek word for "steersman." He set forth his ideas in a highly influential book called *Cybernetics*, published in 1948. While these ideas did not remain central to cognitive science, early work in the field drew attention to the parallels between the human mind and the computer, and brought psychologists and engineers

together in collaborative projects. And Weiner's proposal that the mind participated in controlling action through a feedback process was another argument against the simple stimulus-response theory of behaviorism.

This photograph, taken in about 1958, shows Dr. Norbert Weiner lecturing at M.I.T. Weiner could read and write at the age of three, and by the age of 18 he had received a Ph.D. from Harvard.

that described an approach to grammar in which language exhibited a structure that shared many formal aspects of math.

Behaviorism and cognition

This return to the study of thought did not mean that psychologists rejected behaviorism entirely. While there was some limited use of introspection, cognitive psychologists also found ways to conduct rigorous objective experiments that measured outward behavior but revealed the inner workings of the mind. They also retained the behaviorists' insistence that all thought is carried out by physical mechanisms in the mind and nervous system, and that there is no need to postulate a mystical "mind" that was somehow separate from the body.

> *"The transformations which take place between our ears are the missing links needed to account for the regularities between stimulus and response."*
> — *Owen Flanagan, 1991*

While behaviorists had rejected any idea of mental imagery, cognitive psychologists proposed that thinking begins with the creation of a mental representation of an idea or perception, and that this is the basis for further processing. They assumed that, like a computer, the mind would break each process into a series of steps, and their research sought to find out what those steps might be. Sometimes they drew flow charts to illustrate their theories: For example, between the stimulus and the response observed by the behaviorist the cognitive psychologist might see:

perception ▸ attention ▸ memory retrieval ▸ decision-making ▸ memory storage ▸ action.

According to a cognitive psychologist, a student might look at the top of a desk, perceive a book, focus attention on it, retrieve memories associated with books,

and identify it as a textbook for the day's class, bringing up the memory that an assignment is due. The student then opens the book and begins to study, meanwhile storing in memory the location of the book so that it can be put back later. Of

EXPERIMENT

TOP DOWN AND BOTTOM UP

In identifying what you see or hear, does the mind simply operate on the input until it finds sense, or does it impose its own experience early on in the processing?

• Psychologists generally divide perception into two types— "top-down" and "bottom-up" processing.

• Bottom-up processing is driven by the incoming stimulus, which is processed and fed into consciousness without any attached meaning. Top-down processing involves higher levels of consciousness from the beginning, for example, when we draw on memory to identify the thing perceived.

• Psychologists still debate whether pure bottom-up processing even exists, but it is certainly present in lower animals. In a frog, for example, much visual processing takes place in the retina of the eye, and the image of a fly, or any other small object, will automatically trigger the frog's tongue to attack.

Experiments in top-down processing

The concept of top-down processing is demonstrated by experiments that show that context influences the things people perceive. Thus people look at or listen to other things around the particular thing being perceived and apply their experience to help determine meaning.

In one experiment subjects heard one of the following:
The cobbler said that the *eel was still on the shoe.
The cook said that the *eel was still on the orange.
The projectionist said that the *eel was still on the projector.
The mechanic said that the *eel was still on the car.
In each case the asterisk represents a sound that was edited out of the recording and replaced with a cough. The researchers found that most subjects did not report that anything was missing. Instead, they reported that they heard the words heel, peel, reel, or wheel depending on which sentence they heard.

THEY CHME

Left A partially deformed letter is seen differently depending on the word in which it appears.

course, the actual process is not usually such a straight line. Perception usually involves retrieving information from memory, and attention may be influenced by the results of a decision.

Perception and attention

Perception is the process by which people interpret the stimuli that their sense organs report. As you read this book, your eyes report the page as a pattern of light and dark, but your brain separates the individual words and attaches meaning to them. Psychologists have studied visual perception the most—perhaps because it is accessible and easy to confirm—but it appears that the same general rules also apply to the perception of sound, touch, smell, and taste.

> *"The task of a psychologist trying to understand human cognition is analogous to that of a man trying to discover how a computer has been programmed.... He will not care much how his particular computer stores information...he wants to understand the program, not the hardware."*
>
> — *Ulric Neisser, 1967*

Visual perception is far from simple, as computer scientists trying to build "seeing" robots have discovered. Studies of brain physiology show that tasks such as recognizing vertical and horizontal lines, identifying corners, and detecting motion seem to require the use of separate areas of the brain—thus some psychologists think it is likely that a great deal of processing takes place below conscious awareness. For example, some people with damage to the area of the brain that processes messages from the eye report a total lack of vision, and yet they are able to avoid obstacles of which they are not consciously aware: a phenomenon called "blindsight." In laboratory experiments

Driving requires a great deal of mental processing because the driver has to operate the vehicle and process numerous pieces of information about the roads and traffic. As the driver gains experience, much more of this processing takes place below the level of conscious awareness.

people presented with stimuli so faint or brief as to be unaware of them can still make use of what they have not actively "seen." In one experiment, for example, subjects were presented with brief flashes of images. Although unable to report what they saw, when asked to guess what color an image might have been, more subjects guessed correctly than random chance predicted, indicating that vision might be more than the ability to process information about light.

When people see a book, how do they identify it as a book? One explanation might be that they have stored in memory an image of everything they ever saw and compare the new image with the information in their database until they find a match. But this would probably require far more capacity for memory than even the human brain is capable of.

A popular recognition theory is that people store a sort of general idea of a book, which psychologists call a "schema," a view similar to the ancient philosophical idea of Platonic "Forms" (*see* box p. 13). The fact that people can recognize an object from a simple drawing representing the object provides evidence for this theory. For example, a circle, two dots, and an arc in the proper arrangement are enough to indicate a face.

Another theory proposes that what people store is not an image as such but a list of features. A book, for example, is identified by the fact that it is rectangular, has printing on the spine, and so on. This approach works well in explaining why people can recognize a letter of the alphabet when it is presented in many different sizes, printing fonts, or even scrawled in crayon by a four-year-old.

Attention is usually considered part of perception, but how does an organism concentrate on one sight, sound, or idea more than on others in the immediate environment? In laboratory experiments people presented with two different conversations, one fed to each ear through headphones, were easily able to focus on one conversation and report it in detail while ignoring the other. One theory suggests that as information is processed, some mental activities are limited in terms of how much they can handle. Thus parts of the brain slow processing down, almost forcing us to focus on one thing at a time.

Memory

Adding new information or experiences to your mental supply, storing information, and retrieving information when you need it are all aspects of memory, but cognitive studies mainly attempt to determine how memories are stored. Evidence exists for at least three types of storage: The first is a sort of buffer that holds relatively unprocessed visual and audio data from the sense organs; second is the working or short-term memory, which holds a limited amount of information for a few seconds; and last is long-term memory, which is stored more or less permanently.

You can see a common example of the difference between working and long-term memory when you meet a new person. For example, she says, "Hi, I'm Mary Jones." You reply with your own name, and a conversation begins. A few seconds later you might not be able to recall the name you just heard: It was stored in your working memory and has already been replaced by whatever you are talking about now. However, you will still remember meeting Mary and something

about her, since that information is now part of your long-term memory.

Some psychologists believe that the transfer of information from working memory to long-term storage is the result of attention and rehearsal. So instead of replying immediately with your own name, if you repeat Mary's name a few times, perhaps consciously associating it with something she says about herself, you are more likely to remember her name later. Other researchers suggest that linking new information with previously stored data is the key to long-term storage, while others argue that long-term and working storage occur together.

> *"Among the headache-inducing qualities of cognitive psychology are its tremendous range...the huge volume of published research...and the fragmentary and disorganized nature of much of this research. Cognitive psychology often seems to resemble the messenger in* Alice in Wonderland *who went in all directions at once."*
> — *Michael Eysenck, 1984*

Cognitive psychologists usually test these theories in the laboratory by presenting subjects with lists of words to memorize under various conditions. In one experiment they presented subjects with a short list of words, then asked them to count backward for a few seconds before trying to recall the list. When subjects did not count, they could recall words at the beginning and end of the list more often than words in the middle. However, counting made them forget the words at the end of the list but not those at the beginning, suggesting that the words at the end had been in working memory, but that those at the beginning had moved into long-term storage.

Once information is stored in long-term memory, how is it then retrieved?

Different processes seem to be involved depending on whether the task is to recognize the information or to recall it from scratch. An example of a recognition task would be seeing Mary's name in a list and realizing you had met the person with that name. A recall task would require you to remember her name without any cues. In the first case you presumably search your memory supply for the presented stimulus and then retrieve whatever information is stored along with it. In the recall task you might come up with a few candidates, and you would have to test each one to see if it fitted the definition. Experiments have shown that people can generate only a limited number of candidates at one time, which means that when they are searching for a word, they probably do not search sequentially through all of the thousands of words they know. In one experiment researchers used the definition "an instrument used by navigators to measure the angle between a heavenly body and the horizon." People searching for the word that this definition describes can immediately limit their search to words dealing with navigation, the stars, the sun, and perhaps sailing. Hopefully they will then find the word "sextant." Researchers found that subjects who could not quite remember the word were helped when given the first letter, which narrowed the possibilities available.

Distractions can also interfere with the ability to generate candidates. Subjects have more difficulty unscrambling anagrams when the anagram presented resembles another familiar word. So, if the required answer is "orchestra," research has shown that "carthorse" will take longer to unscramble than "sceahtrro." That is because people are diverted by the meaning of carthorse, while the nonsense word has no distracting meaning.

Language

Cognitive psychologists also try to understand the mechanisms by which people produce and understand language (*see* pp. 118–125). Common theories suggest that there are several distinct steps in speech production. First, the speaker organizes the concepts to be presented; then the grammatical structure of the sentence is mentally laid out; and finally individual words are added into the structure. Understanding is thought to follow a similar series of steps. Theories vary as to the number and complexity of these steps, but experiments have shown that speakers do plan ahead.

Evidence also comes from some of the errors speakers make, such as when they transpose a word from near the end of a sentence into an earlier position, as in "I really like the song of the words." By presenting people with short sentences and measuring the time it took to answer simple questions about the sentences, psychologists learned a great deal about the ways in which people produced and understood language. As with perception, they found that context played a vital role in both speaking and understanding.

Problems and decisions

All the different processes discussed so far—perception, memory, and language—come together in problem solving and decision-making: the processes that are part of what people call thinking. The

Language follows a complex series of rules, but the actual language you learn depends on your immediate social group. For example, the nomadic Bedouin people of the Middle Eastern deserts are organized into independent groups that speak different Arabic dialects.

behaviorists had argued that problem solving was merely a trial-and-error process in which successful solutions were reinforced and preserved. Gestalt psychologists had taken the opposite position, insisting that solutions came in a flash of "insight" when the problem solver understood the whole problem. Research by cognitive psychologists has focused on factors that prevent problem solving.

In typical experiments cognitive researchers present subjects with simple logical statements and ask them to draw conclusions. While ideal logic might dictate a certain answer, subjects will not always choose that answer, but may be distracted by irrelevant information. Consider the following for example: A woman wearing a red dress is reading a 20-page story on a train traveling at 60 mph (100km/h); she finishes the story an hour later just as the train stops; how far has the train traveled? The details of the woman's appearance and her actions are not relevant to the problem; all that really matters are the speed of the train and the length of the journey.

Researchers have also studied the ways in which superior problem solvers differ from other people. Problems in chess, for example, seem to depend on a person examining the position of the pieces on the chess board and then considering possible moves and their likely result. Chess masters were found to consider fewer possible moves than less gifted players, but those they did consider were all good ones. Their superior performance seemed to result from a large memory of possible games and an efficient system for sorting through these memories. Thus problem solving and decision-making seem to parallel the mechanism of memory recall: Possible solutions to a problem or possible outcomes of a decision are generated and then compared with the desired outcome. Following this model, computer scientists have had considerable success in creating programs that can solve limited kinds of problems governed by rules.

CASE STUDY

TESTING THE MIND

There is no way that one person can see what is happening inside another's mind, but cognitive psychologists have devised ways to test the mind's invisible functions. Numerous theories of information processing state that many mental tasks consist of a series of separate operations or "modules." One way to test this is to ask subjects to perform a simple task, then to add some component to this task. If subjects still complete the task in the same amount of time, this might mean that no additional steps are required. If the revised task takes longer, it is likely that an additional processing step has been added.

One example is to present a sentence such as "Star is above plus" or "Star is not above plus" followed by a picture such as

| * |
| + |

or

| + |
| * |

The subject is asked to state whether the sentence is true or false. This task requires at least four steps: determining the meaning of the sentence, perceiving the picture and evaluating it, comparing the two results, and producing a response. In one variation the researchers concluded that a negative sentence such as "Star is not above plus" required an additional step because it took longer to process (measured in microseconds).

Experiments like this were later criticized on the grounds that people who used a visual style of thinking would perform the tasks in different ways from those whose thinking style was primarily verbal.

Historically, cognitive psychologists often assumed that mental processes occurred one at a time and that the mind applied the same learning mechanisms to any problem it encountered. Since the 1980s, however, developments in areas such as artificial intelligence (AI, *see* pp. 126–133), evolutionary psychology (*see* pp. 134–143), and brain-imaging techniques (*see* pp. 96–103) have all led to these assumptions being challenged.

COMPUTER SIMULATIONS

From the late 1950s to the early 1980s most psychological theories were founded on the idea that the mind worked in a manner similar to a digital computer: in other words, it processed symbols (*see* pp.

126–133). To understand this approach it is necessary to understand the concept of a symbol. A symbol represents something else. For example, a road sign containing a curved line symbolizes an approaching bend in the road. Similarly, the Roman numeral "III" and the Arabic-derived "3" symbolize the sum of one plus one plus one, or the word three.

The symbols that computers work with are binary numerals (1s and 0s) or, more precisely, electrical patterns of binary numerals. These binary numerals may represent numbers (for example, 1 and 1 represent two), or they may represent other things. When we type something into a computer, we use mostly letters of the alphabet, numbers, and punctuation marks—but within the computer they are all recoded into patterns of binary numerals. Depending on the way the computer is programmed, a rule may be applied to a binary pattern, transforming it into another binary pattern. At this point another rule may be applied, changing the new pattern into another binary pattern, and so on. The important point is that separate rules cannot be applied simultaneously: They can only be applied one at a time in sequence. When the computer has finished performing transformations on these symbols, it converts them back from binary patterns into the language that we used to type the original input, and we receive our output.

Classical models of cognition

Most early theories of cognition, often referred to as classical theories of cognition, assumed the human mind worked in a similar way. According to these theories, stimuli from the environment had to be transformed into mental symbols before they could be interpreted and processed, and this processing occured in sequence. In 1980 mathematician Allen Newell (1927–1992) argued that intelligent actions could only

This road sign is a symbol: It represents something else. Motorists learn to recognize many signs like this and should know that this one symbolizes that they are not allowed to turn to the left.

be produced by a device capable of processing symbols, a controversial notion since it suggested that computers could behave intelligently like people. An example of a computer program that seemed to exhibit intelligent behavior was the General Problem Solver (GPS, *see* p. 130), developed in 1957 by Newell and his colleagues Herbert Simon (1916–2001) and J. C. Shaw. GPS was able to solve the Tower of Hanoi problem (*see* box p. 113) and other logical puzzles that could be expressed in symbolic form. It was not told how to solve each problem but was programmed with a few general rules. These rules enabled GPS to solve difficult problems by breaking larger tasks into a series of smaller tasks, thus creating subgoals (intermediary goals) that had to be met to reach the main goal. Although GPS ultimately proved somewhat limited in its capabilities, it was a classic example of how a sequence of operations could be applied to a representation to arrive at a practical response—and studies of human problem solvers have indicated that this is what they do, too.

Recent models of cognition

A more recent approach has been to create models of cognition in which numerous things happen at the same time, an idea inspired by the way we now know the human brain is structured. Studies by physiologists have revealed that the brain is composed of millions of interacting neurons (cells that conduct nerve impulses). Brain activity occurs through the transmission of electro-chemical signals from one neuron to another, and a great many neurons send signals at any one time.

The first attempts to create cognitive models inspired by the brain were unsuccessful, but since the early 1980s major advances have been made in this area. In particular, David Rumelhart,

James McClelland, and colleagues have developed parallel distributed processing (PDP) models, also called connectionist models. Just as the brain consists of networks of interconnected neurons, so a PDP model consists of networks of interconnected neuronlike units. And just as neurons send messages to each other, so the connections between PDP units can be activated. Knowledge is not stored in the units themselves, but in the patterns of connections between the units (*see* box p. 114). And just as the more often we think about something, the more likely we are to remember it, these connections can be of different strengths and will become stronger the more they are activated.

One advantage of PDP models is that as long as the data available are sufficient to activate connections in the network, they have the capacity to respond to imperfect information. For example, imagine you are reading a book on rock and roll, and you come across a name that is unclear because the ink has rubbed away: El-is Pres-ey. According to PDP theory, the available letters activate many different connections. Some of these activated patterns will make no sense, and the activation will die down, but the pattern of connections that is sensible should include the missing letters, enabling you to recognize the name Elvis Presley.

Unfortunately, PDP models are less successful at demonstrating the way in which people construct new patterns of connections to represent a single memorable event. Also, although they can perform some perceptual tasks such as word recognition, no PDP models have yet been developed to deal with the kind of problem-solving tasks at which GPS models excel. Thus some psychologists believe that both classical models and PDP models may be necessary for us to fully understand cognition.

TOWER OF HANOI

FOCUS ON

French mathematician Edouard Lucas devised the Tower of Hanoi in 1833. He was inspired by the legend of the Hindu priests who were given a stack of 64 gold disks, each disk a little smaller than the one beneath it, and challenged to transfer them one by one from one of three poles to another, ensuring that no disk was ever placed on top of a smaller one. It was said that when they finished, the temple would crumble to dust, and the world would end.

So how many transfers of single disks would the priests have needed to make? To move the entire tower, the priests would have needed to make $2^{64}-1$ separate moves (18,446,744,073,709,551,615)! So if they had worked day and night, making one move every second, it would have taken them just over 580 billion years to finish the job.

A computer program, the General Problem Solver *(see* p. 130), possessed the logic to solve the Tower of Hanoi problem after being programmed with a few general rules.

How many moves would you need to transfer the blocks from one of the three poles to another?

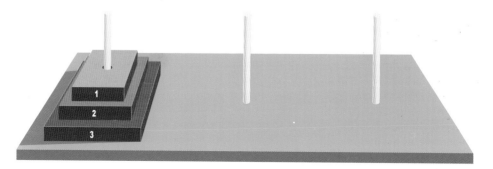

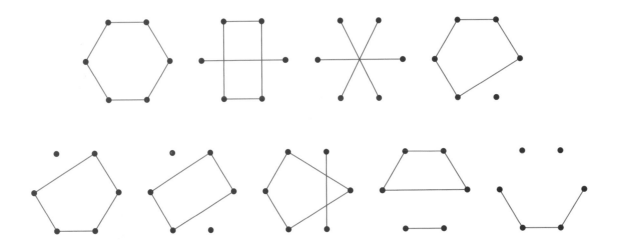

HOW THE BRAIN WORKS

Another question psychologists consider is: Do learning, memory, and perception all work in the same way, regardless of whether the content is verbal, pictorial, musical, or something else? In other words, is the mind made up of a few basic mechanisms that can be applied to all the different tasks we face in everyday life, or are many highly specialized cognitive mechanisms needed to tackle them? "Domain-general" theories suggest that a few basic mechanisms are necessary, while "domain-specific" models suggest that many specialized mechanisms are needed.

To put it another way, some theorists argue that all information in the mind is represented in a few abstract codes similar to the one computers use, while others believe that specific representations are required for words connoting abstract concepts such as "justice" or "peace," but that different kinds of representations are used for objects, sounds, smells, and so on.

To illustrate this distinction, look at the three pairs of objects shown on page 115, and consider which of the shapes on the left is identical to the one on its right. If these shapes were represented in the mind using an abstract code, then the time taken to answer the question should be unrelated to the angle of rotation between the two. In fact, studies show that the bigger the angle of rotation between the two shapes, the longer people take to figure out the answer. This suggests that the shapes are represented in the form of mental images that we rotate mentally to decide whether they are identical. Such representations are called analog (physically quantifiable) representations because they preserve the perceptual features (color, shape, size, and so on) of the things being represented. Information about sounds, smells, and other sensory stimuli may also be stored in analog form.

Evolutionary theory

In 1983 Jerry Fodor published his influential book *The Modularity of Mind* in which he suggested that the mind might be constructed from a variety of information-processing devices, or modules. Fodor suggested that these modules were largely separate from each other and were specialized to deal with language, vision, music, or other kinds of content. In the same year Howard Gardner wrote *Frames of Mind: The Theory of Multiple Intelligences*. Most previous theories had assumed that there were a small number of abilities that interacted and gave rise to intelligence. Gardner proposed that there were eight separate intelligences, each of which was associated with a different cognitive module.

One of the most extreme positions of all on modularity was proposed by Leda

Individual dots are meaningless; but when they are connected, they form recognizable patterns, as the shapes above show. This was the basis of McClelland and Rumelhart's model of cognition, parallel distributed processing (PDP).

Cosmides (*see* p. 141) and John Tooby in the early 1990s. They argued that the human mind evolved to solve problems that recurred in every generation, threatening survival and reproduction. They belived that the mind was more like a Swiss Army knife than a computer, because just as a Swiss Army knife has a different blade for each task, so the mind evolved different modules for solving different adaptive problems.

Social exchange

One of the problems that Cosmides and Tooby referred to was social exchange. Human cooperation is universal and is thought to have been a feature of society since the time of our hunter-gatherer ancestors. Thus it is reasonable to assume that cooperative behavior is important for survival and will be reflected in the organization of the mind. To investigate whether there was evidence of a special mechanism for reasoning about social exchange, Cosmides and Tooby conducted a series of studies involving different versions of Wason's selection task (*see* box p. 142): a reasoning task that people often perform poorly unless it involves some kind of realistic content and context.

What Cosmides and Tooby found was that realistic content only aided reasoning when the problem was phrased in terms of a social exchange involving costs and benefits. Specifically, the social exchange problem required participants to be sensitive to the possibility that a person might cheat on a social arrangement. For example, consider Polynesian people among whom married men are identifiable by their tattoos, and only married men are allowed to eat the aphrodisiac cassava root. Cosmides and Tooby found that when participants were asked to check if people were following the rules, they were particularly alert to the possibility of non-tattooed men eating cassava root. They concluded, therefore, that their subjects possessed inborn mechanisms designed to detect people who might be cheating on a social arrangement, an adaptation that

would give a survival advantage to all those people who inherited it.

Other theorists, such as Fodor, support a more modest version of cognitive adaptability. They believe that certain higher-level processes, such as reasoning, are "all-purpose" and independent of content. However, the research conducted by Cosmides and Tooby suggests that the mind may be more richly structured than previously supposed, and that even reasoning may be influenced by context and evolutionary experience.

Rational analysis

Much cognitive psychology concentrates on mechanisms—that is, the actual cognitive activities and processes that go

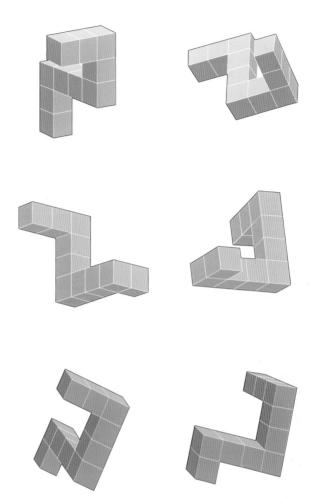

The greater the angle of rotation between two figures, the longer it takes for people to decide whether the shape on the left is identical to the one on the right. This means that you are probably mentally rotating the image to find a match and not examining abstract knowledge to decide which shape is identical to the other.

on in the mind. Generally it is taken for granted that at a simpler or lower level these processes are implemented by the interaction of the brain's neurons. In 1982, however, a highly influential book called *Vision* was published by cognitive scientist and neurophysiologist David Marr (1945–1980). In it he stressed a higher level of explanation, arguing that a proper understanding of cognitive processes could only be achieved by understanding the nature of the problem being solved. Thus to understand cognition, we must understand the principles and laws governing complex mental activity.

> *"Trying to understand perception by studying only neurons is like trying to understand bird flight by studying only feathers."*
> — *David Marr, 1982*

Cognitive psychologist and computer scientist John R. Anderson (born 1947) developed Marr's idea. He contended that instead of studying neurons, researchers should begin by assuming that human behavior was evolutionarily adapted to the environment. Following from this assumption, they then need to specify what the constraints are on behavior for that behavior to be most successful (*see*

Cooperation between people is thought to be universal, and research suggests that we possess inborn mechanisms to detect cheats in social situations, such as at this market in Saint Georges, Grenada, in the Caribbean.

pp. 134–143). Essentially, they need to describe the nature of the environment in which behavior takes place, a procedure that Anderson calls "rational analysis."

Irrationality and statistics

Marr and Anderson had a major effect on the development of psychological theory. Before them researchers assumed that human thought was naturally logical. Therefore the most appropriate method for solving reasoning tasks was through the application of logical rules. However, subsequent studies seemed to show that people often behave irrationally and go against the laws of logic.

In 1994 psychologists Mike Oaksford (born 1956) and Nick Chater (born 1965) attempted to resolve this contradiction by pointing out that our environment is full of uncertainties. Instead of logic, they decided to use probability theory (which is based on uncertainty) to predict how people ought to reason, comparing their results with subjects' actual performance in previous experiments. Using this approach, they tried to predict people's performance on Wason's selection task (*see* p. 142), in which subjects are given a series of problems that require them to decide which items of information to select to test the truth of some rule. The information that subjects typically select is different from the answer suggested by logic, but Oaksford and Chater found that people's performance exactly matched their analysis of probability, suggesting that people are sensitive to information that is likely to reduce uncertainty. In other words, human cognition seeks not logic but certainty.

Fast and frugal heuristics

In a series of papers and a 1999 book, *Simple Heuristics That Make Us Smart*, Gerd Gigerenzer (born 1947) developed a similar approach to the analysis of cognition. Like Oaksford and Chater, he assumed that the mind is adapted to its environment, but he differed slightly because he did not assume that cognition is thereby optimized. Instead, Gigerenzer suggested, many judgments are made by applying mental shortcuts (heuristics).

Consider for example, which city has the larger population: Chicago or Los Angeles? People who do not know the answer might know other things about these cities—whether they have a football team in a major league, whether they are on a national train route, and whether they have a university—and people are more likely to have this information about larger cities than smaller ones. So if they know that Chicago has an art institute but are not sure if Los Angeles has one, they might suggest that Chicago is the larger city. The extra information enables them to give a more informed—though not necessarily accurate—answer. In fact, Chicago ceased to be the "second city" (after New York City) in the United States when its population dropped below that of Los Angeles in the 1980s.

> "Models of rational inference view the mind as if it were a super-natural being."
> — G. Gigerenzer & P. Todd, 1999

As well as using mental shortcuts, people rely on the predictive quality of their information. In other words, some items of information will be more relevant to a problem than others. Although some people might try to solve a problem using all the information at their disposal, this does not guarantee a greater success rate. Gerd Gigerenzer and Daniel Goldstein (born 1969) used computer simulation to show that a judgment based on the single most predictive item of information was as accurate as one integrating several items.

Viewing the brain's activities

A complete theory of cognition must understand both the nature of a given problem and the information-processing mechanism that solves that problem—and like a tool, that information-processing mechanism must be embodied in a physical thing. For people and other animals that thing is the brain.

Developments in medical technology mean that scientists can now examine the structure and activity of people's brains without harming them (see pp. 96–103). These brain-scanning techniques enable psychologists to study people's brains while they are engaged in certain kinds of behavior, such as dreaming, and associate these behaviors with particular forms of brain activity. For example, scanning techniques have been used to shed light on mental representation. One study carried out using functional magnetic resonance imaging (fMRI) found that mental rotation tasks produced activity in the same part of the brain as that used for visual perception. Other research has found that the brain activity that takes place when subjects read a concrete word (for example, "cat") is different from that involved in imagining the object itself.

Practical applications

Research in cognitive science has many practical applications, including computer programming. Studies of perception can aid in the treatment of dyslexia and other perceptual disorders, and can help in the design of everything from road signs to living spaces, while a better understanding of learning and memory contributes to teaching. But basic cognitive research continues to seek simply a better understanding of how the mind works, with a particular focus on consciousness.

CONNECTIONS

Psycholinguistics

"Language is a process of free creation..."

Noam Chomsky

What could be simpler than speaking or understanding speech? Almost all of us do it every day, using words to communicate our ideas, feelings, and moods without any real effort. But how do we acquire language? Do we learn it in the same way that we learn to ride a bicycle? And is it just as easy for people to learn a second language? Psycholinguistics is the study of how people learn and use language, and the job of a psycholinguist is to answer such questions.

Although psycholinguistics is a relatively new field, to understand how it developed, we need to go back more than 2,000 years, to a time when people were intensely interested in studying language (a discipline known as philology or, later, linguistics), but knew little about how people processed it (psycholinguistics). Around 400 B.C. Greek philosophers wondered why objects were named the way they were: why an apple was named "apple" and not "orange." In subsequent centuries they discussed whether word names were randomly assigned to objects by some greater power (one of the gods, for example), or whether they were chosen to fit their meaning or shape. For example, doesn't the word "loop" sound like it refers to something curvy, while "square" sounds like something with sharp edges?

There was also great interest in the rules that people used to assemble words into sentences. We now call these rules grammar or syntax. Such rules allow us to understand the ideas that others want to convey. For example, in English "Mary pushes Peter" and "Peter pushes Mary" have different meanings simply because the word order is reversed.

In ancient times nearly all literate people were fascinated by language: Even political leaders contributed their ideas to the discussion, and it is said that the Roman emperor Julius Caesar (100–44 B.C.) wrote essays on grammatical

KEY DATES

1796 Physiologist Franz Joseph Gall proposes the theory (later known as phrenology) that cognitive functions are organized independently from each other and that they are supported by specific brain structures. He identifies language as one of these functions (*see* p. 37).

1861 Neurologist Paul Broca reports on the first documented case of aphasia, a speech-production disorder (*see* pp. 92–93).

1936 First recorded use of the term psycholinguistics.

1954 Publication of *Psycholinguistics: A Survey of Theory and Research Problems* by Charles Osgood and Thomas Sebeok. The report is seen as a manifesto for collaboration between linguists and psychologists.

1957 Publication of *Syntactic Structures* by linguist Noam Chomsky. Unlike behaviorists (*see* pp.74–89), who considered language to be a simple network of associations, Chomsky claimed language was a unique human skill that involved symbolic computation and mental representation.

1959 Publication of "Review of Skinner's Verbal Behavior," by Noam Chomsky. The article was a deadly blow to pure behaviorist approaches to language, giving psycholinguistics its own academic status.

1986 Connectionism provides new insights into the way in which the brain "remembers" information (*see* pp. 131–132).

1990s onward Technological advances in imaging techniques such as computerized axial tomography (CAT scans), positron emission tomography (PET scans), and functional magnetic resonance imaging (fMRI) allow psychologists to "see through" the brains of patients as they use language, thus pinning down the neurological and anatomical processes involved in language processing (*see* pp. 96–103).

1996 onward Increasing emphasis on the statistical nature of language learning, which suggests that infants and adults pick up regularities in the language they hear without explicit knowledge of any rules or underlying concepts.

regularities while in the middle of a military campaign. The first dictionaries did not appear until the Middle Ages and were very different from those in use today. They remain important to modern linguists, however, because they contain a wealth of information about the languages spoken and written at that time, and also about the way in which invaders assimilated foreign languages, and how languages evolved into their present form.

Words without frontiers
During the 15th and 16th centuries the invention and development of the printing press meant that books could be produced inexpensively and distributed in large numbers. At the same time, the first academies emerged in which thinkers and philosophers gathered to talk about the origin of languages. Among the most prominent and influential were the Italian Accademia della Crusca (founded in 1592) and the French Académie Française (1653). There academicians hotly disputed abstract questions such as "Can thoughts exist without language?" In other words, can we experience the feeling of joy if we do not have a word for it? Similarly, could our eyes and brain distinguish between the colors blue and red if we had only one word for both?

People became more and more interested in the dynamic aspects of language—how it is represented in our minds, how we comprehend it, and how we learn it—and by the early 20th century this interest had led to the birth of psycholinguistics. A great turning point in the development of both linguistics and

Human speech is the result of a complex chain of operations that involves conceptualization, formulation, and articulation (see p. 122). Our accompanying gestures and the tone we adopt may also alter the meaning of what we say.

psycholinguistics came in 1957 with the publication of *Syntactic Structure*, a book by Noam Chomsky that distinguishes between the notions of competence and performance. Competence is the idealized knowledge that we have of our own language, and most of it is expressed in terms of grammatical rules. For example, English-speakers know that in the active form the subject of a sentence should precede the verb, and that the verb should precede the object. For example, "The rabbit (subject) eats (verb) a carrot (object)." Similarly, we know that a

> *"Chomsky did for cognitive science what Galileo did for physical science. We now study the mind as part of the physical world."*
> — *Neil Smith, 2000*

sentence such as "The witness, who saw the man who saw the grocer who saw the victim, left," is grammatically correct. Our knowledge of such grammatical rules constitutes our competence with language.

Performance, meanwhile, refers to the actual use of competence in real-life situations. For example, it is unlikely that anyone would ever say a sentence as inelegant and convoluted as the one just quoted. Similarly, real speech includes many errors or unusual turns of phrase.

The study of linguistics was, and still is, mostly about competence. Chomsky's

Linguistic scholar Noam Chomsky (born 1928) rejected old-style behaviorist ideas (see pp. 74–89) and revolutionized our understanding of language structure.

book was important because it allowed psycholinguistics to emerge from the linguistic tradition, leaving aside competence and concentrating on performance. Thus psycholinguistics is concerned with explicit language behavior, describing how we use language to communicate our ideas with each other.

COMPREHENDING LANGUAGE

According to Chomsky, we comprehend speech by matching the language performance of our interlocutor (the speech produced by another person) to our own language competence (our formal knowledge of linguistic rules).

During the 1970s psycholinguists gained a deeper knowledge of language comprehension by testing Chomsky's theory, devising a range of language experiments from which they gathered empirical evidence (data obtained by observation or experimentation). The availability of computers helped them

> *"No matter what language you're speaking, you're carrying out the same mental computation."*
> — *Noam Chomsky, 1995*

collect vast amounts of information about the competence and speed with which people recognize speech, and the results of their experiments were as follows.

When we listen to speech, we recognize four or five words per second and dozens of sentences every minute. Considering these facts, we might conclude that language comprehension is simple and straightforward. It is not. Consider, for example, this simple sentence: "The girl runs after the duck." We take roughly three steps between hearing these words and understanding the message.

First, we need to recognize the individual speech sounds (phonemes). The word "duck" is composed of three phonemes, each represented by a conventional linguistic symbol: /d/, /ʌ/,

and /k/. This stage, known as phonemic categorization, can be problematic because people pronounce phonemes differently depending on their regional accent, age, health, and mood.

The second step consists of segmenting the string of phonemes into distinct words. Speech segmentation is necessary because, while the written language features plainly visible gaps between each word, speech typically contains no gaps or pauses—it is a continuous flow of sound. Speech segmentation allows successful recognition of the words used. Once this process has been successfully completed, we have accessed the representations of the words in our "mental lexicon" (a term that psycholinguists use to describe the personal dictionary housed in our brains. that contains all the words we know).

The final step in comprehending language consists of making sense of the words or accessing what they mean. This step is termed syntactic and semantic integration (semantics is the study of the relationship between words and their meanings). The meaning of each word is retrieved from our knowledge system— for example, we probably already know that a duck is a bird with a flat bill and shiny feathers that can float, walk, swim, and fly. We interpret the meaning of each word in the context of the sentence, which

KEY TERMS

Grammar or **syntax** The rules that govern the way people use language.

Lexical access The process of retrieving a word from the mental lexicon.

Linguistic competence A theoretical awareness of how language is used.

Linguistic performance The use of language in everyday life.

Linguistics The study of language.

Mental lexicon An individual's personal memory supply of all the words that person knows.

Phonemes Individual speech sounds; not the same as syllables.

Psycholinguistics The study of how people learn, understand, and produce language.

Semantics The scientific study of the meaning of words and changes in the meanings of words.

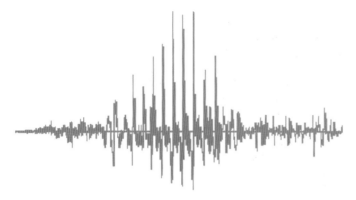

The acoustic signal (or waveform) of speech has no clear boundaries between words. To decode it, we first need to segment the waveform into words. The diagram shown is the waveform for the word "How ?"

is where our knowledge of grammatical rules helps us distinguish between "The girl runs after the duck" and "The duck runs after the girl."

Fast work

The sequence of events described above takes place in less than half a second and seems easy to us. That is because we have learned to make our mental processes more and more automatic over years of practice. Because we recognize words effortlessly, we can devote our attention to other tasks, such as thinking and planning responses. For people who learn foreign languages as adults, each step is much harder, requiring time and concentration. Chomsky's original ideas did not include notions of recognition speed, automatic recognition, and other aspects of performance. These ideas were developed later by psycholinguists who used experimentation as their research tool.

Accessing the mental lexicon

At birth we all start out with an empty mental lexicon. This memory store of words grows quickly in the first years of life, from 100 words at around one year to about 50,000 words in adulthood.

When we hear speech, we recognize each word almost immediately, accessing the right word in our mental lexicon in less than half a second. The process of retrieving a word in our lexicon is known as lexical access. Sometimes, lexical access

fails, and we retrieve the wrong word, such as "carrot" instead of "parrot." Psycholinguists claim that this kind of mistake reveals that words that sound the same are filed close together in the brain.

The structure of the lexicon could also be based on the semantic properties of the words (what they mean). According to this theory, words that are connected by their meaning will be close to each other, for example, "carrot" will be close to "lettuce" because they are both vegetables. Experimenters can test this hypothesis by measuring whether people recognize the word "carrot" faster when it is preceded by "lettuce" than when it is preceded by "parrot." The scientific term for this mental process is called priming.

> *Since priming occurs in tasks where memory...is not required...it is assumed to be an involuntary and...unconscious phenomenon."*
> *— Harvey G. Schulman, 1997*

SPEAKING MACHINES

Speech sounds are complex, and most attempts to generate them artificially have failed, although at the end of the 18th century the Russian physiology professor Christian Kratzenstein and the German inventor Wolfgang von Kempelen both built tube-and-pipe "speaking machines" that were capable of producing intelligible speech sounds, words, and even short sentences (*see* p. 122).

Over the past two centuries speech synthesis has developed into a fascinating discipline involving psycholinguists, speech engineers, phoneticians (scientists who study vocal sounds), physiologists, and computer scientists. Some researchers have constructed artificial lung and mouth devices in their efforts to mimic human speech sounds as closely as possible. We also have speaking computers; but while they are efficient, they do not sound the same as real human speech.

COMPETENCE AND PRODUCTION

One of the obstacles facing speech synthesists is that no one knows exactly how people produce speech. Obviously, language production is not just about the generation of sound but involves the whole production process from thinking to articulation. Chomsky suggested that if thinking is described in terms of syntactically organized relationships

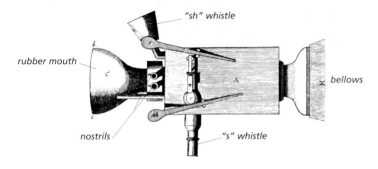

"sh" whistle

rubber mouth

bellows

nostrils

"s" whistle

between concepts expressed in words (language competence), then language production is the process of transforming language competence into language performance—a theory that provided a rich starting point for the study of thinking in the 1950s. Once again psychologists needed empirical evidence to build a solid theory, and by the end of the 20th century they had established that speech production involves a division of labor within the brain.

The "wind box" from Wolfgang von Kempelen's speaking machine: a hand-operated device that let air flow through resonance tubes and organ pipes. It was capable of producing various speech sounds, some words, and short sentences.

The operations involved in speaking are the same for everyone regardless of age or nationality. Speaking begins with an idea that we want to express. For example, we may want to communicate our surprise as we come face to face with a large dog. This is known as the conceptualization stage. Thoughts are translated into concepts (surprise/large/dog) that can be expressed in words. Once the conceptual structure of the message is ready, we then need to retrieve the right words from our mental lexicon—the same mental lexicon that we use during speech comprehension. We also want the words to be assembled into a syntactically correct and meaningful sentence. This is known as the formulating stage; and if anything goes wrong during this part of the process, we may end up with a sentence such as "I've never seen such a big rat" (lexical mistake) or "I've never saw such a big dog" (grammatical mistake). The result of the formulating stage is not yet real speech. It is internal speech, which is the silent voice you hear inside your head when you think.

We are now ready to voice the internal speech. But we need more than our mouths to do this. Our lungs, larynx, tongue, nose, and lips collaborate to produce the clear and audible sentence "I've never seen such a big dog!" This stage is termed articulation because it involves the muscular programs necessary

HOW DO WE KNOW ALL THIS?

FOCUS ON

Psycholinguists use several methods to study language. They gather data on static aspects (familiarity with words, dialectal variations, and so on) and use rating scales ("How familiar are you with the word 'femur'?"), questionnaires, population surveys, and samples of real speech or writing.

The study of the dynamic aspects of language (how processing stages interact with each other) requires more ingenious and indirect techniques. One of the most popular consists of measuring reaction times. It is thought that a mental operation, such as recognizing a word, takes longer if it involves many steps than if it involves only a few. Thus it takes longer to recognize an infrequent word, such as "scalp," than a frequent one, such as "school," because, presumably, words are looked up by order of frequency. To measure reaction times, participants sit in a quiet room and listen to speech over headphones or read material on a computer monitor. They are instructed to perform a task—for example, to detect a certain sound or decide if what they hear is a word—as fast as they can. A computer measures how long it takes them to push the button. Reaction time differences can be as small as 15 or 20 milliseconds (one-fiftieth of a second).

to utter the phonemes that make up each word. It is at this stage of the model that people make the strangest speech errors, such as "I've never seen such a dig bog!" in which two phonemes are swapped. Speaking machines such as those of Kratzenstein, von Kempelen, and modern engineers focus on this step.

Fortunately, real people accomplish the above operations very quickly. Imagine if we had to think each step through before talking. The simple sentence "Watch out!" addressed to a friend about to cross a busy road would come too late. Speech production (speaking) is not as easy and automatic as speech comprehension (understanding speech), however. People differ greatly in how well they speak and how swiftly they can articulate ideas, and these individual differences can originate in any of the three stages described.

William Archibald Spooner, a 19th-century English clergyman and scholar, became famous for his articulatory mishaps. His "slips of the tongue" were so humorous—for example, "half-warmed fish" instead of "half-formed wish"—that speech errors of this type became known generically as spoonerisms.

LANGUAGE DEVELOPMENT
People have wondered for hundreds of years how we acquire language. One of the earliest, though totally unethical, experiments on language acquisition was carried out in the 16th century. The greatest of the Mughal emperors of India, Akbar (1542–1605), believed that people acquired language by hearing others speak. To test his hypothesis, he confined several newborn babies to a mansion isolated from civilization and guarded by mute nurses. Four years later he returned and found, as expected, that the children could not emit a single speech sound.

There have also been many reports of wild or isolated children who have experienced years of language deprivation and consequently never learn more than a few words. And if they are able to learn words, they usually cannot master the

W. A. Spooner (1844–1930) was famous for mixing up the beginnings of his words. According to one famous story, he supposedly told a lazy college student: "You have tasted a whole worm!" instead of "You have wasted a whole term!"

rules of grammar. Recovery seems to depend on the age at which language learning began. Psycholinguist Eric Lenneberg (1921–1975) suggested there might be a critical period for language learning (ending before puberty) after which such learning is seriously impaired.

> *"The natural ability for acquiring language normally diminished rapidly somewhere around the age of puberty. There is a critical age for acquiring fluent native language."*
> — *Eric Lenneberg, 1967*

For most of us language acquisition comes naturally, beginning early in life and requiring almost no formal training. If someone asked us when we learned the word "sun," and what muscles we flex to articulate it, we would probably be unable to answer. Contemporary psycholinguists, who have access to modern speech laboratories, divide this learning process into several stages.

Mother tongue
People learn the typical intonation (prosody) of their native language before they are born. From inside the womb a

fetus can hear the low frequencies of its mother's voice and the voices of people close by. The sound quality is poor, but it is enough for the fetus to become familiar with many of the noises of language. Once born, infants will show a preference for the voices of the people who spent a lot of time near their mother during pregnancy. They also show a clear preference for what is known as their mother tongue.

In the first few months of life infants become familiar with the speech sounds of their environment. Before long (around

> "Infants learn to recognize speech by picking up sound pattern regularities in their environment."
> — Peter W. Jusczyk, 1997

six months) they learn a few words, usually those that occur often in their environment (for example, "mommy," "daddy," "dog," "light"). It is possible to tell that infants recognize the meaning of these words because they show a preference for photographs of their mothers when they hear the word "mommy" and for photographs of their fathers when they hear the word "daddy." By the time they reach their first birthday they usually have a large repertoire of phonemes and a few true words.

The first words infants produce may be difficult to understand—they will say "ba" for "ball," for example. But at around one year they develop a small vocabulary that helps them communicate their intentions. It is still not always clear what they mean, however. If they say "ball," do they mean the ball itself, the spinning of the ball, the color of the ball, or the action of playing with it? Thus the communicative value of the one-word stage is limited because words do not yet have a clear meaning.

The telegraphic stage
The two-word stage, or telegraphic stage, brings the infant closer to producing real sentences. This stage generally occurs at

the end of the second year and coincides with a lexical explosion (a sharp rise in the number of words children know). With a few hundred words in their vocabulary it becomes easier to express ideas, like "daddy shoe" and "throw ball." But many two-word sentences are still ambiguous. For example, "No eat!" could mean "I don't want to eat," or "You can't eat," or even "Don't eat me!"

Only at the syntactic stage, at around two and a half years, do children start saying real sentences. They contain verbs, prepositions, adverbs, and so on, and follow syntactical rules. This is when children learn the importance of word order in sentences, for example, "the car pulls the trailer" is quite different from "the trailer pulls the car."

Is language an inborn skill?
One of the most intriguing questions in studying how people learn language concerns the nature of the grammatical knowledge that children develop at around two years of age. Do children learn a list of rules? Since Chomsky's *Syntactic Structures* many scientists have tried to answer this question, but they have not yet come up with a satisfactory answer. Syntax is so complex, and yet so easy to learn,

A human fetus in utero. Research shows that we start to learn our native language or mother tongue before we are born.

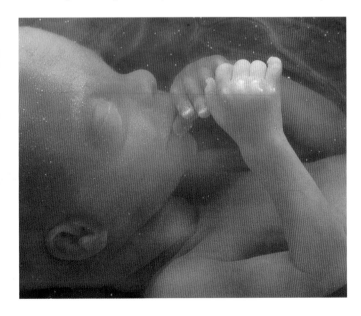

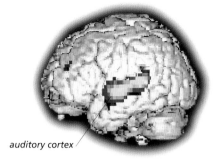

auditory cortex

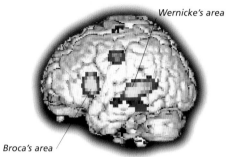

Wernicke's area

Broca's area

PET scans of human brain activity (showing a left view of the brain with the front to the left). Top left: inward thought lights up part of the auditory cortex. Top right: figuring out word meanings lights up areas of the temporal lobe. Lower left: repeating words lights up Broca's area for generating speech, Wernicke's area for comprehending language, and a motor region. Lower right: hearing speech lights up the auditory cortex.

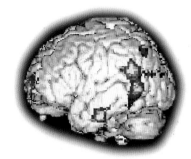

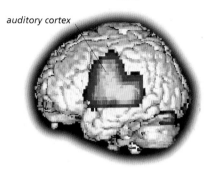

auditory cortex

however, that it seems likely that people are born with a predisposition, or inborn talent, to learn language.

LANGUAGE IN THE BRAIN

One way or another, everything we do originates from our brain. Language is no exception, and a complete understanding of how language is controlled by our brain requires knowledge of neurology.

Pathologist Paul Broca (1824–1880) first established that in most people the areas of the brain that control language comprehension and production are located in the left hemisphere, behind the left ear. He discovered this by performing autopsies on patients who had lost the capacity to speak (aphasia) and found that they had lesions (injuries) in their left hemispheres, on an area of the brain that is now named after him (*see* pp. 96–97). Carl Wernicke (1848–1905) discovered that damage in an area slightly farther back from Broca's area was responsible for difficulty in comprehending speech. These two discoveries started a research program that is still continuing today.

There have been many subsequent attempts to map language areas in the

brain. The aim is to find out which part of the brain controls which language ability. Neurolinguistic researchers are trying to identify the exact location of the mental lexicon and the area of the brain that controls syntax. They also hope to discover how these areas differ from those involved in the perception of music, and how language is represented in the brains of bilingual speakers. If scientists can find the answers to these questions, they may be able to build an accurate model of language processing in the brain, which will help surgeons during operations on the brain. It will also provide computer scientists with a model that can be used to build machines capable of recognizing and producing authentic-sounding speech.

CONNECTIONS

- Neuropsychology: pp. 90–95
- Brain-imaging Techniques: pp. 96–103
- Computer Simulation: pp. 126–133
- Learning by Association: Volume 3, pp. 44–63
- Language Processing: Volume 3, pp. 114–135
- Communication: Volume 5, p. 72–93

Computer Simulation

—————— *"If a computer could think, how could we tell?"* ——————

Alan Turing

One important reason for the so-called cognitive revolution in psychology during the 1950s and 1960s was the development of the computer—work that began in earnest during World War II (1939–1945). The computer soon became a valuable research tool, enabling psychologists to create programs and systems that tried to simulate human brain activity and mental processes.

Before the computer was developed, behaviorism had dominated psychology for several decades (see pp. 74–89), emphasizing observation or measurement of the outward behavior of a person or animal. But as interest in computers grew, another line of thought emerged. Computers, it appeared, could carry out tasks similar to those performed by people, and this led some psychologists to view the mind as a powerful computer. While physiologists continued studying the mechanics or anatomy of the brain, these cognitive psychologists began to try to figure out how the brain worked, or how it was "programmed."

Both the mind and the computer are information-processing systems that can read, output, store, and compare symbols. The mind uses nerve cells to carry out such tasks, while the computer completes these processes using microchips—but there are parallels in the way they work.

Built by Professor Max Newman at Manchester University, UK, the Manchester Mark 1 was the first fully electronic stored-program computer. It was completed in June 1949 and was a great success. It also had a huge influence on the psychological theories of the 1950s.

Consequently psychologists can test their theories of what goes on in the mind by writing computer programs to simulate the way they think mental processes work. First they try to find out how people solve a particular complex problem, then they use the information as a guide in programming a computer to solve the same problem. If the computer's output matches the performance of the people, then this suggests that the way the computer solves the problem may be the way a person would go about the task.

The mind and the machine

The simulation of mental processes should not be confused with artificial intelligence (*see* Vol. 2, pp. 140–163), although the lines between the two are blurred and were especially so when this type of research began. Psychologists are trying to understand how the human or animal mind works and create computer

THE TURING TEST AND THE DOCTOR

EXPERIMENT

British mathematician and computer scientist Alan Turing (1912–1954) suggested the following test for artificial intelligence: Let a person have a conversation by typing at a console. In the next room, out of sight, are a person and a computer, and the tester will converse with both of them without being told which is which. If the tester cannot tell the difference, the computer can be said to be intelligent.

Alan Turing suggested that a machine could be considered intelligent if it could imitate a person— but this is not the only way that a machine can demonstrate intelligence.

Since then computer programers have written many programs that can hold a fairly acceptable conversation. A program named Doctor, for example, offers what appears to be psychiatric advice simply by looking for keywords and bouncing them back at the patient. If someone types: "I'm having a problem with my parents," Doctor might respond: "What is the problem with your parents?" The person might then write: "I don't think they love me any more," to which the computer will reply: "Why do you

think that?" and so on. Doctor parodies psychotherapy, but other programs using a more sophisticated keyword approach have produced far more realistic conversations. None have been totally convincing, however.

In 1990 the Cambridge Center for Behavioral Studies offered $100,000 to anyone who wrote a conversation program that could fool a person. At the end of 2001 it remained unclaimed. As a consolation, the Institute offers $2,000 annually for the program that does the best job.

---

programs that work in the same way. Researchers in artificial intelligence (AI) are usually trying to build an "intelligent" machine that will accomplish a particular task. Whether it does the task in the same way as a person is unimportant, although an AI programmer would almost certainly be overjoyed if the machine did the job faster or more efficiently than a person.

Nevertheless, an AI experiment that has no psychological goals may still give psychologists useful insights. In particular, AI can often demonstrate "sufficiency." That is, if a computer can accomplish a particular task with certain resources, then a person would not need to have any more resources to accomplish the same task.

When work in this area began, computers were slow and had very little memory space compared to the machines we have on our desktops today. But even the most up-to-date computers have nothing remotely approaching the capacity of the human brain, although they can do some things faster and more accurately than people. As a result computer simulation of mental processes has been limited to fairly simple tasks, or

smaller components of tasks, that programmers understand well enough to put into programs. Even some of the abilities possessed by two-year-olds are too complex to be programmable.

> *"The study is to proceed on the basis of the conjecture that every aspect of learning or any other feature of intelligence can, in principle, be so precisely described that a machine can be made to simulate it."*
> — *John McCarthy, 1956*

The most common criticism of computer simulation as a tool in psychological research is that computers do not work in the same way as the brain, so any comparison between the two will be inexact. In particular, most theories of cognition recognize that human thinking, from the simple perception of objects to the understanding of spoken language, draws heavily on a vast storehouse of

Alan Turing and his colleagues working on the Ferranti Mark I computer in 1951. Turing was involved in the construction of the world's first electronic computer during World War II.

knowledge, something that even the most powerful computers we have today can never match. Nevertheless, this has not prevented scientists from trying.

The logic theorist

One of the earliest efforts to create a program that would simulate human thought was called the Logic Theorist. Developed by Herbert Simon, Allen Newell, and J. C. Shaw (*see* box opposite), it used symbolic logic—a system for writing logical statements in the form of variables related by operators (link words such as AND, OR, and NOT). These relationships are naturally built into the architecture of a digital computer, which operates by using electronic "gates" that either conduct or do not conduct current. If two gates are wired in series so that both of them have to be on for current to pass through, that is equivalent to an AND. But if two gates are wired in parallel so that current passes through when either one is on, that is equivalent to an OR. A NOT circuit reverses the state of a gate, turning it on if it is off, and off if it is on.

The Logic Theorist was given a few axioms (statements that were assumed to be true), a series of rules for performing logical operations on these axioms, and a mathematical theorem to prove. Logical operations governed by rules are called operators. In mathematics, for example, common operators are plus, minus, divide, and multiply. By applying operators to the

axioms, the Logic Theorist generated new statements in sequence until the result matched the theorem it had set out to prove. It then printed out the sequence it had used. In this way it produced proofs of several theorems from the standard text of *Principia Mathematica*, a book on mathematical logic written by Sir Isaac Newton in 1687. In one case it even produced a proof that was considered more "elegant"—a word mathematicians use to describe simplicity and ingenuity—than the one in the 17th-century book.

A new logic theory

Simon conducted extensive studies of people solving similar logic problems while "thinking aloud," and ultimately his analysis convinced him that their thought processes were very different from the procedure used by the Logic Theorist.

In response to this work Simon developed a new theory to describe problem solving. He defined the place where a problem existed in the real world as the "task environment." The problem solver, he said, began by creating a mental representation of the problem called the problem space, which might or might not contain all the elements needed to solve the problem. In this space would be a representation of the starting conditions (the way things were), the goal (the way things would be if the problem were solved), and a set of operators that the solver could apply. Thus problems were solved by applying operators to the initial object until it could be changed into the desired final object. Sometimes the change could not be accomplished directly and had to be divided into various subtasks.

According to Simon's theory, a program could also solve a problem by searching the problem space for operators, applying them to objects, and then testing the results. If necessary, it could also break down the major task into various subtasks to which the same process is applied— something that computer programmers call "recursive" processing.

One example Simon used was the problem of taking children to school. The object that needs to be modified is the time taken to travel from home to school, while an operator that can be applied here is the car. But if the car has broken down or needs gas, then various other operators —such as a mechanic or a gas station— might have to be applied to modify the car object until it becomes an effective operator that can solve the larger problem. One barrier to success might be an improper selection of the problem space, which may fail to include all the objects and operators needed to achieve the goal. Therefore a possible strategy when no solution can be found could be to redefine the problem space. In this example the problem space might be expanded to include bus or bicycle operators.

PIONEERS IN COMPUTATIONAL COGNITION

BIOGRAPHY

Neither Herbert Simon (1916–2001) nor Allen Newell (1927–1992) was a psychologist, but they are generally considered the first important workers in artificial intelligence and computer simulation of mental processes. Their work played a major role in launching the "cognitive revolution" of the 1950s and 1960s.

Simon obtained a degree in political science and, as professor at the Carnegie Institute of Technology (now Carnegie Mellon University), studied the behavior of big businesses. He came to the conclusion that large organizations reach decisions by thought processes similar to those used by individuals. His findings, set out in the book *Administrative Behavior*, earned him the 1978 Nobel Prize for Economics.

In 1952 Simon went to work as a consultant at the Rand Corporation, a think-tank in Santa Monica, California. There he met Allen Newell, who had dropped out of graduate school in mathematics to apply mathematical game theory to organizational behavior. Newell had studied physics and mathematics but wanted to do applied rather than theoretical work.

Simon and Newell worked together on a government-funded study of air defense organizations, for which Newell created a computer program that simulated the images of planes on a radar screen. When Simon saw it, he realized that computers, previously used almost entirely for number crunching, could also manipulate symbols. He already believed this was how the human mind worked.

Herbert Simon won the 1978 Nobel Prize for Economics. Together with his colleague Newell he made a significant contribution to theories on how the brain functions.

Simon and Newell, together with Rand programmer J.C. Shaw, then created the Logic Theorist, a program that could prove mathematical theories. They demonstrated it at the historic Dartmouth conference on AI in 1956. They went on to write the General Problem Solver, from which Newell derived SOAR, an even more general program for AI. Most cognitive scientists and AI researchers now regard this work as seminal.

separate from the details of each task, however, which was why the program was called the General Problem Solver. As well as processing logic problems, it could solve a variety of other tasks, including puzzles in chess and mathematics.

Start, Objects, and Response

Newell went on to expand the problem-solving theory and create a program called SOAR (an acronym of "Start, Objects, and Response"), which he described as both a unified theory of cognition and a tool for AI. He argued that all human cognition could be represented as problem solving in a problem space, so theoretically SOAR could model any thought process. Since it was unveiled in 1983, SOAR has undergone many revisions and is still widely used.

SOAR can be programmed for various different tasks by supplying it with the appropriate decision-making rules. It is also capable of learning as it goes along by a process known as "chunking." In human terms chunking occurs when we gather several pieces of information together into something we can think about and

The General Problem Solver

Simon, Newell, and Shaw developed a computer program called the General Problem Solver (GPS) based on this research. GPS treated the initial situation and the goal as objects and began by measuring the difference between them, before looking for an operator that could reduce the difference. AI programmers call such operators "production systems." The simplest production system is a rule of the form: "If A AND B are both true, then C happens." Production systems can also use operators such as OR, NOT, and IMPLIES.

Like Logic Theorist, GPS worked with statements of symbolic logic, so all the problems had to be translated into this form. Thus the problems and the tools to solve them had to be input into the program as simple definitions expressed as relationships between words. The section of the program that carried out the problem-solving operation was kept

> *"The talents of the brain and the computer complement each other, rather than mimic each other, and we should be wary of using one as a metaphor for the other."*
> — *J. A. Anderson, 1977*

remember as a single item. An example is the way we gather several letters of the alphabet together and think of them as a single word. By chunking, SOAR can assimilate old rules into new ones, thereby expanding its knowledge base.

SOAR is one of the programs that have been used to create expert systems: systems that store large collections of rules about a subject and can apply them to reach conclusions about a particular situation. Expert systems usually establish their decision-making rules after extensive "interviews" with knowledgeable people:

A human operator inputs the information, and the expert system asks questions, adjusting its subsequent responses to reflect previous answers. In a way, this is also a simulation of the way people work.

Expert systems are not intended to replace people, but to serve as intelligent assistants to trained professionals. The first, called DENDRAL, was written in 1965 by Bruce Buchanan, an AI researcher at the Stanford Research Institute. It helped chemists interpret the results of mass spectrometry analysis. Buchanan also helped develop MYCIN, another system begun by Edward Shortliffe that assisted medical diagnosis, oil exploration, and chemical analysis. PROSPECTOR, which analyzed information about the geology of an area and suggested the best places to find mineral deposits, was developed by their colleague Richard Duda in 1976. Like many programs, these systems evolved over the years, and some are still in regular use.

HEARSAY
Another expert system called HEARSAY was designed to recognize speech, even when the initial recognition of sounds was poor. Several versions of the system were created in the 1970s and 1980s, and they provided psychologists with new ideas about speech recognition in humans.

HEARSAY has several different modules that operate separately on the incoming data, but which also share data and compare notes: an approach known as parallel processing. The first module to analyze the sound input generates guesses about what phones (vowel and consonant sounds) are present and passes them to other modules that guess what syllables and words they form. Meanwhile, other modules generate guesses about the syntax (sentence structure) and meaning of the possible words. All these modules continually compare hypotheses, assigning them various reliability scores, until eventually the system chooses what seems to be the most likely sentence. Even early versions of HEARSAY were about 90

percent accurate, but many cognitive psychologists still took the view that it was not a very good simulation of the way people process speech because it was so heavily "top-down" (it generated hypotheses about meaning early on in the processing process). They argued that the brain could not do all this processing fast enough to understand speech in real time and relies on a more "bottom-up" approach: organizing the information before trying to understand it.

PROCESSING APPROACHES
All of the computer programs described so far use "symbol-processing" methods. Objects or ideas in the real world are represented by symbols that the computer manipulates, usually serially—that is, one part of the program performs an operation then passes the results on to another. Critics, however, believe that the brain probably does not work in this way.

Even in the 1950s physiologists believed the brain was a vast parallel processing system, and research since then has tended to confirm this hypothesis. Memories are stored and thought processes carried out by establishing complex patterns of connections among the neurons (brain cells specialized to conduct nerve impulses). These connections are not established instantly, in the way that an

World chess champion Garry Kasparov in New York in May 1997, competing with Deep Blue: a program similar to an expert system developed at IBM by three students from Carnegie Mellon University. By drawing on a huge supply of information about chess and examining the possible outcomes of moves, Deep Blue defeated Kasparov.

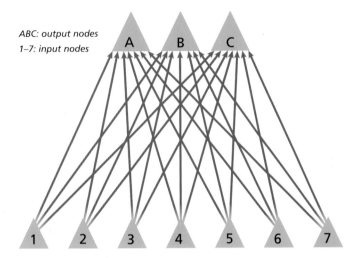

ABC: output nodes
1–7: input nodes

electronic switch opens and closes in a computer, but seem to be formed by repetition. If a neuron (nerve cell) fires repeatedly, it eventually causes a nearby neuron to fire. A chemical change then takes place that amounts to a lowering of the resistance between the two neurons. As a result the second neuron will now fire at the same time as the first one.

Connectionism

In the 1950s both psychologists and AI researchers began to think about simulating this process, creating what became known as artificial neural networks: systems that simulated the physiology of the brain, rather than its thought processes. This approach is known as connectionism because it emphasizes the connections between a situation and a response.

In its simplest form an artificial neural network consists of several input nodes connected to some output nodes. There may or may not be intermediate layers between them. Usually, each input node is connected to several nodes in an adjoining layer. When a stimulus activates an input node, a signal is sent to every node to which it is connected. But the signals are weighted—their effect diminishes as they reach nodes farther away.

A common application of neural networks is in visual pattern recognition,

A simple illustration of a neural network. The signals sent by the numbered input nodes are "weighted" according to their distance from the three output nodes. Thus node 2 sends strong signals to node A, medium signals to node B, and weak signals to node C. The output nodes fire depending on the total amount of signal they receive. For example, a few signals from 3, 4, or 5 might cause B to fire or many signals from nodes 1 and 7. In this way the system can learn repeated patterns even if they are not identical.

in which the input nodes are arranged on a grid representing the pixels of an image. Through repeated exposure to the same pattern the weightings (that is, the values) placed on some of the connections to the output nodes are adjusted as the desired output pattern is gradually achieved. The device can then be set to report success whenever a match is identified. Because a success rating depends on the total value of several nearby connections, a neural network of this kind can also deal with "fuzzy" situations, such as recognizing visual patterns that have the same general design but are not identical.

There are two types of neural network: supervised and unsupervised. In a supervised network the operator adjusts the weightings. In an unsupervised network the system adjusts its own weightings, a process known in other contexts as "learning."

The Perceptron

The first artificial neural network was a machine built by Frank Rosenblatt in 1957 at the Cornell Aeronautical Laboratory in Buffalo, New York. He called it the Perceptron. The first Perceptron was not an electronic computer but a mechanical device that used real weights to adjust the values of connections. Rosenblatt demonstrated the Perceptron publicly in 1960, impressing scientists with its ability to recognize simple patterns. His idea was quickly re-created in the form of computer programs, in which "weights" were represented by variables: numerical values assigned to the connecting nodes.

In 1969 computer scientist Marvin Minsky (cofounder of the MIT Artificial Intelligence Laboratory and a major figure in the cognitive revolution, born 1927) and Seymour Papert (a mathematician at MIT) wrote a book entitled *Perceptrons: An Introduction to Computational Geometry*. In it they pointed out serious limitations of the Rosenblatt Perceptron, explaining that it could not perform various tasks of which symbol-processing systems were already capable. As a result research on neural networks was set aside for 15 years. Minsky has since admitted that he was "too harsh" in his criticism.

The original Perceptron had only one input layer and one output layer. The imperfections identified by Minsky and Papert were later ironed out by adding an intermediate or "hidden" layer and by allowing the intermediate and final layers to send signals back to the first layers, a technique known as "back propagation." A variation, named the Hopfield network, used only a single layer of nodes.

Pandemonium

A new program named Pandemonium combined cognitive theories with the neural network approach. Developed by Oliver Selfridge at MIT, Pandemonium was made up of four layers that modeled what some theorists saw as the structure of human perception. The first layer, corresponding to the sense organs, simply accepted the input, stored it, and passed it on. The next layer consisted of "demons" (as in pan-demon-ium) that performed computations on the input data to refine it, then passed the results to the third layer. The third layer contained further "demons" that evaluated the data and reported their findings to the final layer. Each demon in the third layer would "shriek" at those in the fourth layer in proportion to the value of its evidence, and the fourth layer had to decide which demons were shrieking the loudest.

Pandemonium incorporated a "genetic" algorithm that allowed it to modify itself for improved performance. (An algorithm is a logical arithmetical or computational procedure that ensures the solution of a problem. For example, to determine whether a number is even or odd, divide it by two.) At the beginning of each task the

KEY DATES

1956 The Logic Theorist, a theorem-proving program, is written. A conference at Dartmouth College brings together psychologists and computer scientists.

1957 The General Problem Solver is introduced.

1958 Frank Rosenblatt designs the Perceptron.

1958 LISP, the first programming language for AI, is created.

1965 DENDRAL, the first expert system, is created to help chemists interpret data from mass spectrometry.

1969 Marvin Minsky and Seymour Papert publish a criticism of the Perceptron that stalls research on neural networks.

1971 The first version of HEARSAY is written.

1973 MYCIN becomes the first useful medical diagnosis expert system.

1974 The backpropagating form of Perceptron revives interest in neural networks.

1987 The launch of SOAR, which was described as a "unified theory of cognition."

program would use a supervised learning approach in which a human operator trained it to achieve an approximation of the correct result. Then it would select the second-layer demons that seemed to be doing the best job, delete the others, and create new copies of the successful demons. In this way Pandemonium was able to recognize hand-written characters.

Current approaches

Today neural networks are used widely in pattern-recognition applications, such as optical character and speech recognition, and in "optimization" problems in which the goal is to find the most economical or efficient combination of interacting variables. But while symbol-processing systems are still widely used in AI, most cognitive scientists have moved away from this approach as a simulation of thought —they have even been known to call symbol processing GOFAI (Good Old-Fashioned Artificial Intelligence.)

CONNECTIONS

• Cognitive Psychology: pp. 104–117
• Perception: Volume 2, pp. 62–85

• Artificial Minds: Volume 2, pp. 140–163
• The Human Computer: Volume 3, pp. 6–23
• Representing Information: Volume 3, pp. 64–87
• Problem Solving: Volume 3, pp. 136–163

Evolutionary Psychology

———— *"Nothing in biology makes sense except in the light of evolution."* ————

T. Dobzhansky

Evolutionary psychology is one of the most recent approaches to the study of behavior, in which researchers combine a knowledge of biology and the history of our species to develop new ideas about human nature. Much of their work builds on the theories of the English naturalist Charles Darwin (1809–1882), who developed the theory of evolution by natural selection.

The publication in 1859 of Charles Darwin's book *On the Origin of Species* revolutionized people's understanding of the natural world. Before Darwin no convincing scientific account had existed to explain why organisms were the way they were and what caused differences and similarities between them. Today, no serious biologist would try to understand any species without considering it in the context of Darwin's theory of natural selection. In 1995 the philosopher Daniel Dennett summed up Darwin's impact: "In a single stroke, the idea of evolution by natural selection unifies the realm of life, meaning, and purpose with the realm of space and time, cause and effect."

Darwin's idea was relatively simple. Observing that some organisms seemed to reproduce more successfully than others, he assumed that some of these reproductive differences were the result of differences in the individuals' inherited traits. For example, finches with beaks that were strong enough to crack open seeds survived and procreated more than finches with beaks that were too narrow or weak. Environmental forces such as drought, said Darwin, "selected" certain traits, such as strong beaks. Individuals with these traits were then more likely to survive, reproduce, and pass these traits to

This photograph of Charles Darwin dates from about 1870. Between 1868 and 1872 he published three important works, all of which were continuations of the theories he had propounded in On the Origin of Species.

their offspring. Thus differences that led to greater reproductive success were passed down from one generation to the next, Darwin reasoned, until they spread throughout a population as individuals with the more successful traits in each generation out-reproduced individuals with less successful traits.

One of the main attractions of this simple idea is that it explains why organisms seem so well-adapted to survive and reproduce in their environments. All organisms need to accomplish certain tasks—such as finding food, avoiding predators, attracting mates, and so on—and small changes in certain traits that enable them to perform these tasks more efficiently than competitors gradually accumulate. As they do, the organisms gradually appear better "designed" to flourish in their environments.

To test his theory, Darwin bred pigeons using artificial (as opposed to natural) selection methods, mating birds with desired traits to produce each subsequent generation. In this way he established that specific traits could be passed down from parent to offspring, although he did not understand the mechanism that enabled this. That was because he did not yet know about genes, the microscopic units of information found in the nucleus of cells. Gregor Mendel studied inheritance in pea plants in the 1860s, but it was not until 1900 that his work was rediscovered independently by Erich Tschermak von Seysenegg, Hugo de Vries, and Carl Erich Correns. In 1909 the Danish biologist Wilhelm Ludvig Johannsen proposed the term "genes" to describe the responsible factors. This discovery lead to a greater understanding of how traits are inherited and a refinement of Darwin's theory.

> *"In the future I see open fields for far more important researches. Psychology will be securely based on the foundation...of the necessary acquirement of each mental power and capacity by gradation."*
> — *Charles Darwin, 1859*

African honeybees cover a honeycomb that has been removed from their hive. Researchers studying bee colonies sought to explain the existence of nonreproductive drones, which produce no offspring and appear to contradict Darwin's theories about natural selection and evolution.

Dawkins and the selfish gene

Darwin thought about the evolutionary process at the level of the individual, believing that the key lay in the number of surviving offspring that each individual produced. Biologist Richard Dawkins (born 1941) disputed this, however, in his book *The Selfish Gene* (1976), arguing that it was what happened to different genes, rather than to different individuals, that was crucial to understanding evolution.

Dawkins proposed that, in essence, evolution was a "feedback loop." Thus genes had certain effects on the organisms in which they were found, and the way in which they influenced each individual determined how many copies of each gene made it to the next generation. In this way exact copies of different genes passed from parent to offspring. So although all individual organisms died, genes were "immortal" in the sense that their copies traveled from generation to generation.

One important illustration that seems to support this theory is the process of kin selection, which biologist William D. Hamilton (1936–2000) studied. Hamilton knew that in some species of insect, colonies included many nonreproductive drones that left no offspring at all, which was a puzzle from the standpoint of traditional Darwinism. How could natural selection produce individuals that did not leave any descendants? Hamilton offered a solution to this problem in the 1970s, when he pointed out that more of the drones' genes survive in their sisters than would be the case in any offspring they had of their own. Thus in evolutionary

KEY DATES

1859 Publication of Charles Darwin's *On the Origin of Species*.
1976 Publication of Richard Dawkins' *The Selfish Gene*.
1994 The field achieves greater academic respectability when the Center for Evolutionary Psychology opens in Santa Barbara, California.
1999 David Buss publishes an evolutionary psychology textbook.

terms it is better for them to help the queen reproduce than do so themselves.

Darwin's theory of evolution by natural selection revolutionized biology. Today his theory has been improved and refined, but its underlying logic remains essentially unmodified. So why have scientists been so reluctant to apply his theory to people?

EVOLUTION AND HUMANS

When Darwin's theory first became public, many people reacted strongly against it, largely because of the apparent conflict between the concept of evolution and the Biblical story of creation. For some people this is still a problem today.

Among the first to apply Darwin's ideas to people were individuals with political agendas who wanted to justify unpalatable social and political policies, such as social Darwinism and eugenics (*see* p. 24).

> *"Religion had to be explained as a material process.... It had to be embraced by the single grand naturalistic image of man."*
> — *Edward O. Wilson, 1994*

Unfortunately, their attempts were burdened by a deep confusion about the true role of biology in politics and human social affairs. Theories of evolution also became associated with Hitler's policy of genocide (mass murder) during World War II, causing hostile reactions to more recent attempts to integrate evolution into our understanding of human behavior.

In 1975 Harvard biologist Edward O. Wilson (born 1929) published a book entitled *Sociobiology: The New Synthesis* in which he described how evolution helped explain animal social behavior. In his final chapter he applied the same ideas to human social life, generating fierce opposition from people who objected to the way he applied biological ideas to humans. Despite this hostility, several other scientists (*see* box right and p. 138) have since attempted to use evolutionary

theory to understand human behavior. From their work a new field called evolutionary psychology has emerged, which is now recognized as a scientific discipline rather than a political movement with an evolutionary label. Evolutionary psychology applies a modern understanding of the evolutionary principles of natural selection to human behavior and to the organ that generates this behavior, the human brain. Although not all evolutionary psychologists share the same ideas, there are some principles on which they generally agree. Some of the basic principles that most researchers in the area agree on are as follows.

Cognition

Evolutionary psychology begins with the same basic premise as other branches of psychology: that the human brain produces human behavior. In particular, many evolutionary psychologists agree with cognitive psychologists (*see* pp. 104–117) in viewing the brain as an

FAMILY VIOLENCE

PSYCHOLOGY & SOCIETY

Martin Daly and Margo Wilson, a husband-and-wife team of psychologists at McMaster University in Canada, have studied an issue of profound importance to society: family violence. In 1988 they published *Homicide*, which took an evolutionary approach to violence, particularly in the context of family. Starting from the theory of kin selection (*see* p. 135), they predicted that parents' biological children would be less likely to be abused than nonbiological (adopted or step-) children. After combing through a wide range of historical and anthropological records, they reached some startling conclusions. They found that in the United States and Canada stepchildren were more than 50 times as likely to be fatally abused by their parents than biological children.

The couple also gathered a great deal of evidence confirming several other hypotheses surrounding violence and murder, generated from the evolutionary point of view. They did not conclude that a child should always fear a step-parent, however, but rather that blended families are in some ways new and challenging to human nature. Thus parenting behavior must be learned if such families are to adapt successfully.

information-processing device much like a computer. Thus they see the brain as an organ that takes information from the various senses, processes it, and then produces behaviorial responses.

The cognitive view of the brain implies that one important task of psychology is to identify the programs that constitute the brain's circuitry. The evolutionary view adds the idea that programs in the brain are products of evolution by natural selection, and this provides important clues when researchers are trying to understand these circuits, or pathways.

Adaptations and by-products

According to Darwinian theory, the process of evolution preserves genes that enable individuals to perform tasks that promote survival and reproduction. These tasks—such as finding food, avoiding predators, and so on—are called "adaptive problems." Thus an adaptive problem is any difficulty faced by a species that has affected its reproductive success.

Because natural selection is a slow process, often requiring hundreds or thousands of generations for significant changes to occur, the only adaptive problems that matter are those that a given species faces repeatedly during its evolutionary history. If only a few generations face a problem, natural selection will generally not have time to select the genes that solve the problem.

This suggests that the programs that constitute human psychology evolved because they helped our ancestors solve problems during human evolutionary history. Of course, people today can do many things our ancestors never dreamed of doing, such as driving automobiles and flying airplanes. But even though our brains are able to produce these behaviors, the systems that enable us to behave in these ways did not evolve over time. These behaviors are rather by-products of the cognitive systems that evolved to perform other tasks that early people needed to accomplish to survive. And the fact that these genetically produced behaviors

produce so many new actions and abilities only demonstrates how flexible the human brain really is. Evolution, therefore, is not a rigid script; instead, it is much more like a library of forms and behaviors that has many unanticipated uses.

In his book *Adaptation and Natural Selection* (1966) biologist George Williams elaborated on the concept of cognitive evolution. He argued that evolution occurred because the traits of some organisms worked better than those of others. Over time the traits that functioned more efficiently in solving specific adaptive problems were selected over others, so an organism became better at performing the required functions. For instance, an organism with eyes that saw better than the eyes of other organisms of the same species would find it easier to catch food and avoid predators. Thus it would be more likely to survive and might pass the genes for better eyesight to the next generation. Such traits (the parts of organisms that are filtered by natural selection to perform specific, vital tasks) are called adaptations.

In contrast, by-products are accidental consequences of these adaptations. For example, the fact that bones are white is not a trait that was selected over time because it made bones function any better. Bones are actually white as an

A surfer rides the crest of a wave in Hawaii. Although this specific behavior is not a product of evolution, the skills required, such as balance and physical coordination, have evolved over many hundreds of generations. Evolution, therefore, has many unexpected outcomes.

KEY WORKS

• In 1859 Charles Darwin published the groundbreaking *On the Origin of Species*.
• In 1871 Darwin published *The Descent of Man and Selection in Relation to Sex*, which added the controversial theory of sexual and reproductive selection to the ideas he had set out in *On the Origin of Species*.
• In 1964 William D. Hamilton published his theory of kin selection.
• In 1976, after the flood of protest against Edward O. Wilson's book *Sociobiology: The New Synthesis* (1975), Richard Dawkins wrote *The Selfish Gene*.
• The next great landmark in evolutionary theory applied to human behavior was *The Evolution of Human Sexuality* (1979) by anthropologist Don Symons.
• One of the key works of the next decade was Leda Cosmides' 1985 dissertation. Titled

"Deduction or Darwinian Algorithms? An Explanation of the 'Elusive' Content Effect on the Wason Selection Task," Cosmides' thesis explored "cheater detection" (*see* p. 142).
• Another important book of the 1980s was *Homicide* (1988) by psychologists Martin Daly and Margo Wilson.
• In 1994 Steven Pinker announced his arrival with *The Language Instinct*.
• *The Moral Animal*, a popular treatment of evolutionary psychology by journalist Robert Wright, was also published in 1994.
• In 1997 the journal *Ethnology and Sociobiology* changed its name to *Evolution and Human Behavior*.
• In 1998 Steven Pinker published *How the Mind Works*.
• In 1999 David Buss published the first textbook on evolutionary psychology.

accidental consequence of the fact that calcium phosphate (the material that makes bones strong) is white.

Domain specificity

Perhaps the most important principle of evolutionary psychology is the concept of domain specificity, which is the idea that evolution tends to create organisms with different parts, each designed to solve a particular problem. For example, the human liver is designed to filter blood, the lungs enable air exchange, the muscles enable movement, and so on. These organs exist in their present forms because different problems required different solutions.

The selected traits of every organism depend entirely on the lifestyle of each organism, and biologists have made similar observations across the natural world. Birds have wings designed for flight, fish have fins designed for an aquatic lifestyle, and so on. Darwin made his discovery by observing different species of finch on the Galápagos Islands. He noticed that the finches had beaks that were specific to the kind of foraging they did: Birds that needed to reach into

shallow crevices had long, narrow beaks, while those that needed to crack open nuts had shorter, stouter beaks more appropriate to this task. It was this observation that organisms had features suited to their way of life that led to his insight about the nature of evolution.

Evolutionary psychologists believe that human brains develop along the same lines and for the same reason. Organs like the heart and liver need to be structured differently because they accomplish different tasks—the liver cannot pump blood, and the heart cannot filter it. Similarly, pathways in the brain must be able to solve different kinds of problems, and the problems that they solve are information-processing problems.

Consider the pathways in the brain associated with vision. Light-sensitive cells in the retina of the eye communicate the information they have gathered to specific parts of the brain, and that is all they do. They cannot be used for hearing, tasting, or deciding whom to date. This type of specialization is not found just at the level of perception. Evolutionary psychologists believe the brain consists of specialized pathways at every level. Their central premise is that the brain consists of a vast number of these specialized pathways that solve the adaptive problems faced by our ancestors during human evolutionary history—finding food, avoiding predators, hunting, attracting mates, and so on.

The ancestral past

We cannot, of course, know precisely what human evolutionary history was like, but we can make guesses using archaeological and anthropological evidence. The picture below shows the classic linear view of evolution, which has now been discredited. Discoveries in more recent decades have indicated that the human family tree has many different branches, although the exact path from early hominid to modern *Homo sapiens sapiens* is still unclear.

It is generally thought that some 500,000 years ago our ancestors were hunter-gatherers who lived in roving bands of perhaps 50 to 150 individuals, obtaining their food by hunting wild animals and collecting edible plants, fruits, and nuts. Our modern way of life, which includes agriculture, is very new in evolutionary terms, so evolutionary psychologists would not expect people to have specific adaptations suited to functioning in these environments. Instead, they would expect human adaptations to function best in ancestral environments.

For example, over human evolutionary history hunting was a difficult and dangerous enterprise. Meat, therefore, was scarce and hard to obtain. But because meat is high in protein, individuals who had a taste for it and ate it whenever it was available stored more calories than those who disliked or failed to obtain meat. Thus the desire for meat was probably very adaptive. These days meat is plentiful, but our inherited appetite for it leads to a multitude of health problems.

> *"The key to understanding how the modern mind works is to realize that its circuits were not designed to solve the day-to-day problems of a modern American."*
> — *Tooby and Cosmides, 2001*

The importance of understanding human evolutionary history explains why evolutionary psychologists work closely with anthropologists, who study the origins and nature of people. Information about the past helps these psychologists develop hypotheses about possible adaptations of the human mind. Hunter-gatherer cultures still exist around the world, providing additional clues to this lifestyle, although they should not be

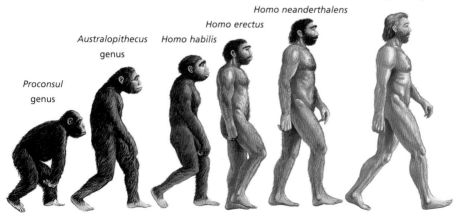

Homo sapiens sapiens

Homo neanderthalens

Homo erectus

Homo habilis

Australopithecus genus

Proconsul genus

23–15 million years ago

4–2.5 million years ago

2.5 million years ago

1.5 million years ago

200,000 years ago

100,000 years ago

This diagram depicts the classic view of human evolution. It starts with Proconsul, which was similar to an African ape, and ends with Homo sapiens sapiens (modern humans), although the place of Homo neanderthalens is uncertain. However, new discoveries point to a much more complex story.

seen as duplicates of ancestral cultures. Studying them simply helps researchers develop ideas about what the lives of our ancestors might have been like.

Learning

Biological approaches to the study of behavior were often thought to leave no room for learning, which is why the nature-nurture debate raged for so long (*see* pp. 22–29). Throughout history people tended to believe that behavior was caused either by instinct (biology, or nature) or by learning (culture, or nurture). Likewise scholars traditionally favored one side of the debate over the other, arguing over which position was correct. Evolutionary psychologists, however, believe that every aspect of an organism is produced by the interaction between its genes and the environment— so neither nature nor nurture is sufficient to explain behavior by itself.

Language learning illustrates this idea. Babies cannot speak a language when they are born, but acquire it by listening to and interacting with the adults in their lives. However, they are equipped to learn language through an innate cognitive system that is adapted to the purpose. Building on the work of linguist Noam Chomsky (*see* pp. 119–122), Steven Pinker (*see* box above) referred to this capacity as an instinct—suggesting that the specific cognitive capacity for learning language evolved over the course of human history.

Evolutionary psychologists regard evolution as a process that adds more "instincts to learn," and that these extra mechanisms allow organisms greater flexibility. This approach suggests that learning mechanisms are likely to be domain-specific (related to a specific function of the brain), which conflicts with the view favored by behaviorists of a general learning mechanism (*see* pp. 74–89). So just as Chomsky suggested there was an innate "language organ," evolutionary psychologists believe that other "mental organs" exist to learn and reason about other specific domains.

STEVEN PINKER

BIOGRAPHY

One of the great modern popularizers of science, Steven Pinker has made the fields of evolutionary psychology and language acquisition accessible to the public, especially in his bestselling books *The Language Instinct* (1994), *How the Mind Works* (1997), and *Words and Rules: The Ingredients of Language* (1999). Born on September 18, 1954, in Montreal, Canada, he studied first at McGill University, before completing a psychology doctorate at Harvard in 1979. He is currently on the faculty of the Massachusetts Institute of Technology in the Department of Brain and Cognitive Sciences. His main research is in the area of visual cognition and language, but he lectures widely on evolutionary matters.

Cultural differences

A frequent criticism of the evolutionary approach is that it cannot explain why people differ, and some have even argued that biological explanations of behavior assume that everyone is the same. This is due to a common misunderstanding about biology, however, and a simple example makes this clear. Consider calluses, the layers of dead skin cells that form when you rub a particular area of skin repeatedly. Every person has the same mechanism for producing calluses, but some expose their hands, feet, or other areas to more friction than others, and it is these individuals who develop calluses. So, although everyone has the same mechanism, there is still a great deal of difference among individuals in terms of who has calluses and who does not.

Evolutionary psychologists believe that the same is true of the human brain, suggesting that there is a universal human cognitive design (although males and females may differ in certain ways). Behavior is variable, however, because people develop in different environments. For example, everyone has the same language acquisition mechanisms, but the language people learn depends entirely on the language those around them speak.

Thus evolutionary approaches do not predict uniform behavior. Evolutionary psychologists believe that the human brain consists of many mechanisms that interact in various ways with their environments. So even though people are born with the same evolved mechanisms, the way that they behave can vary greatly depending on circumstances.

EVOLUTIONARY RESEARCH

Evolutionary psychology differs from traditional approaches in various important ways, but probably the most significant is the idea that the brain consists of many information-processing mechanisms specific to particular domains. One of the earliest experimental programs in the field illustrated this difference in perspectives.

Leda Cosmides was interested in using evolutionary reasoning to investigate the human ability to reason logically, which according to traditional approaches was one of the small number of general human cognitive capacities. In 1985, for her doctoral dissertation, Cosmides used an experiment that was already well known to cognitive psychologists, the Wason selection task (*see* box on p. 142). She started with the idea suggested by historical studies of different cultures that social exchange—the trading of one good for another—has a long history among people. She expected, therefore, that people would have a specific cognitive mechanism necessary for trade: the ability to detect when they are being cheated, or a "cheater-detection" mechanism.

She tested her hypothesis by giving her experimental subjects two different versions of the same logical reasoning problem. In one case the problem was phrased in terms of a social exchange, and in one case it was not. Her results showed that when the problem involved a social exchange, people were good at choosing the answer that would correctly identify any cheaters. This contrasted with the

People may not consciously choose a mate on the basis of reproductive potential or their ability to acquire resources, but research has shown that evolutionary-driven requirements such as these do play a major role in our selection of a mate.

answers given to the problem that did not involve any form of social exchange.

Cosmides ran a considerable number of these experiments, and through a rigorous research program she eliminated various other explanations for her results. In this way she showed that her subjects' good performance was not due simply to the problems being familiar or to the social contract facilitating clear thinking. In short, she provided evidence for a specific cognitive adaptation: cheater-detection. This indicated that cheater-detection was so important to human survival that we inherited it from ancestors who possessed this domain-specific ability—and who out-reproduced others who could not detect cheaters as efficiently.

Mating

Another prominent example of research in evolutionary psychology is David Buss's work on human mating, which began with a few ideas from evolutionary theory. The first of them is that in species like humans in which females usually provide parental care, males can increase their reproductive success by mating with many females. Mating with multiple males will not lead to more offspring for females, however. This concept led Buss to suspect that males had evolved preferences for mating with multiple females. A second factor important to reproductive success in human males is the age of the female with whom the male mates. As a woman

gets older, the number of children she may produce in the future decreases. Thus Buss hypothesized that men would have evolved a preference for younger women. Finally, Buss considered the preferences that evolutionary theory would predict for women. He reasoned that an important mating factor for women would be the quantity of resources that a man could invest in his offspring and predicted that females would prefer males who displayed a greater ability to acquire these resources.

Buss tested his hypotheses by surveying thousands of subjects in 37 different cultures, trying to establish whether his predicted differences between the sexes could be found cross-culturally (*see* pp.

152–161). Working with collaborators, he gave his subjects questionnaires that asked them about their preferences in mates. Buss's monumental collection of cross-cultural data generated strong support for his evolutionary hypotheses, showing that differences between the sexes in mating preferences are remarkably consistent across many cultures. His influential book *The Evolution of Desire* (1995) was partly responsible for ensuring that evolutionary psychology and cross-cultural studies of sex differences in mating were included in many college psychology courses. Critics, however, argue that there are many other reasons for the behavior he studied, such as cultural values and social conditioning.

THE WASON SELECTION TASK

EXPERIMENT

After studying reasoning for decades, without being able to explain how people made deductions, researchers in the 1960s decided that people had a mental logic. In 1966, however, British psychologist Peter Wason devised his famous selection task and discovered that adults regularly made predictable kinds of logical errors. When logic problems were put into certain kinds of social contexts, however, more people made the correct selections. Leda Cosmides developed this theory by introducing the concept of cheater-detection, which comes into play in social situations involving an element of trade.

Try to solve the following problem. You read a report on the habits of Cambridge residents that says: "If a person goes into Boston from Cambridge, then that person takes the subway." The cards shown below are printed with information about four Cambridge residents, each card representing one person. One side of each card tells you where that person went, and the other side tells you how that person got there. So which card(s) would you definitely need to turn over to test whether the report is true or not?

Now try to solve the following problem. You are working in a bar, and your job is to enforce the rule: "If a person drinks beer, then that person must be more than 18 years old." The cards shown below are printed with information about four patrons, each card representing one person. One side of the card tells you how old that person is, and the other side of the card tells what they are drinking. Indicate which card(s) you definitely need to turn over to see if any of these people are violating the rule.

Person 1   Person 2   Person 3   Person 4

The correct answer to both problems is that you must turn over the second and last cards. In the first problem you must find out if the person who went to Boston took the subway, and where the person who took the cab went. In the second problem you must find out if the person drinking beer is over 18, and what the 14-year-old is drinking. Although the problems are identical in terms of logical form, most people answer the first one incorrectly. However, the second problem requires you to find out who is cheating, and most people answer it correctly.

Person 1   Person 2   Person 3   Person 4

CRITICISMS

Evolutionary psychologists have been criticized for telling "just-so" stories, a reference to Rudyard Kipling's whimsical tales about how organisms came to have their particular traits. Such critics are implying that hypotheses in evolutionary psychology cannot be tested and are therefore unscientific. However, research programs like those of Cosmides (who used experimental methods) and Buss (who used survey techniques) show that evolutionary theory can be tested using scientific principles (*see* pp. 141–142).

> *"Magnificent things in the future aside, we will still be trying to understand it all with a brain… whose function is to mate, eat, and smell the roses."*
> — *Robert L. Solso, 1998*

Another misunderstanding concerns the fact that evolutionary ideas have previously been used to justify political agendas. This represents a fundamental misunderstanding of science, often called the "naturalistic fallacy." As a science, evolutionary psychology might give us insight into human nature, but it cannot tell us what is, or ought to be, "good."

Evolutionary psychologists are also accused of believing that people want to produce as many offspring as possible, another misrepresentation that stems from confusion about evolution. It is the selection of traits that lead to reproductive success, not a deliberate bid for numerical superiority. The human mind consists of those mechanisms that were historically adaptive. In modern environments, these mechanisms may have many effects, some

This Mormon man from Utah has five wives. Polygyny (marriage to more than one wife at a time) was once a common practice in much of the world. Although there can be economic advantages for both sexes, it is becoming increasingly rare and is illegal in western countries.

adaptive, and some—such as the human taste for meat—potentially maladaptive.

Finally, some people believe that the theories of evolutionary psychology imply genetic determinism: the idea that behavior is inflexible because it is totally determined by genetic influence. In reality, however, the evolutionary view holds that behavioral adaptations, created by genes, lead to flexible behavior. Thus evolution is a process by which organisms change so that they can respond more adaptively to their environments.

THE FUTURE

Psychology as a field has been slow to accept evolutionary approaches to behavior, but that is changing. A few U.S. universities now offer specializations in evolutionary psychology, and textbooks have been produced for evolutionary psychology courses. Scientists in related disciplines such as political science and economics are also beginning to incorporate evolutionary thinking into their research. Currently researchers are using evolutionary ideas to research areas such as reasoning, language, emotion, mating, violence, Darwinian medicine, economic behavior, and esthetics.

CONNECTIONS

- Nature and Nurture: pp. 22–29
- Cognitive Psychology: pp. 104–117
- Research Methods: pp. 162–163
- History of the Brain: Volume 2, pp. 6–19
- Perception: Volume 2, pp. 62–85.
- Problem Solving: Volume 3, pp. 136–163

Nonwestern Theories of the Mind

"A redefinition of psychology is needed..."

K. Owusu-Bempah & D. Howitt

Mainstream psychology developed in Europe and the United States during the late 19th century, which means that current theories and research projects are deeply rooted in western culture. However, people in other cultures have also produced theories about psychological questions such as how the mind works, why people engage in certain behaviors, and how to treat people with mental problems—and many of them have a much longer history than western theories.

In Asian cultures psychology is strongly related to religion and spirituality. This Buddhist monk is meditating in front of a small stone altar.

Western psychologists sometimes claim that nonwestern theories of the mind are invalid, partly because they are not based on scientific experiments, and partly because they often include religious and philosophical ideas. Anthropologists, however, have shown that nonwestern theories of the mind are at least as complex as their western equivalents, and that it is important for scientists to study these theories if they wish to gain an understanding of their own and other communities.

Indigenous psychologies

In both nonwestern countries and the western world, researchers have recently begun to promote the study of so-called indigenous psychologies. The term indigenous means native or homegrown, but most psychologists use it to mean culturally appropriate. An indigenous psychology is formulated along western lines, integrating western standards about research methodology and data analysis, but attempts to take account of cultural norms and values. For example, an indigenous Chinese psychology would be more concerned with community life than standard U.S. psychology. Essentially, however, indigenous psychologies are western psychologies that have been corrected for cultural values—and they do not always allow for a proper appreciation of truly "homegrown" ideas.

Endogenous psychologies

An endogenous psychology, on the other hand, is entirely produced within the cultural heritage of a country and does not rely on western models and research methods. Thus endogenization means that all psychological ideas come from inside the community and, in most cases, have been part of the culture for thousands of years. People in India, Japan, or China would not use the word psychology, but their endogenous views deserve to be called psychologies because they include important ideas on the mind, or psyche.

Endogenous psychologies are often so strongly linked with folklore and cultural rites that they cannot be separated from religion, spirituality, and art. In Asian cultures, for example, the philosophical and religious writings of Hinduism and Zen Buddhism provide the starting point

ZEN BUDDHISM

Buddhism began in India in about the sixth century B.C. when a Nepalese prince called Siddhartha Gautama left his life of luxury to become a wandering holy man. After many years he believed he had found the ultimate truth and became known as the Buddha, or Enlightened One.

Buddhism is different from most major religions because it does not require the worship of a god but is entirely focused on the realization of nirvana, a state of mind in which an individual overcomes all pain and suffering and attains a state of complete happiness. Zen Buddhism is a type of Buddhism that accords central value to silent internal prayer, and it informs many Asian theories of the mind. In Zen Buddhism nirvana is achieved through prolonged meditation—the term "zen" coming from the Chinese word *chan*, which in turn derives from the Sanskrit word *dhyana*, which refers to meditation.

The principles of Zen Buddhism spread across Japan during the 12th century A.D., influencing many aspects of Japanese culture, such as painting and the decorative arts, and becoming a way of life. Zen Buddhism also contributed to the development of Asian combat techniques such as jujitsu, kung fu, and karate.

and background for many people's views on the mind, behavior, and healing.

People who grew up within a western community often find it difficult to study endogenous psychologies. They may find it hard to set aside their own norms and values to understand nonwestern ideas, and may even need to learn another language or learn something about a culture's religious and spiritual beliefs. Without knowing about Zen Buddhism (*see* box above) or being able to read Sanskrit, for example, it is almost impossible to understand many Asian views on the mind.

In parts of Africa and Asia such studies are especially difficult, since westerners imposed their own psychological ideas on the local people during the course of colonization in the 20th century, driving many endogenous psychologies into the background. As a result, these psychologies were forgotten or abandoned as western psychologies replaced them.

Another problem is that endogenous psychologies may not be taught in published writings, but through oral tradition, kept alive by the tales and myths that people share during family gatherings and religious ceremonies. Westerners hoping to study the psychology of a particular community must therefore gain the respect of the local people before they will share this information.

This image from the late 1950s shows a Christian missionary working with children in Central Africa. Missionary activity and political colonization often went hand in hand in Africa, and both were guilty of imposing western ideas at the expense of different local cultures.

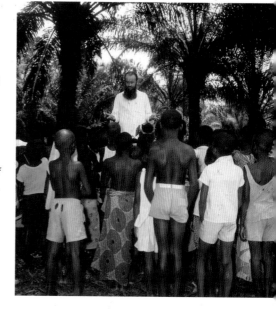

- Western theories about the workings of the mind have been developed in the western world and reflect western experiences.
- Western psychologists have tried to modify their theories by adding ideas from other cultures, but these indigenous psychologies still use western notions and methods as their basis.
- Endogenous psychologies can help us understand nonwestern cultures, enabling professionals in the west to work effectively within a multicultural environment.
- Although endogenous psychologies are different from mainstream psychologies, they are not inferior. Indeed, western psychology is endogenous from a nonwestern viewpoint.

our body), the social self (how we present ourselves to others), the ideal self (the individual we would like to be), and the self-concept (the way we think about ourselves). Many explanations have been given for how the self and the subselves develop. Social constructionists, for example, have claimed that culture creates the self, while radical essentialists argued that the self is an inborn phenomenon. These definitions of the self, the subselves, and the personality are relatively easy for westerners to grasp because they reflect the ideals, private experiences, and the cultural context in which they live.

The definition of the self as a unity, the psychological distinctions between the self and the nonself, and the distinctions between bodily self and self-concept have been developed by western psychologists studying western people in western cultures. In nonwestern cultures few of these definitions and distinctions apply. An Asian person would probably find western psychologies of the self bizarre for at least two reasons.

First, Asian thought does not always distinguish between the self and the nonself, between what is part of ourselves and what belongs to the outside world. In the *Mandukaya Upanishad*, one of the most important philosophical books of Hinduism, the self is described as a synthesis between the subjective and the objective. This means that the self is not opposed to the outside world (the nonself, the objective), but is a combination of an individual's private experiences (the subjective) and the community in which he or she lives. Sometimes western psychologists have argued that the self is not important within Asian thought, but that is not true: Asian and western notions of self are just different.

The second reason why an Asian person would probably find western ideas about the self strange is that in much eastern thought there is no distinction between the mind and the body. The principle whereby the mind and the body always work together is called monism and is

In some Asian cultures "native" researchers have sought to overcome these problems by undertaking their own studies of endogenous psychologies, but in Africa such studies have hardly even begun. Unlike India and China, the poorer African countries offer few opportunities for people to train as researchers and investigate the psychological knowledge of their own culture.

In modern western culture the individual is all important, and people focus on their sense of self as something separate from the world around them. But in many nonwestern cultures the mind and body are thought to work together, and the self is viewed as part of the environment.

> *"Africa claims pride of place as the birthplace of humanity, but remains the least known part of our planet in terms of psychological knowledge."*
> — *Bame Nsamenang, 1993*

The western concept of self

In western psychologies the notion of the "self" usually refers to the individual person; it does not mean the same thing as personality. Western psychologists have argued that the self can only emerge if children are able to distinguish between themselves and the outside world, the self emerging in opposition to the "nonself."

Western psychologists have unraveled the self into a whole series of subselves, such as the bodily self (our awareness of

derived from the Greek term for single. It is opposed to dualism, which means double or twofold. While most western psychologies are based on a dualism of body and mind, most Asian systems of thought promote a monism of the body-mind working as a single unit—and this unity underpins many therapeutic and meditative techniques, such as yoga (*see* box below) and Chinese medicine.

Once researchers start investigating endogenous psychologies, they soon discover that people in every community, no matter how simple or complex their lives, have certain ideas about what makes a person different from other life forms.

> *"It is not possible to live as a human being without having an idea of what it is to be human."*
> — *Paul Heelas, 1981*

Until the 1940s most western researchers believed that endogenous ideas were inferior to western views and that they reflected an underdeveloped and primitive way of thinking. The work of social anthropologists such as Claude Lévi-Strauss (born 1908) proved that this was a misguided interpretation. After extensive fieldwork in Brazil and among Native American communities Lévi-Strauss concluded that the notion of the primitive mind was a myth.

In a nonindustrialized society systems of thought are often much more complex than those adopted in the developed world. Endogenous concepts of the self are not inadequate just because they are based on stories and spiritual beliefs rather than experiments. In fact, they enable people to live and function quite successfully within their own cultures.

Buddhist theory of emotion

Even concepts of emotion vary outside western society, and one such example occurs in Buddhist cultures. Although there are different schools of Buddhism, the Buddhist tradition generally refers to a basic list of primary mental events called *kleshas*. A *klesha* is similar to an extreme affect, passion, or emotional reaction.

The six primary *kleshas* are pride, anger, desire, doubt, ignorance, and mistaken views—and they always emerge in response to a mental disturbance. So when people experience one or more of the six *kleshas*, they suffer from a deficiency in personality. According to the Buddhist psychology of emotions, *kleshas* require treatment and must be addressed by meditation and spiritual reflection.

Looking at the Buddhist theory of emotions from a western viewpoint, the list of *kleshas* seems to include mental

YOGA

FOCUS ON

The technique of yoga is one of the six systems of Indian philosophy. Yoga practitioners (yogis) have to learn to control the body-mind by canceling all thoughts and feelings, and when this is achieved, consciousness becomes empty and pure. Yogis try to reach this state of purity through moral and physical discipline. As part of the moral discipline they have to abstain from violence and any type of sexual activity. For the physical discipline a specific posture and a particular type of breathing are important. Seated with their hands on their legs or knees, yogis keep their chin parallel to the ground and close their eyes. Then they concentrate on a point between their eyebrows and control their breathing until it becomes deep, regular, and slow. In this way yogis may reach the state of pure consciousness, where the distinction between self and nonself disappears, and the mental world merges with the physical world. Experienced practitioners are allegedly able to lower their heart rate to four beats per minute, which is essentially miraculous according to western medical knowledge. In the 20th century yoga also became popular in the west, but not all westerners are aware of its philosophical basis.

events that would never be described as emotions within western psychology. Western psychologists, for example, would probably classify ignorance and doubt as cognitive states (mental events related to thinking) rather than emotional experiences. They would be unlikely to regard the *kleshas* as signs of a mental disturbance requiring treatment unless they became compulsive or extreme. Anger, for example, is not considered a problematic mental event and only becomes a problem when it veers into aggression, violence, and destruction.

However, some of these apparent differences between Buddhist and western theories of emotion may stem from a bad translation of the original Sanskrit terms. "Emotion," "passion," and "affect" are poor translations of *klesha* and may not convey the meaning of the word effectively.

According to stress psychologist Richard Lazarus there are also some significant similarities between Buddhist theory and western cognitive views of emotion. Both theories state that emotions originate from various cognitive (thought) processes. While Buddhists see the nature of emotion as either instinctive or acquired, westerners see it as concious or unconscious. Last, according to Buddhist theory, emotions influence the mind and body, while western theory states that emotions affect mind, body, and actions. Modern western psychologists are still seeking explanations for the origin, nature, and influence of emotions, so it is valuable to see that ancient Buddhist tradition comes to the same conclusions.

The Indian tradition

India also has a rich intellectual tradition concerning the origin and nature of emotions. Unlike western psychologies, however, Indian ideas did not rely on the results of experiments, but came from reflections on religion, philosophy, and art. The oldest Indian theory of emotion is the *rasa* theory (*see* box below), which distinguishes between 8 aesthetic moods, 8 major emotions, and 33 minor emotions.

Some of the major aesthetic moods in the *rasa* tradition, such as love and horror, are immediately recognizable as important emotions within western culture, while others, such as pathos and marvel, would

---

 ## THE RASA TRADITION

The Sanskrit term *rasa*, meaning "aesthetic relish," refers to the theory of emotions developed by the Brahman sage and priest Bharata sometime between the fifth century B.C. and the second century A.D. Bharata discussed the key principles of *rasa* in the *Natyasastra*, a book concerned mainly with the art of performance, the theory of staged drama, and the techniques of acting. Consequently,

Indian dancers perform a sacred dance of love called the rasa lila, *which depicts a scene from the famous epic poem* Ramayana.

Bharata composed his theory of emotions within the context of a general discussion of dramaturgy (the theory of how to write, direct, and perform a play).

The eight basic *rasas* in Bharata's work are primarily "aesthetic moods." He distinguished between love, comedy, pathos, fury, heroism, horror, hatred, and marvel, and linked each of these *rasas* with a major durable emotion: respectively, erotic feeling, mirth, sorrow, anger, energy/mastery, fear, disgust, and astonishment. Some of the *rasas* would also qualify as basic emotions in western psychologies—but they might be expressed in different ways than what we would expect.

Alongside the major emotions Bharata listed 33 minor emotions, such as despair, pride, jealousy, and indignation. He believed that they were minor because they were less durable than the major emotions and did not occur in humans and nonhuman animals alike.

be unlikely to enter a western classification of emotions. The major aesthetic moods may also be expressed in very different ways than those seen in the United States and Europe. One of the *rasa* moods is horror, which is universally understood as an emotion, but a Westerner might not recognize it as expressed in an Indian drama. This contrast between expressions of similar emotions makes it clear that emotional expression is influenced by social customs and by biological factors.

> *"In the Indian traditions, major contributions to the study of emotion came from aesthetics."*
> — A. C. Paranjpe & G. S. Bhatt, 1997

In the western world the idea that emotions are socially constructed did not gain prominence until the 20th century. However, the author of the *rasa* theory had realized that sociocultural rules played a crucial part in the emergence and expression of emotion some 3,000 years before. So *rasa* theory already included the explanations of emotion that western psychologists and anthropologists allegedly discovered, after much hard work, during the 1970s and 1980s.

An example from Africa
Relatively little original documentation exists about endogenous psychologies on the African continent, since much of the early literature about local myths and religions was written by outsiders. Nonetheless, some writers have provided interesting accounts of the ways that people in these communities think about the mind and the emotions.

In a book called *Casting out Anger* Grace Harris describes how people of the Taita community in Kenya think about the nature of emotions, and anger in particular. According to the Taita, every person can experience good and bad emotions. Good emotions are those that contribute to the survival of the individual

Emotions are influenced by social customs as well as biological factors, so different people may express the same emotions in different ways. But there is no mistaking the sorrowful feelings of this Palestinian woman on the West Bank.

and the community, while bad emotions lead to the destruction of the individual and his social relationships. The Taita believe that anger, which they call the "angry heart," is a bad emotion, and they try to replace it with a good emotion whenever it occurs.

The Taita do this by performing purification rituals in which the affected individuals are relieved from the bad emotions they are enduring, and good emotions (such as love and respect) are restored. In a sense the goals of these rituals are similar to those of western psychotherapeutic practices: In both cases people suffering from mental problems and antisocial tendencies are returned to an acceptable level of social competence.

Therapy in the west
The word therapy is derived from the Greek *therapeia*, which means service, worship, religion, care, and healing. Nowadays it is used as a synonym for

"treatment," usually in combination with a prefix that indicates the method through which the healing process occurs, such as physiotherapy or psychotherapy (*see* pp. 52–65). The original meanings of the word make it clear that for the ancient Greeks (*see* pp. 10–15) treatment could take place within various contexts: magical, religious, or scientific. Each was associated with a particular type of healer—the sorcerer-magician, the priest, or the physician—but often the same person performed all these roles. Spiritual healers still operate in contemporary western cultures, but most professionals believe that it is better to heal physical and mental problems with scientifically proven treatments. Thus western medicine is often believed to be more effective than alternative treatments.

Chinese medicine
Outside the western world communities still rely on treatment processes with a philosophical or religious basis. Chinese medicine, for example, is based on the Taoist vision of a universe ruled by two equal but opposite forces, yin and yang. Yin is passive and reflective, while yang is active and dynamic. According to the Taoists, everything in the world can be explained in terms of the two. Illness is thought to be the result of an imbalance of the two forces within the body.

The task of practitioners of Chinese medicine is much more complex than that of western doctors because they must consider the patient as a whole, taking the

> "*Healing is a question of knowing how harmony can be restored; and the task of the physician is as much philosophical as technical.*"
> — *Roy Porter, 1997*

state of body, mind, and spirit into account. Treatments might include diet, herbs, exercises such as tai chi chuan, meditation, and massage. Another popular therapy is acupuncture, which involves inserting hot or cold needles at key points along the body's meridians: channels through which the body's energy (chi) is thought to circulate. Acupuncture frees the chi, which balances the yin and yang.

Traditional healing
Nonwestern communities often have quite different beliefs about what constitutes a mental problem, and they also have their

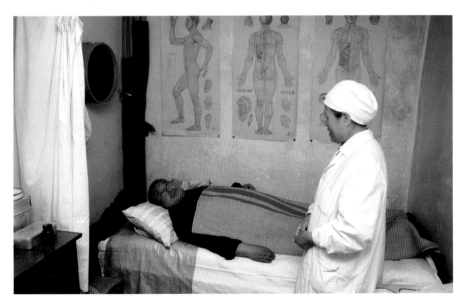

A Chinese patient and a medical practitioner in Beijing, China. Traditionally, Chinese practitioners treat the whole person rather than just a specific complaint, so a consultation with the doctor is not limited to when a person feels ill, but is also seen as an important part of staying in good health.

own techniques for curing them. Some treat mental disorders by applying ritual forms of healing in which religious and magical beliefs converge; in traditional healing ceremonies witch doctors and shamans may perform elaborate rituals in which they appeal to a natural force or to one of the gods.

Western psychiatrists often find it difficult to believe that these practices are effective, or as effective as drug therapy, but this may just be another example of western narrow-mindedness. Researchers have already discovered that western people can feel better when they take an inactive drug simply because they believe that the drug works. This is called the "placebo effect," and it suggests that the patient's belief in the power of the drug and the authority of the healer should not be underestimated. A similar effect may be at work in traditional forms of healing.

New models

Faced with such a huge diversity of western and nonwestern psychologies, and all the differences between them, some researchers have tried to create new models of the mind that can be applied to all cultures. Not everyone working in the fields of psychology and psychotherapy agrees with this approach, however. The main problem is that it tends to focus on the things that people have in common, while minimizing those aspects that make people different from each other.

Instead of an integration of western and nonwestern theories into a unitary model, some researchers now advise psychologists and psychotherapists to learn about alternative psychologies. Hopefully, this should enable them to recognize the limits of their own views

The witch doctor shown above has gone into a deep trance as part of his sacred ritual. Witch doctors play an import role in the religion of the Azande people of Central Africa, acting as religious officials, healers, and therapists.

and help people belonging to ethnic minorities by using their own endogenous psychologies. However, an awareness of cross-cultural variety does not mean it is essential for patients to be treated by people of their own community. As psychologists K. Owusu-Bempah and Dennis Howitt stated, "Having a few black professionals to deal with black people...should be seen as a rejection of responsibility rather than its acceptance."

A genuine awareness of such alternative psychologies should help professional psychologists ensure that the same services are available to all people, without considerations of race, western cultural bias, and implicit discrimination. In reality, of course, this is a complex task, and many psychological services still appear to have few beneficial effects beyond the boundaries of western psychology. Professional training in alternative psychologies is therefore a prerequisite for creating multicultural awareness among western psychologists.

CONNECTIONS

Cross-cultural Psychology

——————— *"...studies [of] variability among...societies and cultural groups..."* ———————

Smith & Bond

Cross-cultural psychologists study the thought processes, social attitudes, motivations, and beliefs of people in different societies, comparing and contrasting any influences on behavior. When used judiciously, such findings can offer valuable insights into the human mind that may have been overlooked in traditional western psychology—although it is important to avoid the numerous pitfalls that can lead to unfounded value judgments about what is right and wrong.

Culture can be defined as the attitudes, values, beliefs, and behaviors shared by a group of people with a common history, which are passed down from generation to generation, principally through language, but also through other forms of communication, such as art. In psychology cultural studies are important for two main reasons. First, psychologists need to know whether their findings apply to all people of all cultures or are applicable only to some people in some cultures. Second, studies of other cultures

> *"Until recently, most of the data in psychology were derived from predominantly middle-class, white, introductory psychology students."*
> — *David Masumoto, 1994*

Anthropologist Margaret Mead interviews a mother from the Admiralty Islands of Papua New Guinea in the Pacific Ocean during a visit in 1953. Studies of remote civilizations such as this have had a huge influence on western psychology.

can provide valuable new approaches to understanding human behavior. Cross-cultural psychology helps psychologists understand the relationships between culture and behavior, teaching them how the two areas relate to one another at both the individual and the group level.

Cross-cultural psychology overlaps with anthropology in several areas, but the two disciplines tend to focus on different aspects of a civilization. For example, anthropologists have traditionally been concerned with matters such as kinship, land distribution, and ritual—topics that

generally do not concern psychologists. When anthropologists turn their attention to psychological matters, they tend to focus on collecting data through direct observation of behavior and customs, such as child-rearing practices or the age of weaning. However, there is no significant body of anthropological data on many of the more abstract questions commonly addressed by psychologists, such as notions of intelligence. Indeed, cross-cultural psychology has greatly influenced measurements of intelligence (*see* Vol. 5, pp. 118–141). The earliest IQ tests were heavily biased in favor of people who knew the same songs, read the same books, and worshiped the same gods as the examiners, while modern tests of this type strive to be culturally neutral.

As global travel and communication have become common, and a rise in migration has led to increased numbers of people from different cultures living together in a single location, cross-cultural psychology has entered the mainstream of scientific research. By learning about different cultures, psychologists hope to acquire new insights into the way in which people think and conduct their lives. One of the biggest obstacles in the path of cross-cultural research, however, is the difficulty of achieving true scientific objectivity. Researchers must be mindful of their own cultural bias and resist any temptation to impose it on their subjects.

Ethnocentrism

Historically, the study of psychology has its roots in the western world (*see* pp. 10–15) and has thus been criticized for ethnocentrism: the assumption that an indivdual's own culture is "right" or "best." Ethnocentrism can result in a failure to understand the behavior and thoughts of people from other backgrounds, and in viewing behaviors they regard as normal

CULTURAL DIFFERENCES

FOCUS ON

Research carried out in the 1970s by Stanley Sue, a professor at the University of California, appeared to show that psychotherapy was excluding large sections of the U.S. population. Although many North Americans of European descent benefited from analysis, Asian Americans and Native Americans were less likely to seek counseling, and those who did were less likely to find it helpful or even to complete their therapy courses. These results were replicated in a later study in the 1990s, and it was concluded that the problem was caused by the insensitivity of standard treatment methods to the needs of different cultures.

KEY TERMS

- **Culture** A set of attitudes, values, beliefs, and behaviors shared by a group of people.
- **Dependent variable/ independent variable** Used in psychological experiments to measure change, for example, in measuring the effect of heat on someone's ability to perform a task. In this instance the independent variable would be the change in temperature, which may or may not influence the number of errors made—the dependent variable.
- **Ethnocentrism** People's inability to ignore their own cultural background when making judgments about behavior.
- **Stereotypes** Widely held beliefs that people belonging to a particular group have certain characteristics.

as unacceptable, and that may lead to bias. For example, babies in China do not wear diapers, and their parents may allow them to defecate in the street. This behavior would be frowned on in the west, but it does not mean that the Chinese have fewer concerns about hygiene than other nationalities. Similarly, public expressions of grief in Islamic and Jewish cultures are often less restrained than those of northern Europeans, many of whom have been brought up to show nothing more than a stiff upper lip in times of sorrow. This does not mean that a wailing Muslim widow is hysterical or has lost her reason, however, any more than it indicates that a reticent European widow feels no emotion at a funeral.

Ethnocentric western psychology can also fall into the trap of stereotyping: a belief that people's behavior is defined by their culture. The idea that all Africans are good athletes, that all Irishmen are good talkers, or that white people are useless at basketball are all examples of stereotyping. At its worst, stereotyping is racist and discriminatory. Contemporary cross-cultural psychology tries to avoid prejudice of this type, discouraging the groundless assumption that any alien practice is somehow inferior to a person's own traditions—or that it is deviant. It strives to be sensitive to the different peoples of the world and to recognize that each grouping has its own special needs.

Primitive thought

It was not always this way. During the 19th and early 20th centuries anthropologists, psychologists, and sociologists typically graded different societies on a scale that ranged from "modern" to "primitive." Given that most of the scientists making these assessments were Europeans and North Americans, it is hardly surprising that they classified their own cultures in the former category and regarded communities with different standards of living as backward. Some of the poorest and remotest cultures, such as those of the Polynesian Islands in the Pacific Ocean, were additionally described as "heathen" (they did not worship the God of the Bible). These observations were clearly ethnocentric. The Polynesians have their own gods and their own ways of life, and to judge their societies by western standards was unhelpful and unjust.

Causes and effects

The main research method cross-cultural psychologists use is called comparative analysis: A researcher obtains data from a sample of people in a particular culture and compares it with other known data or values. A known behavior or value is called a dependent variable: It is an observed, established behavior event or pattern. The researcher is then free to ask which factors might account for the dependent variable and to decide which of these potential causes or influences to test. These factors are the independent variables in the research study. The researcher then collects data that might support the link between cause and effect.

Research on observed effects is easier when psychologists are studying cultures similar to their own because they can make educated guesses about independent variables. When they are studying different cultures, however, it is more difficult to come up with useful theories about cause and effect—and it is here that generalizations might be made or findings blurred by ethnocentrism and stereotyping. To avoid this, researchers

need to collect as much data as possible about independent and dependent variables before coming to conclusions.

For example, the people of southern Spain habitually take longer lunchbreaks than workers in New York City, but what accounts for this cultural difference? An uninformed researcher might decide that this observation constitutes evidence to suggest that Mediterranean people are lazy by nature. However, further research would reveal that in Spain and other southern European cultures the midday sun makes lunchtime an uncomfortably hot time to work. Consequently, businesses and shops close for three or four hours in the middle of the day, but stay open later at night. Thus researchers would agree that this difference between the behavior of New Yorkers and Spaniards has nothing to do with genetics or personality, but is a culture-based behavior pattern reflecting the influence of climate in Mediterranean cultures rather than personality or work ethics.

Wearing elaborate costumes, men of the Mekeo tribe of Papua New Guinea play drums during a ceremony. Cross-cultural psychologists have been fascinated by the similarities and differences between cultures such as this and those of the western world.

Ingroups and outgroups

People are naturally social creatures, and their day-to-day lives are made up of almost constant interaction with others. Social psychologists examine people's behavior in a social context, observing how they influence each other and how others affect their thoughts, feelings, and actions. Culture creates the rules that tell people which social behaviors and interactions are appropriate, and these rules vary between cultures.

In their efforts to understand people's relationships with others, both social psychologists and sociologists have commonly distinguished between two categories of social groups: ingroups and

> *"The ultimate challenge…is the development of a theory that can explain individual differences within and across culture."*
> — M. Guyll & S. Madon, 1999

outgroups. Ingroup relationships are formed with the people we feel closest to and involve various levels of intimacy, trust, or familiarity. Thus a person's ingroups might include family, friends, and work associates. Outgroups are groups to which we feel we don't belong, such as other families, rival sports teams, or different departments at work. Generally we are positively predisposed toward our ingroups, experiencing feelings of pride, familiarity, affection, and loyalty. In contrast, we regard outgroups and their members with neutral to negative feelings, including caution, mistrust, superiority, prejudice, and even hostility.

Although the ingroup–outgroup classification is important, social relationships can seldom be neatly pigeonholed: There are many different levels of intimacy and familiarity, both between and within the different groups a person experiences. As children grow, they gradually learn the rules and standards of their society and culture—and as part of

this process they learn which people are members of their ingroups and which people form part of their various outgroups. This happens in all the usual social contexts: at school, at work, in clubs, while playing team games, and so on.

Such selections continue throughout life, as adults assess almost everyone they meet to see whether new aquaintances are outgroup or ingroup material. By "testing" new people, they decide whether these people will continue to be acquaintances or whether there is a chance that they may form closer relationships with them. Although these decisions might be unconscious, they are always being made, because social distinctions form a vital part of social interaction.

To date, most studies in this area have dealt almost exclusively with European and North American societies—there is much work still to be done on ingroups and outgroups in other cultures. Yet despite the persistence of ethnocentricity (preference for one's own ethnic group), there is already abundant evidence that many ingroup and outgroup relationships differ significantly from their equivalents

Members of a basketball team at a school in Celestun on the Gulf coast of the Yucatán Peninsula, Mexico. These young men form part of the same ingroup—their sports team—but each of them will also belong to other, different ingroups.

in the western world. For example, in some Asian and collectivist cultures, such as kibbutzim in Israel, group membership tends to be more fluid than in the west, changing with circumstance and need. Thus people may be ingroup members in some situations, but find themselves relegated to an outgroup in others. One example from Asian cultures is that business people see each other as competitors when discussing domestic issues, but may form an ingroup when issues become international. This concept is sometimes hard for westerners to understand, because their ingroups and outgroups tend to be more rigidly delineated—but a similar phenomenon has also been noted in western cultures, although research is still too sketchy for any firm conclusions to be reached.

Individualism and collectivism
Sometimes the theory of individualism–collectivism (IC) is used to explain the cultural differences in ingroup–outgroup relationships. IC is a scale that measures how much a particular society promotes individual needs, wishes, desires, and values above group goals. In 1994 an influential study by David Matsumoto showed that individualistic (generally western) cultures are less concerned with

> "In a society in which it is a moral offense to be different from your neighbor your only escape is never to let them find out."
> — Robert A. Heinlein, 1961

people's social responsibilites, encouraging people to achieve power and success in their own right. Collectivistic cultures tend to emphasize the needs of society as a whole, identifying individuals through their membership in a group rather than their position, rank, or personal qualities.

Although the composition of ingroups and outgroups in collectivistic cultures varies from time to time, people generally belong to fewer ingroups than those in individualistic nations, such as the United States or Germany. Consequently, people in collectivistic cultures show a greater commitment to their ingroups, since these ingroups are essential to the individual's identity. In individualistic cultures people feel at greater liberty to flit from one ingroup to another.

Collectivistic communities also demand greater harmony, cooperation, and cohesion ("togetherness") within their ingroups, and individuals are expected to conform and identify with the group. Individualistic societies emphasize values at the opposite end of the spectrum, encouraging individuals to achieve autonomy, pursue personal goals, and to

People practice Tai chi chuan (a Chinese system of calisthenics) in Shanghai, China. The approach to group activities in a collectivistic society such as this is notably different from that of people in individualistic western societies, such as the United States.

depend less on the group. This means people are under less pressure to conform, and less importance is attached to group harmony. Or at least that is how it appears in the absence of a significant body of research—perhaps these judgments are based on unwarranted ethnocentric western preconceptions about collectivism and communist ideals.

Standards of behavior

Generally, within their own ingroup members in any culture will feel safe to show emotion, while immersion in an outgroup leads individuals to be much more restrained and reticent. However, interpersonal behavior in and between groups appears to differ widely according to whether the predominant culture is individualistic or collectivistic.

In individualistic ingroups members make fewer sacrifices for the sake of the group, while collectivistic ingroup members commonly subordinate their own needs to those of the majority and try harder to cooperate with other members. Members of individualistic ingroups therefore feel freer to express their own opinions, attitudes, and feelings than collectivistic ingroup members, who are generally not encouraged to give voice to their concerns in the interests of harmony. Consequently, individualistic ingroup members are less fearful of the effects of uncensored self-expression, while collectivistic ingroup members may

Business may be international, but in conduct it is often extremely parochial (narrow in outlook). Executives of all nationalities may experience difficulties when dealing with different cultural approaches.

The 1985 Boy Scout World Jamboree held at Fort Hill, Virginia. This international movement is typical of the ingroups to which individualistic westerners belong.

be reluctant to bring up interpersonal concerns because they fear that expressing them may damage the organic structure of which they are a part.

When it comes to outgroups, however, people in an individualistic society tend to treat outgroup members more equally, making fewer distinctions between their ingroups and outgroups. In collectivistic communities, despite the greater fluidity of roles, people tend to feel aloof and even hostile toward outgroup members. These differences in ingroup and outgroup relationships also influence the emotions expressed in social situations. People in individualistic societies are more likely to suppress any negative feelings about outgroups, while people in collectivistic societies will be more critical, exhibiting little of the relationship-building behaviors that occur with outgroups in individualistic communities.

CULTURE-BOUND ILLNESSES

When psychologists are dealing with behavioral problems, they must look at every aspect of the individual seeking help. Although the main cause of any disturbance is often an unhappy personal history or physical ill-health, culture may also plays an important role—and not only may it be partly responsible for the condition itself, but it may also influence the psychologist's response to the illness. Indeed, what is considered normal or abnormal behavior varies considerably from culture to culture.

Marie Smith Jones, an elderly Eyak from Alaska. Studies of cultures such as hers have given western psychologists new insights into the differences and similarities between various cultures.

Cross-cultural psychology has various aims, one of which is to help find ways of providing better treatment for everyone regardless of creed, race, nationality, or geographical location. In the 1980s psychologists A. Kleinmann and Wolfgang M. Pfeiffer claimed that it was impossible to use the existing western system of medical classification to understand disorders that were culture-specific. Today, such illnesses are called culture-bound syndromes, and researchers have shown that cross-cultural perspectives can help in the diagnosis of these conditions.

Comparative studies have revealed that anorexia nervosa (*see* Vol. 6, pp. 20–67) is a culture-bound syndrome, since this psychological disorder has so far been observed only in the west and not in developing countries. This eating disorder occurs mainly in women, although men can suffer from it too, and there are several theories about its possible causes. Some researchers have suggested that it is a psychosomatic reaction to the way in which western cultures associate physical attractiveness with slimness; others believe it is an adverse physical response to a restricted sex role or an external manifestation of a fear of losing control or of taking on adult responsibilities.

Unusual reactions

Among the various conditions that cannot be diagnosed according to the western classification system is *witiko* (also called *windigo*), a disorder that appears to affect only Algonquins in Canada. The main symptom is the sufferers' belief that they are possessed by a human-eating spirit (the *witiko*). This produces first a desire to eat human flesh, then guilt as the person struggles with these cannibalistic urges—sometimes resulting in suicidal tendencies.

Other culture-specific illnesses include *koro* (impotence caused by fear that the penis is retracting), which is suffered by

A photographer's image of one of the classic symptoms of anorexia nervosa— a thin girl convinced that she is fat despite all the evidence to the contrary.

some Southeast Asian men; *latah* (symptoms of which include hysteria, hypersensitivity to sudden fright, and dissociative or trancelike behavior), seen primarily in Malay women; and *susto* (depression and apathy thought to reflect "soul loss"), observed in Amer-Indians of the Andean highlands.

Although psychologists do not really understand why such conditions are localized rather than widely distributed

> "If African healers were transplanted to this country, they would be surprised by the odd symptoms of patients here."
> — H. I. Kaplan, 1994

across many cultures, there are several plausible hypotheses. One is that these conditions are caused by particular types of stress found only in certain societies. They may include pressures from family and specific environmental conditions.

Research also appears to suggest that culture-bound illnesses have culture-bound cures. For example, although some western doctors have diagnosed *susto* as a form of liver disease or diabetes, several people were observed to have been cured after a native healer performed a sacrifice to appease the Earth so that it would return their lost souls.

RESEARCH METHODOLOGY

It is tempting to conclude from this that both the mind itself and the psychological analysis of it may be influenced—and sometimes even governed—by the local culture. However, it is easier to accept this idea than to prove it. One of the problems with culture is that it is a sociological concept, not a biological one, and as such very hard to define. Even if it is agreed that culture is a combination of values, attitudes, behaviors, and beliefs communicated from one generation to another through language and art, this still leaves a huge range of variables that

Cultures are not static but constantly evolve: Anne Heche (left) and Ellen de Generes went public about their relationship in the late 1990s. The fact that they felt able to do so reflected a significant shift in U.S. cultural attitudes—30 years previously the two actresses would not have dared admit their love for each other.

must be measured accurately if they are to be scientifically meaningful. In their efforts to satisfy this requirement psychologists have often found themselves with no option but to classify people in easy-to-measure categories, such as their nationality, even though culture does not necessarily equate with country of birth.

Nevertheless, researchers have shown that these pitfalls can be avoided and have produced valuable information about the psychological significance of various cultural differences. In one study researchers found evidence that human perceptual processes develop differently depending on the particular shapes and angles to which people are exposed daily in their environment. People living in the United States, where many buildings contain 90-degree angles, are susceptible to different optical illusions than people in rural African villages, where structures are more usually curvilinear.

Other cross-cultural studies have led to a reconsideration of older questions, particularly about what constitutes normal human sexuality. Homosexuality, long considered pathological behavior in the United States, is approved of in some cultures, for example, and may even be encouraged as a sexual outlet before entry into heterosexual marriage.

In the 1920s anthropologist Bronislaw Malinowski (1884–1942) carried out a study of the young boys of the Trobriand Islands of Papua New Guinea in the Solomon Sea, observing in them the type of hostility that Freud had described in his Oedipus complex (*see* p. 55). According to Malinowski's findings, however, the boys

> *"Every civilization, custom, material object, idea, and belief fulfills a vital function, represents an indispensable part with a working whole."*
> —Abram Kardiner, 1961

did not direct their ill-feeling at their fathers but at maternal uncles who were assigned the role of family disciplinarian. This observation presented a challenge to Freud's theory by raising the possibility that a boy's tense relations with his father at a certain period in his life may be a reaction to discipline rather than sexual jealousy. Although doubts have been expressed about Malinowski's observations

and interpretations, the questions raised by his work are a good example of the valuable contribution that cross-cultural research can make to psychology.

Cross-cultural psychology may also examine the relationship between a dominant culture and any subcultures contained within it. In this instance a subculture is defined as a group of people whose experiences differ from those of the majority culture. A subculture may be constituted in different ways and is often an ethnic, racial, or religious group, although any group that develops its own customs, norms, jargon, and behavior may be so defined, including groups of drug dealers or criminal gangs.

Research problems
The greatest problem faced by cross-cultural psychologists is that of finding representative samples of people to study. For their research to be valid, they need to obtain information about one culture and compare it either with data collected in exactly the same way from another culture or with known values from past research. Yet it is notoriously difficult to obtain a

An Inuit drives his dog team ashore after a day's hunting on the ice-covered seas along the coast of Greenland. Research suggests that people in cultures such as this one may suffer different physical and psychological illnesses from people in other parts of the world. Why this should be is still unclear, however.

sample that truly reflects a particular society because it is so hard to define a culture and the people who represent it.

Researchers also need to ensure that the samples they compare are demonstrably equivalent. Thus all subjects must be of the same educational level and come from the same socioeconomic group and social background; otherwise, it is impossible to tell whether any differences between the groups being studied have a cultural origin or another socioeconomic cause.

Response sets and translation

Another problem encountered by cross-cultural psychologists is that subjects within one cultural group often answer questions in a particular way because of their culture's norms. A completed test that reflects or appears to reflect a set of governing attitudes in this way is called a response set. For example, response sets may occur when individualistic and collectivistic cultures are compared: When asked to put a value on something, members of an individualistic society may make a conscious effort to stand out (possibly by going for high-rating scores on a scale), while collectivistic society members may be self-effacing and thus score lower. The researcher has no way of knowing whether an individual's scores reflect the person's personality or a motivation to express the culture's values. In other circumstances (*see* Vol. 5, pp. 28–49) even members of an individualistic society may make a conscious effort to fit

in, giving answers they know are wrong to conform with the majority view.

Some cross-cultural research projects have also been invalidated by defective translation of tests or surveys, which meant that subjects answered questions that were different from those the researchers meant to ask. To avoid this, a procedure known as back-translation is often used to ensure that questions are equivalent in the various languages. Thus a question in English might be translated into French and then back into English by another translator. Problems are indicated by comparing key differences between the two English versions. This minimizes unintended meanings, ambiguities, and cultural misconceptions.

Cross-cultural psychology is a critical field in psychologists' efforts to understand human behavior worldwide. But as we have seen, it is also one of the most difficult fields to study accurately.

CONNECTIONS

- Nonwestern Theories of the Mind: pp. 144–151
- Research Methods: pp. 162–163
- The Mind: Volume 2, pp. 40–61
- Language Processing: Volume 3, pp. 114–135
- People as Social Animals: Volume 5, pp. 6–27
- Relating to Others: Volume 5, pp. 28–49
- Relating to Society: Volume 5, pp. 50–71
- What Is Abnormality?: Volume 6, pp. 6–19
- Mental Disorders and Society: Volume 6, pp. 142–163

Research Methods

———— *"Science will...bring...objective results to our subjective world."* ————

Ivan Pavlov

Whatever approach modern psychologists prefer, they all follow scientific methods and research guidelines to test their theories. The main methods researchers use are experimental, observational, and correlational—and ethics are an important consideration in all three.

A hypothesis is a statement that can be tested. Psychologists may come up with a hypothesis by observing the phenomenon being studied or by reading scientific literature, which keeps them up to date with scientific theory. Sometimes they will also work with scientists in other disciplines to study psychological phenomena. Having posed a hypothesis, they use several methods to test it.

Experimental method

The main scientific method psychologists use is to conduct experiments to test their predictions (*see* pp. 74–89). These experiments can take place in either a laboratory setting (a controlled environment) or a field setting (a natural environment). Conducting an experiment in a laboratory allows the researcher greater control over the conditions, but the findings cannot be generalized since the volunteers and conditions may differ in important ways from real life. The experiment can only prove or disprove the original theory, which may then be revised or extended. It is not a process of proving truth, but of testing outcomes.

Scientists are seldom satisfied with the results of a single experiment. To prove their conclusions, other scientists must be able to repeat the experiment and produce the same results, which is difficult when people are involved, since their responses may be influenced by all kinds of stimuli. An experiment performed on a few people produces less reliable results, so psychologists try to do their experiments with as many individuals as possible.

One method used in well-designed experiments is to divide subjects into two randomly assigned groups and to isolate the condition or behavior being measured: Thus each group has the same experiences except for one element. To test the effect of noise on test-taking, for example, two groups might be asked to take an identical test, one in a noisy room and the other in a quiet room. The scores of the people in the noisy room (the experimental group) would then be compared with those in the quiet room (the control group).

Unfortunately, no matter how carefully the groups are matched, there will still be variations, so the group that produces the best test may not have done so because of lack of noise. Research like this can only narrow down the likelihood of different explanations for a particular effect. To estimate how likely it is that a difference between two groups is a result of the experimental conditions rather than just a chance occurrence, psychologists use statistics. The analysis of data, such as test scores, comes from statistics: a branch of mathematics based on probabilities.

Correlation and observation

Sometimes a controlled experiment may not be appropriate, for example, when studying conditions that already exist but cannot be induced in a group of people, such as depression or anorexia. Another research tool psychologists use in these cases is to compare or correlate the behavior of two different groups of people. For example, they might analyze the effects of sleeplessness by comparing

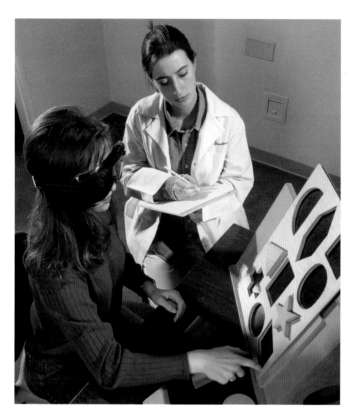

the performance of a certain task by people who have slept for only two hours with those who have slept for nine hours.

Observational investigations can be conducted in a laboratory but usually involve indirect research such as surveys, questionnaires, or interviews. This method is useful when studying more personal aspects of behavior such as political opinion. For the results to be valid, the people chosen must be a representative sample of the population. The drawback is that they tend to bias the results: For example, a questionnaire about health is likely to see subjects overstating the healthiness of their lifestyle.

Psychology experiments and studies are usually conducted using groups of people rather than individuals, but case studies also have an important part in the history of psychology. A case study is a detailed account of a person's feelings and life history. Sigmund Freud based most of his theories on his observation of individual

Only 13 percent of all psychologists in the United States work in research, the results of which are applied within the society in which we live. This researcher is observing a blindfolded girl taking a tactile performance test.

patients (*see* pp. 52–57). The drawbacks are that each person is unique, and the conclusions cannot be generalized to the population as a whole. However, case studies can be used to formulate a theory that can be scientifically tested.

Ethics

Psychological studies usually rely on volunteers, who give informed consent when they take part in an experiment. The American Psychological Association sets standards to regulate the treatment of these volunteers and has strict guidelines governing the privacy of people that relate to the way in which researchers collect, store, and use psychological data. In some cases the research topic may make it necessary for the subject not to know what an experiment is about, for example, if a psychologist is researching the effects of an emotion such as anger. In such cases the psychologists conducting the research must agree that the benefits to society will outweigh the individual discomfort caused by the experiment. After the experiment is finished, it is also essential that participants are told which emotions were being manipulated and measured.

If animals are used in research, any painful or harmful procedures must be justified in terms of the knowledge to be gained. American Psychological Association rules also govern the living conditions and care of any animals used in experiments.

Why we do research

Just as the results of research about the physical world can be used to develop useful technology, so the results of psychological research can help improve society. There are about 100,000 psychologists in the United States, but only about 13 percent work primarily in research. Others work in business, industry, and education, and by far the largest group work as therapists or counselors. Those who work in hospitals or clinics are called clinical psychologists, and they make up more than 40 percent of all professional psychologists.

Set Glossary

abnormality Within abnormal psychology abnormality is the deviation from normal or expected behavior, generally involving maladaptive responses and personal distress both to the individuals with abnormal behavior and to those around them.

abnormal psychology The study and treatment of mental disorders.

acquisition The process by which something, such as a skill, habit, or language, is learned.

adaptation A change in behavior or structure that increases the survival chances of a species. Adjective: adaptive

addiction A state of dependence on a drug or a particular pattern of behavior.

adjustment disorder A mental disorder in which a patient is unable to adjust properly to a stressful life change.

affect A mood, emotion, or feeling. An affect is generally a shorter-lived and less-pronounced emotion than mood.

affective disorder A group of mental disorders, such as depression and bipolar 1 disorder, that are characterized by pronounced and often prolonged changes of mood.

agnosia A group of brain disorders involving impaired ability to recognize or interpret sensory information.

Alzheimer's disease A progressive and irreversible dementia in which the gradual destruction of brain tissue results in memory loss, impaired cognitive function, and personality change.

amnesia A partial or complete loss of memory.

amygdala An almond-shaped structure located in the front of the brain's temporal lobe that is part of the limbic system. Sometimes called the amygdaloid complex or the amygdaloid nucleus, the amygdala plays an important role in emotional behavior and motivation.

anorexia nervosa An eating disorder in which patients (usually young females) become obsessed with the idea that they are overweight and experience dramatic weight loss by not eating enough.

antidepressants A type of medication used to treat depression.

antianxiety drugs A type of medication used to treat anxiety disorders.

antipsychotic drugs A type of medication used to treat psychotic disorders such as schizophrenia. Sometimes known as neuroleptics.

anxiety disorder A group of mental disorders involving worry or distress.

anxiolytics *See* antianxiety drugs

aphasia A group of brain disorders that involve a partial or complete loss of language ability.

arousal A heightened state of awareness, behavior, or physiological function.

artificial intelligence (AI) A field of study that combines elements of cognitive psychology and computer science in an attempt to develop intelligent machines.

attachment theory A theory that describes how infants form emotional bonds with the adults they are close to.

attention The process by which someone can focus on particular sensory information by excluding other, less immediately relevant information.

attention deficit disorder (ADD) A mental disorder in which the patient (usually a child) is hyperactive, impulsive, and unable to concentrate properly.

autism A mental disorder, first apparent in childhood, in which patients are self-absorbed, socially withdrawn, and engage in repetitive patterns of behavior.

automatization The process by which complex behavior eventually becomes automatic. Such a process may be described as having automaticity or being automatized.

autonomic nervous system A part of the nervous system that controls many of the body's self-regulating (involuntary or automatic) functions.

aversion therapy A method of treating patients, especially those suffering from drink or drug addiction, by subjecting them to painful or unpleasant experiences.

axon Extension of the cell body of a neuron that transmits impulses away from the body of the neuron.

behavioral therapy A method of treating mental disorders that concentrates on modifying abnormal behavior rather than on the underlying causes of that behavior.

behaviorism A school of psychology in which easily observable and measurable behavior is considered to be the only proper subject of scientific study. Noun: behaviorist

bipolar I disorder A mental (affective) disorder involving periods of depression (depressed mood) and periods of mania (elevated mood).

body image The way in which a person perceives their own body or imagines it is perceived by other people.

body language The signals people send out to other people (usually unconsciously) through their gestures, posture, and other types of nonverbal communication.

Broca's area A region of the brain (usually located in the left hemisphere) that is involved with processing language.

bulimia nervosa An eating disorder in which patients consume large amounts of food in binges, then use laxatives or self-induced vomiting to prevent themselves putting on weight.

CAT scan *See* CT

causality The study of the causes of events or the connection between causes and effects.

central nervous system The part of the body's nervous system comprising the brain and spinal cord.

cerebellum A cauliflower-shaped structure at the back of the brain underneath the cerebral hemispheres that coordinates body movements.

cerebral cortex The highly convoluted outer surface of the brain's cerebrum.

cerebrum The largest part of the brain, consisting of the two cerebral hemispheres and their associated structures.

classical conditioning A method of associating a stimulus and a response that do not normally accompany one another. In Pavlov's well-known classical conditioning experiment dogs were trained so that they salivated (the conditioned response or CR) when Pavlov rang a bell (the conditioned stimulus or CS). Normally, dogs salivate

(an unconditioned response or UR) only when food is presented to them (an unconditioned stimulus or US).

clinical psychology An area of psychology concerned with the study and treatment of abnormal behavior.

cognition A mental process that involves thinking, reasoning, or some other type of mental information processing. Adjective: cognitive

cognitive behavioral therapy (CBT) An extension of behavioral therapy that involves treating patients by modifying their abnormal thought patterns as well as their behavior.

cognitive psychology An area of psychology that seeks to understand how the brain processes information.

competency In psycholinguistics the representation of the abstract rules of a language, such as its grammar.

conditioned stimulus/response (CS/CR) *See* classical conditioning

conditioning *See* classical conditioning; instrumental conditioning

connectionism A computer model of cognitive processes such as learning and memory. Connectionist models are based on a large network of "nodes" and the connections between them. Adjective: connectionist

consciousness A high-level mental process responsible for the state of self-awareness that people feel. Consciousness is thought by some researchers to direct human behavior and by others simply to be a byproduct of that behavior.

cortex *See* cerebral cortex

cross-cultural psychology The comparison of behavior, such as language

acquisition or nonverbal communication, between different peoples or cultures.

cross-sectional study An experimental method in which a large number of subjects are studied at a particular moment or period in time. Compare longitudinal study

CT (computed tomography) A method of producing an image of the brain's tissue using X-ray scanning, which is commonly used to detect brain damage. Also called CAT (computerized axial tomography).

culture-specific A behavior found only in certain cultures and not observed universally in all humankind.

declarative knowledge A collection of facts about the world and other things that people have learned. Compare procedural knowledge

declarative memory *See* explicit memory

defense mechanism A type of thinking or behavior that a person employs unconsciously to protect themselves from anxiety or unwelcome feelings.

deficit A missing cognitive function whose loss is caused by a brain disorder.

delusion A false belief that a person holds about themselves or the world around them. Delusions are characteristic features of psychotic mental illnesses such as schizophrenia.

dementia A general loss of cognitive functions usually caused by brain damage. Dementia is often, but not always, progressive (it becomes worse with time).

Dementia of the Alzheimer's type (DAT) See Alzheimer's disease

dendrite A treelike projection of a neuron's cell body that conducts nerve impulses toward the cell body.

dependency An excessive reliance on an addictive substance, such as a drug, or on the support of another person.

depression An affective mental disorder characterized by sadness, low self-esteem, inadequacy, and related symptoms.

desensitization A gradual reduction in the response to a stimulus when it is presented repeatedly over a period of time.

developmental psychology An area of psychology concerned with how people develop throughout their lives, but usually concentrating on how behavior and cognition develop during childhood.

discrimination In perception the ability to distinguish between two or more stimuli. In social psychology and sociology unequal treatment of people based on prejudice.

dysgraphia A brain disorder involving an ability to write properly.

dyslexia Brain disorders that disrupt a person's ability to read.

eating disorders A group of mental disorders that involve disturbed eating patterns or appetite.

echoic memory See sensory memory

ego The central part of a person's self. In Freudian psychology the ego manages the balance between a person's primitive, instinctive needs and the often conflicting demands of the world around them.

egocentric A person who is excessively preoccupied with themselves at the expense of the people and the world around them.

eidetic An accurate and persistent form of visual memory that is generally uncommon in adults (often misnamed "photographic memory").

electroconvulsive therapy (ECT) A treatment for severe depression that involves passing a brief and usually relatively weak electric shock through the front of a patient's skull.

electroencephalogram (EEG) A graph that records the changing electrical activity in a person's brain from electrodes attached to the scalp.

emotion A strong mood or feeling. Also a reaction to a stimulus that prepares the body for action.

episodic memory A type of memory that records well-defined events or episodes in a person's life. Compare semantic memory

ethnocentricity The use of a particular ethnic group to draw conclusions about wider society or humankind as a whole.

event-related potential (ERP) A pattern of electrical activity (the potential) produced by a particular stimulus (the event). EVPs are often recorded from the skull using electrodes.

evoked potential See event-related potential (ERP)

evolution A theory suggesting that existing organisms have developed from earlier ones by processes that include natural selection (dubbed "survival of the fittest") and genetic mutation.

evolutionary psychology An approach to psychology that uses the theory of evolution to explain the mind and human behavior.

explicit memory A type of memory containing information that is available to conscious recognition and recall.

flashbulb memory A very clear and evocative memory of a particular moment or event.

fMRI (functional magnetic resonance imaging) An MRI-based scanning technique that can produce images of the brain while it is engaged in cognitive activities.

functionalism An approach to psychology that concentrates on the functions played by parts of the mind and human behavior.

generalized anxiety disorder (GAD) A type of nonspecific anxiety disorder with symptoms that include worry, irritability, and tension.

genes A functional unit of the chromosome that determines how traits are passed on and expressed from generation to generation. Adjective: genetic

Gestalt psychology A psychology school that emphasizes the importance of appreciating phenomena as structured wholes in areas such as perception and learning, as opposed to breaking them down into their components. Most influential in the mid-1900s.

gray matter The parts of the nervous system that contain mainly nerve cell bodies.

habituation See desensitization

hallucination A vivid but imaginary perceptual experience that occurs purely in the mind, not in reality.

heritability The proportion of observed variation for a trait in a specific population that can be attributed to genetic factors rather than environmental ones. Generally expressed as a ratio of genetically caused variation to total variation.

hippocamus A part of the limbic system in the temporal lobe that is thought to play an important role in the formation of memories.

Humanism A philosophy that stresses the importance of human interests and values.

hypothalamus A small structure at the base of the brain that controls the autonomic nervous system.

hysteria A type of mental disturbance that may include symptoms such as hallucinations and emotional outbursts.

implicit memory A type of memory not normally available to conscious awareness. Sometimes also known as procedural or nondeclarative memory. Compare explicit memory

imprinting A type of learning that occurs in a critical period shortly after birth, such as when chicks learn to accept a human in place of their real mother.

individual psychology An approach to psychology that focuses on the differences between individuals. Also a theory advanced by Alfred Adler based on the idea of overcoming inferiority.

information processing In cognitive psychology the theory that the mind operates something like a computer, with sensory information processed either in a series of discrete stages or in parallel by something like a connectionist network.

ingroup A group whose members feel a strong sense of collective identity and act to exclude other people (the outgroup).

innate A genetically determined trait that is present at birth, as opposed to something that is acquired by learning.

instinct An innate and automatic response to a particular stimulus that usually involves no rational thought.

instrumental conditioning A type of conditioning in which reinforcement occurs only when an organism makes a certain, desired response. Instrumental

conditioning occurs, for example, when a pigeon is trained to peck a lever to receive a pellet of food.

internalize To make internal, personal, or subjective; to take in and make an integral part of one's attitudes or beliefs:

introspection A behaviorist technique of studying the mind by observing one's own thought processes.

language acquisition device (LAD) According to linguist Noam Chomsky, a part of the brain that is preprogrammed with a universal set of grammatical rules that can construct the rules of a specific language according to the environment it is exposed to.

libido The sexual drive.

limbic system A set of structures in the brain stem, including the hippocampus and the amygdala, that lie below the corpus callosum. It is involved in emotion, motivation, behavior, and various functions of the autonomic nervous system.

long-term memory A type of memory in which information is retained for long periods after being deeply processed. Generally used to store events and information from the past. Compare short-term memory

longitudinal study An experimental method that follows a small group of subjects over a long period of time. Compare cross-sectional study

maladaptive Behavior is considered maladapative or dysfunctional if it has a negative effect on society or on a person's ability to function in society.

medical model A theory that mental disorders, like diseases, have specific underlying medical causes, which must be addressed if treatment is to be effective.

mental disorder A psychiatric illness such as schizophrenia, anxiety, or depression.

metacognition The study by an individual of their own thought processes. *See also* introspection

mnemonic A technique that can be used to remember information or improve memory.

modeling The technique by which a person observes some ideal form of behavior (a role model) and then attempts to copy it. In artificial intelligence (AI) people attempt to build computers that model human cognition.

modularity A theory that the brain is composed of a number of modules that occupy relatively specific areas and that carry out relatively specific tasks.

morpheme The smallest unit of a language that carries meaning.

motor neuron *See* neuron.

MRI (magnetic resonance imaging) A noninvasive scanning technique that uses magnetic fields to produce detailed images of body tissue.

nature–nurture A long-running debate over whether genetic factors (nature) or environmental factors (nurture) are most important in different aspects of behavior.

neuron A nerve cell, consisting of a cell body (soma), an axon, and one or more dendrites. Motor (efferent) neurons produce movement when they fire by carrying information *from* the central nervous system *to* the muscles and glands; sensory (afferent) neurons carry information *from* the senses *to* the central nervous system.

neuropsychology An area of psychology that studies the connections between parts of the brain and neural processes, on one hand, and different cognitive processes and types of behavior, on the other.

neurotransmitter A substance that carries chemical "messages" across the synaptic gaps between the neurons of the brain.

nonverbal communication The way in which animals communicate without language (verbal communication), using such things as posture, tone of voice, and facial expressions.

operant conditioning *See* instrumental conditioning

outgroup The people who do not belong to an ingroup.

parallel processing A type of cognition in which information is processed in several different ways at once. In serial processing information passes through one stage of processing at a time.

peripheral nervous system All the nerves and nerve processes that connect the central nervous system with receptors, muscles, and glands.

personality The collection of character traits that makes one person different from another.

personality disorder A group of mental disorders in which aspects of someone's personality make it difficult for them to function properly in society.

PET (positron emission tomography) A noninvasive scanning technique that makes images of the brain according to levels of metabolic activity inside it.

phenomenology A philosophy based on the study of immediate experiences.

phobia A strong fear of a particular object (such as snakes) or social situation.

phoneme A basic unit of spoken language.

phrenology An early approach to psychology that studied the relationship between areas of the brain (based on skull shape) and mental functions. Phrenology has since been discredited.

physiology A type of biology concerned with the workings of cells, organs, and tissues.

positive punishment A type of conditioning in which incorrect responses are punished.

positive reinforcement A type of conditioning in which correct responses are rewarded.

primary memory *See* short-term memory

probability The likelihood of something happening.

procedural knowledge The practical knowledge of how to do things ("know-how"). Compare declarative knowledge

prosody A type of nonverbal communication in which language is altered by such things as the pitch of someone's voice and their intonation.

psyche The soul or mind of a person or a driving force behind their personality.

psychiatry The study, classification, and treatment of mental disorders.

psychoanalysis A theory of behavior and an approach to treating mental disorders pioneered by Austrian neurologist Sigmund Freud. Adjective: psychoanalytic

psychogenic A mental disorder that is psychological (as opposed to physical) in origin.

psycholinguistics The study of language-related behavior, including how the brain acquires and processes language.

psychosurgery A type of brain surgery designed to treat mental disorders.

psychotherapy A broad range of treatments for mental disorders based on different kinds of interaction between a patient and a therapist.

psychosis A mental state characterized by disordered personality and loss of contact with reality that affects normal social functioning. Psychosis is a feature of psychotic disorders, such as schizophrenia. Adjective: psychotic

reaction time The time taken for the subject in an experiment to respond to a stimulus.

recall The process by which items are recovered from memory. Compare recognition

recognition The process by which a person realizes they have previously encountered a particular object or event. Compare recall

reductionism A philosophy based on breaking complex things into their individual components. Also, an attempt to explain high-level sciences (such as psychology) in terms of lower-level sciences (such as chemistry or physics).

reflex An automatic response to a stimulus (a "knee-jerk" reaction).

reflex arc The neural circuit thought to be responsible for the control of a reflex.

rehearsing The process by which a person repeats information to improve its chances of being stored in memory.

representation A mental model based on perceptions of the world.

repression In psychoanalysis an unconscious mental process that keeps thoughts out of conscious awareness.

response The reaction to a stimulus.

reuptake The reabsorption of a neurotransmitter from the place where it was produced.

risk aversion A tendency not to take risks even when they may have beneficial results.

schema An abstract mental plan that serves as a guide to action or a more general mental representation.

schizophrenia A mental disorder characterized by hallucinations and disordered thought patterns in which a patient becomes divorced from reality. It is a type of psychotic disorder.

secondary memory *See* long-term memory

selective attention *See* attention

self-concept The ideas and feelings that people hold about themselves.

semantic memory A type of long-term memory that stores information based on its content or meaning. Compare episodic memory

senses The means by which people perceive things. The five senses are vision, hearing, smell, touch, and taste.

sensory memory An information store that records sensory impressions for a short period of time before they are processed more thoroughly.

sensory neuron *See* neuron

serotonin A neurotransmitter in the central nervous system that plays a key role in affective (mood) disorders, sleep, and the perception of pain. Serotonin is also known as 5-hydroxytryptamine (5-HT).

shaping A type of conditioning in which behavior is gradually refined toward some ideal form by successive approximations.

short-term memory A memory of very limited capacity in which sensory inputs are held before being processed more deeply and passing into long-term memory. Compare long-term memory

social cognition An area of psychology that combines elements of social and cognitive psychology in an attempt to understand how people think about themselves in relation to the other people around them.

social Darwinism A theory that society behaves according to Darwinian principles, with the most successful members thriving at the expense of the least successful ones.

social psychology An area of psychology that explores how individuals behave in relation to other people and to society as a whole.

sociobiology A theory that seeks to explain social behavior through biological approaches, notably the theory of evolution. *See also* evolutionary psychology

somatic Something that relates to the body as opposed to the mind; something physical as opposed to something mental.

stereopsis The process by which the brain assembles one 3-D image by combining a pair of 2-D images from the eyes.

stimulus A type of sensory input that provokes a response.

subject The person studied in a psychological experiment.

synapse The region across which nerve impulses are transmitted from one neuron to another. It includes the synaptic cleft (a gap) and the sections of the cell membranes on either side of the cleft. They are called the presynaptic and postsynaptic membranes.

synesthesia A process by which the stimulation of one sense (such as hearing a sound) produces a different kind of sensory impression (such as seeing a color).

thalamus A structure in the forebrain that passes sensory information on to the cerebral cortex.

theory of mind The realization by an individual (such as a growing child, for example) that other people have thoughts and mental processes of their own. It is universally accepted that humans have a theory of mind, and research has shown that some other animals, such as chimpanzees and dolphins, might also have a theory of mind, but this is still debated. Theory of mind is of interest to developmental psychologists since it is not something people are born with, but something that develops in infancy.

tranquilizers A type of medication with sedative, muscle-relaxant, or similar properties. Minor tranquilizers are also known as antianxiety or anxiolytic drugs; major tranquilizers are also known as antipsychotic drugs.

unconditioned stimulus/response (US/UR) *See* classical conditioning

unconscious In psychoanalytic and related theories the area of the mind that is outside conscious awareness and recall but that informs the contents of such things as dreams. In general usage *unconscious* simply refers to automatic cognitive processes that we are not aware of or the lack of consciousness (that is, "awareness") at times such as during sleep.

working memory *See* short-term memory

Resources

Further Reading

Altmann, G. T. M. *The Ascent of Babel: An Exploration of Language, Mind, and Understanding.* Cambridge, MA: Oxford University Press, 1999.

American Psychiatric Association. *Diagnostic and Statistical Manual of Mental Disorders, 4th edition, Text Revision.* Washington, DC: American Psychiatric Press, 2000.

Argyle, M. *The Psychology of Interpersonal Behaviour (5th edition).* London, UK: Penguin, 1994.

Asher, S. R. and Coie, J. D. (eds.). *Peer Rejection in Childhood.* Cambridge, UK: Cambridge University Press, 1990.

Atkinson, R. L. *et al. Hilgard's Introduction to Psychology (13th edition).* London, UK: International Thomson Publishing, 1999.

Barnouw, V. *Culture and Personality.* Chicago, IL: Dorsey Press, 1985.

Baron, J. *Thinking and Deciding.* Cambridge, UK: Cambridge University Press, 1994.

Barry, M. A. S. *Visual Intelligence: Perception, Image, and Manipulation in Visual Communication.* Albany, NY: State University of New York Press, 1997.

Beck, J. *Cognitive Therapy: Basics and Beyond.* London, UK: The Guildford Press, 1995.

Bickerton, D. *Language and Species.* Chicago, IL: The University of Chicago Press, 1990.

Blackburn, I. M. and Davison, K. *Cognitive Therapy for Depression and Anxiety: A Practitioner's Guide.* Oxford, UK: Blackwell, 1995.

Boden, M. A. *Piaget (2nd edition).* London, UK: Fontana Press, 1994.

Brehm, S. S., Kassin, S. M., and Fein, S. *Social Psychology (4th edition).* Boston, MA: Houghton Mifflin, 1999.

Brody, N. *Intelligence (2nd edition).* San Diego, CA: Academic Press, 1997.

Brown, D. S. *Learning a Living: A Guide to Planning Your Career and Finding a Job for People with Learning Disabilities, Attention Deficit Disorder, and Dyslexia.* Bethesda, MD: Woodbine House, 2000.

Bruhn, A. R. *Earliest Childhood Memories.* New York: Praeger, 1990.

Buunk, B. P. "Affiliation, Attraction and Close Relationships." *In* M. Hewstone and W. Stroebe (eds.), *Introduction to Social Psychology: A European Perspective.* Oxford, UK: Blackwell, 2001.

Cacioppo, J. T., Tassinary, L. G., and Berntson, G. G. (eds.). *Handbook of Psychophysiology (2nd edition).* New York: Cambridge University Press, 2000.

Cardwell, M. *Dictionary of Psychology.* Chicago, IL: Fitzroy Dearborn Publishers, 1999

Carson, R. C. and Butcher, J. N. *Abnormal Psychology and Modern Life (9th edition).* New York: HarperCollins Publishers, 1992.

Carter, R. *Mapping the Mind.* Berkeley, CA: University of California Press, 1998.

Cavan, S. *Recovery from Drug Addiction.* New York: Rosen Publishing Group, 2000.

Clarke-Stewart, A. *Daycare.* Cambridge, MA: Harvard University Press, 1993.

Cohen, G. *The Psychology of Cognition (2nd edition).* San Diego, CA: Academic Press, 1983.

Cramer, D. *Close Relationships: The Study of Love and Friendship.* New York: Arnold, 1998.

Daly, M. and Wilson, M. *Homicide.* New York: Aldine de Gruyter, 1988.

Davis, R. D., Braun, E. M., and Smith, J. M. *The Gift of Dyslexia: Why Some of the Smartest People Can't Read and How They Can Learn.* New York: Perigee, 1997.

Davison, G. C. and Neal, J. M. *Abnormal Psychology.* New York: John Wiley and Sons, Inc., 1994.

Dawkins, R. *The Selfish Gene.* New York: Oxford Universty Press, 1976.

Dennett, D. C. *Darwin's Dangerous Idea: Evolution and the Meanings of Life.* Carmichael, CA: Touchstone Books, 1996.

Dobson, C. *et al. Understanding Psychology.* London, UK: Weidenfeld and Nicolson, 1982.

Duck, S. *Meaningful Relationships: Talking, Sense, and Relating.* Thousand Oaks, CA: Sage Publications, 1994.

Durie, M. H. "Maori Psychiatric Admissions: Patterns, Explanations and Policy Implications." *In* J. Spicer, A. Trlin, and J. A. Walton (eds.), *Social Dimensions of Health and Disease: New Zealand Perspectives.* Palmerston North, NZ: Dunmore Press, 1994.

Eliot, L. *What's Going on in There? How the Brain and Mind Develop in the First Five Years of Life.* New York: Bantam Books, 1999.

Eysenck, M. (ed.). *The Blackwell Dictionary of Cognitive Psychology.* Cambridge, MA: Blackwell, 1991.

Faherty, C. and Mesibov, G. B. *Asperger's: What Does It Mean to Me?* Arlington, TX: Future Horizons, 2000.

Fernando, S. *Mental Health in a Multi-Ethnic Society: A Multi-Disciplinary Handbook.* New York: Routledge, 1995.

Fiske, S. T. and Taylor, S. E. *Social Cognition (2nd Edition).* New York: Mcgraw-Hill, 1991.

Franken, R. E. *Human Motivation (5th edition).* Belmont, CA: Wadsworth Thomson Learning, 2002.

Freud, S. and Brill, A. A. *The Basic Writings of Sigmund Freud.* New York: Modern Library, 1995.

Gardner, H. *The Mind's New Science: A History of the Cognitive Revolution.* New York: Basic Books, 1985.

Garnham, A. and Oakhill, J. *Thinking and Reasoning.* Cambridge, MA: Blackwell, 1994.

Gaw, A. C. *Culture, Ethnicity, and Mental Illness.* Washington, DC: American Psychiatric Press, 1992.

Giacobello, J. *Everything You Need to Know about Anxiety and Panic Attacks.* New York: Rosen Publishing Group, 2000.

Gazzaniga, M. S. *The Mind's Past.* Berkeley, CA: University of California Press, 1998.

Gazzaniga, M. S. (ed.). *The New Cognitive Neurosciences (2nd edition).* Cambridge, MA: MIT Press, 2000.

Gazzaniga, M. S., Ivry, R. B., and Mangun, G. R. *Cognitive Neuroscience: The Biology of the Mind (2nd edition).* New York: Norton, 2002.

Gernsbacher, M. A. (ed.). *Handbook of Psycholinguistics.* San Diego, CA: Academic Press, 1994.

Gigerenzer, G. *Adaptive Thinking: Rationality in the Real World.* New York: Oxford University Press, 2000.

Goodglass, H. *Understanding Aphasia.* San Diego, CA: Academic Press, 1993.

Gordon, M. *Jumpin' Johnny Get Back to Work! A Child's Guide to ADHD/Hyperactivity.* DeWitt, NY: GSI Publications Inc., 1991.

Gordon, M. A *I Would if I Could: A Teenager's Guide to ADHD/Hyperactivity.* DeWitt, NY: GSI Publications Inc., 1992.

Goswami, U. *Cognition in Children.* London, UK: Psychology Press, 1998.

Graham, H. *The Human Face of Psychology: Humanistic Psychology in Its Historical, Social, and Cultural Context.* Milton Keynes, UK: Open University Press, 1986.

Grandin, T. *Thinking in Pictures: And Other Reports from my Life with Autism.* New York: Vintage Books, 1996.

Greenberger, D. and Padesky, C. *Mind over Mood.* New York: Guilford Publications, 1995.

Groeger, J. A. *Memory and Remembering: Everyday Memory in Context.* New York: Longman, 1997.

Gross, R. and Humphreys, P. *Psychology: The Science of Mind and Behaviour.* London, UK: Hodder Arnold, 1993.

Halford, G. S. *Children's Understanding: The Development of Mental Models.* Hillsdale, NJ: Lawrence Erlbaum Associates, 1993.

Harley, T. A. *The Psychology of Language: From Data to Theory (2nd edition).* Hove, UK: Psychology Press, 2001.

Harris, G. G. *Casting out Anger: Religion among the Taita of Kenya.* New York: Cambridge University Press, 1978.

Hayes, N. *Psychology in Perspective (2nd edition).* New York: Palgrave, 2002.

Hearst, E. *The First Century of Experimental Psychology.* Hillsdale, NJ: Lawrence Erlbaum Associates, 1979.

Hecht, T. *At Home in the Street: Street Children of Northeast Brazil.* New York: Cambridge University Press, 1998.

Hetherington, E. M. *Coping with Divorce, Single Parenting, and Remarriage: A Risk and Resiliency Perspective.* Mawah, NJ: Lawrence Erlbaum Associates, 1999.

Higbee, K. L. *Your Memory: How It Works and How to Improve It (2nd edition).* New York: Paragon 1993.

Hinde, R. A. *Individuals, Relationships and Culture: Links between Ethology and the Social Sciences.* Cambridge, UK: Cambridge University Press, 1987.

Hogdon, L. A. *Solving Behavior Problems in Autism.* Troy, MI: Quirkroberts Publishing, 1999.

Hogg, M. A. (ed.). *Social Psychology.* Thousand Oaks, CA: Sage Publications, 2002.

Holden, G. W. *Parents and the Dynamics of Child Rearing.* Boulder, CO: Westview Press, 1997.

Holmes, J. *John Bowlby and Attachment Theory.* New York: Routledge, 1993.

Hughes, H. C. *Sensory Exotica: A World Beyond Human Experience.* Cambridge, MA: MIT Press, 1999.

Hyde, M. O. and Setano, J. F. *When the Brain Dies First.* New York: Franlin Watts Inc., 2000.

Ingersoll, B. D. *Distant Drums, Different Drummers: A Guide for Young People with ADHD.* Plantation, FL: A.D.D. WareHouse, 1995.

Jencks, C. and Phillips, M. *The Black-White Test Score Gap.* Washington, DC: Brookings Institution Press, 1998.

Johnson, M. J. *Developmental Cognitive Neuroscience.* Cambridge, MA: Blackwell, 1997.

Johnson, M. H. and Morton, J. *Biology and Cognitive Development. The Case of Face Recognition.* Cambridge, MA: Blackwell, 1991.

Johnson-Laird, P. N. *The Computer and the Mind: An Introduction to Cognitive Science.* Cambridge, MA: Harvard University Press, 1988.

Jusczyk, P. W. *The Discovery of Spoken Language.* Cambridge, MA: MIT Press, 1997.

Kalat, J. W. *Biological Psychology (7th edition).* Belmont, CA: Wadsworth Thomson Learning, 2001.

Kaplan, H. I. and Sadock, B. J. *Synopsis of Psychiatry: Behavioral Sciences, Clinical Psychiatry.* Philadelphia, PA: Lippincott, Williams and Wilkins, 1994.

Karen, R. *Becoming Attached: First Relationships and How They Shape Our Capacity to Love.* New York: Oxford University Press, 1998.

Kirk, S. A. and Kutchins, H. *The Selling of DSM: The Rhetoric of Science in Psychiatry.* New York: Aldine de Gruyter, 1992.

Kinney, J. *Clinical Manual of Substance Abuse.* St. Louis, MO: Mosby, 1995.

Kleinman, A. *Rethinking Psychiatry: From Cultural Category to Personal Experience.* New York: Free Press, 1988.

Kosslyn, S. M. and Koenig, O. *Wet Mind: The New Cognitive Neuroscience.* New York: Free Press, 1992.

Kutchins, H. and Kirk, S. A. *Making Us Crazy: DSM: The Psychiatric Bible and the Creation of Mental Disorders.* New York: Free Press, 1997.

LaBruzza, A. L. *Using DSM-IV; A Clinician's Guide to Psychiatric Diagnosis.* St. Northvale, NJ: Jason Aronson Inc., 1994.

Leahey, T. A. *A History of Psychology: Main Currents in Psychological Thought (5th edition).* Upper Saddle River, NJ: Prentice Hall, 2000.

LeDoux, J. *The Emotional Brain.* New York: Simon and Schuster, 1996.

Levelt, W. J. M. *Speaking: From Intention to Articulation.* Cambridge, MA: MIT Press, 1989.

Lewis, M. and Haviland-Jones, J. M. (eds.). *Handbook of Emotions (2nd edition).* New York: Guilford Press, 2000.

Lowisohn, J. H. *et al. Substance Abuse: A Comprehensive Textbook (3rd edition).* Baltimore, MD: Williams & Wilkins, 1997.

McCabe, D. *To Teach a Dyslexic.* Clio, MI: AVKO Educational Research, 1997.

McCorduck, P. *Machines Who Think: A Personal Inquiry into the History and Prospects of Artificial Intelligence.* San Francisco: W. H. Freeman, 1979.

McIlveen, R. and Gross, R. *Biopsychology (5th edition).* Boston, MA: Allyn and Bacon, 2002.

McLachlan, J. *Medical Embryology.* Reading, MA: Addison-Wesley Publishing Co., 1994.

Manstead, A. S. R. and Hewstone M. (eds.). *The Blackwell Encyclopaedia of Social Psychology.* Oxford, UK: Blackwell, 1996.

Marsella, A. J., DeVos, G., and Hsu, F. L. K. (eds.). *Culture and Self: Asian and Western Perspectives.* New York: Routledge, 1988.

Matlin, M. W. *The Psychology of Women.* New York: Harcourt College Publishers, 2000.

Matsumoto, D. R. *People: Psychology from a Cultural Perspective.* Pacific Grove, CA: Brooks/Cole Publishing, 1994.

Matsumoto, D. R. *Culture and Modern Life.* Pacific

Grove, CA: Brooks/Cole Publishing, 1997.

Mazziotta, J .C., Toga, A. W., and Frackowiak, R. S. J. (eds.). *Brain Mapping: The Disorders.* San Diego, CA: Academic Press, 2000.

Nadeau, K. G., Littman, E., and Quinn, P. O. *Understanding Girls with ADHD.* Niagara Falls, NY: Advantage Books, 2000.

Nadel, J. and Camioni, L. (eds.). *New Perspectives in Early Communicative Development.* New York: Routledge, 1993.

Nobus, D. *Jacques Lacan and the Freudian Practice of Psychoanalysis.* Philadelphia, PA: Routledge, 2000.

Oakley, D. A. "The Plurality of Consciousness." *In* D. A. Oakley (ed.), *Brain and Mind,* New York: Methuen, 1985.

Obler, L. K. and Gjerlow, K. *Language and the Brain.* New York: Cambridge University Press, 1999.

Ogden, J. A. *Fractured Minds: A Case-study Approach to Clinical Neuropsychology.* New York: Oxford University Press, 1996.

Owusu-Bempah, K. and Howitt, D. *Psychology beyond Western Perspectives.* Leicester, UK: British Psychological Society Books, 2000.

Paranjpe, A. C. and Bhatt, G. S. "Emotion: A Perspective from the Indian Tradition." *In* H. S. R. Kao and D. Sinha (eds.), *Asian Perspectives on Psychology.* New Delhi, India: Sage Publications, 1997.

Peacock, J. *Depression.* New York: Lifematters Press, 2000.

Pfeiffer, W. M. "Culture-Bound Syndromes." *In* I. Al-Issa (ed.), *Culture and Psychopathology.* Baltimore, MD: University Park Press, 1982.

Pillemer, D. B. *Momentous Events, Vivid Memories.* Cambridge, MA: Harvard University Press, 1998.

Pinel, J. P. J. *Biopsychology (5th edition).* Boston, MA: Allyn and Bacon, 2002.

Pinker, S. *The Language Instinct.* New York: HarperPerennial, 1995.

Pinker, S. *How the Mind Works.* New York: Norton, 1997.

Porter, R. *Medicine: A History of Healing: Ancient Traditions to Modern Practices.* New York: Barnes and Noble, 1997.

Ramachandran, V. S. and Blakeslee, S. *Phantoms in the Brain: Probing the Mysteries of the Human Mind.* New York: William Morrow, 1998.

Ridley, M. *Genome: The Autobiography of a Species in 23 Chapters.* New York: HarperCollins, 1999.

Robins, L. N. and Regier, D. A. *Psychiatric Disorders in America.* New York: Free Press, 1991.

Robinson, D. N. *Toward a Science of Human Nature: Essays on the Psychologies of Mill, Hegel, Wundt, and James.* New York: Columbia University Press, 1982.

Rugg, M. D. and Coles, M. G. H. (eds.). *Electrophysiology of the Mind: Event-Related Brain Potentials and Cognition.* Oxford, UK: Oxford University Press, 1995.

Rutter, M. "The Interplay of Nature and Nurture: Redirecting the Inquiry." *In* R. Plomin and G. E. McClearn (eds.), *Nature, Nurture, and Psychology.* Washington, DC: American Psychological Association, 1993.

Sarason, I. G. and Sarason B. R. *Abnormal Psychology: The Problem of Maladaptive Behavior (9th edition).* Upper Saddle River, NJ: Prentice Hall, 1998.

Savage-Rumbaugh, S., Shanker, S. G., and Taylor, T. J. *Apes, Language, and the Human Mind.* New York: Oxford University Press, 1998.

Schab, F. R., & Crowder, R. G. (eds.). *Memory for Odors.* Mahwah, NJ: Lawrence Erlbaum Associates, 1995.

Segal, N. L. *Entwined Lives: Twins and What They Tell Us about Human Behavior.* New York: Plume, 2000.

Seeman, M. V. *Gender and Psychopathology.* Washington, DC: American Psychiatric Press, 1995.

Seligman, M. E. P. *Helplessness: On Depression, Development, and Death.* San Francisco, CA: W. H. Freeman and Co., 1992.

Shorter, E. *A History of Psychiatry: From the Era of Asylum to the Age of Prozac.* New York: John Wiley and Sons, Inc., 1997.

Siegler, R. S. *Children's Thinking (3rd edition).* Englewood Cliffs, NJ: Prentice Hall, 1998.

Simpson, E. M. *Reversals: A Personal Account of Victory over Dyslexia.* New York: Noonday Press, 1992.

Singer, D. G. and Singer, J. L. (eds.). *Handbook of Children and the Media.* Thousand Oaks, CA: Sage Publications, 2001.

Skinner, B. F. *Science and Human Behavior.* New York: Free Press, 1965.

Slavney, P. R. *Psychiatric Dimensions of Medical Practice: What Primary-Care Physicians Should Know about Delirium, Demoralization, Suicidal Thinking, and Competence to Refuse Medical Advice.* Baltimore, MD: The Johns Hopkins University Press, 1998.

Smith McLaughlin, M., Peyser Hazouri, S., and Peyser Hazouri, S. *Addiction: The "High" That Brings You Down.* Springfield, NJ: Enslow publishers, 1997.

Sommers, M. A. *Everything You Need to Know about Bipolar Disorder and Depressive Illness.* New York: Rosen Publishing Group, 2000.

Stanovich, K. E. *Who Is Rational? Studies of Individual Differences in Reasoning.* Mahwah, NJ: Lawrence Erlbaum Associates, 1999.

Symons, D. *The Evolution of Human Sexuality.* New York: Oxford University Press, 1979.

Symons, D. "Beauty is in the Adaptations of the Beholder: The Evolutionary Psychology of Human Female Sexual Attractiveness." *In* P. R. Abramson and S. D. Pinkerton (eds.), *Sexual Nature, Sexual Culture.* Chicago, IL: University of Chicago Press, 1995.

Tavris, C. *The Mismeasure of Women.* New York: Simon and Schuster, 1992.

Triandis, H. C. *Culture and Social Behavior.* New York: McGraw-Hill, 1994.

Tulving, E and Craik, F. I. M. *The Oxford Handbook of Memory.* Oxford, UK: Oxford University Press, 2000.

Vygotsky, L. S. *Mind in Society: The Development of Higher Psychological Processes.* Cambridge, MA: Harvard University Press, 1978.

Weiten, W. *Psychology: Themes and Variations.* Monterey, CA: Brooks/Cole Publishing, 1998.

Werner, E. E. and Smith, R. S. *Overcoming the Odds: High-Risk Children from Birth to Adulthood.* Ithaca, NY: Cornell University Press, 1992.

White, R. W. and Watt, N. F. *The Abnormal Personality (5th edition).* Chichester, UK: John Wiley and Sons, Inc., 1981.

Wickens, A. *Foundations of Biopsychology.* Harlow, UK: Prentice Hall, 2000.

Wilson, E. O. *Sociobiology: A New Synthesis.* Cambridge, MA: Harvard University Press, 1975.

Winkler, K. *Teens, Depression, and the Blues: A Hot Issue.* Springfield, NJ: Enslow publishers, 2000.

Wolman, B. (ed.). *Historical Roots of Contemporary Psychology.* New York: Harper and Row, 1968.

Wrightsman, L. S. and Sanford, F. H. *Psychology: A Scientific Study of Human Behavior.* Monterey, CA: Brooks/Cole Publishing, 1975.

Yap, P. M. *Comparative Psychiatry: A Theoretical Framework.* Toronto, Canada: University of Toronto Press, 1974.

Zarit, S. H. and Knight, B. G. *A Guide to Psychotherapy and Aging.* Washington, DC: American Psychological Association, 1997.

Useful Websites

Amazing Optical Illusions
http://www.optillusions.com
See your favorite optical illusions at this fun site.

Bedlam
http://www.museum-london.org.uk/MOLsite/exhibits/bedlam/f_bed.htm
The Museum of London's online exhibition about Bedlam, the notorious mental institution.

Bipolar Disorders Information Center
http://www.mhsource.com/bipolar
Articles and information about bipolar 1 disorder.

Brain and Mind
http://www.epub.org.br/cm/home_i.htm
An online magazine with articles devoted to neuroscience, linguisitics, imprinting, and a variety of related topics.

Exploratorium
http://www.exploratorium.edu/exhibits/nf_exhibits.html
Click on "seeing" or "hearing" to check out visual and auditory illusions and other secrets of the mind.

Freud and Culture
http://www.loc.gov/exhibits/freud
An online Library of Congress exhibition that examines Sigmund Freud's life and key ideas and his effect on 20th-century thinking.

Great Ideas in Personality
http://www.personalityresearch.org
This website looks at scientific research programs in personality psychology. Pages on attachment theory, basic emotions, behavior genetics, behaviorism, cognitive social theories, and more give concise definitions of terms as well as links to further research on the web.

Jigsaw Classroom
http://www.jigsaw.org
The official web site of the Jigsaw Classroom, a

cooperative learning technique that reduces racial conflict between schoolchildren. Learn about its history and how to implement the techniques.

Kidspsych
http://www.kidspsych.org/index1.html
American Psychological Association's childrens' site, with games and exercises for kids. Also useful for students of developmental psychology. Follow the "about this activity" links to find out the theories behind the fun and games.

Kismet
http://www.ai.mit.edu/projects/humanoid-robotics-group/kismet/kismet.html
Kismet is the MIT's expressive robot, which has perceptual and motor functions tailored to natural human communication channels.

Neuroscience for Kids
http://faculty.washington.edu/chudler/neurok.html
A useful website for students and teachers who want to learn about the nervous system. Enjoy activities and experiments on your way to learning all about the brain and spinal cord.

Neuroscience Tutorial
http://thalamus.wustl.edu/course
The Washington University School of Medicine's online tutorial offers an illustrated guide to the basics of clinical neuroscience, with useful artworks and user-friendly text.

Psychology Central
http://emerson.thomsonlearning.com/psych
Links to many useful articles grouped by subject as well as cool, animated figures that improve your understanding of psychological principles.

Schizophrenia.com
http://www.schizophrenia.com
Information and resources on this mental disorder provided by a charitable organization.

Seeing, Hearing, and Smelling the World
http://www.hhmi.org/senses
A downloadable illustrated book dealing with perception from the Howard Hughes Medical Institute.

Sigmund Freud Museum
http://freud.t0.or.at/freud
The online Sigmund Freud Museum has videos and audio recordings of the famous psychoanalyst—there are even images of Freud's famous couch.

Social Psychology Network
http://www.socialpsychology.org
The largest social psychology database on the Internet. Within these pages you will find more

than 5,000 links to psychology-related resources and research groups, and there is also a useful section on general psychology.

Stanford Prison Experiment
http://www.prisonexp.org
A fascinating look at the Stanford Prison Experiment, which saw subjects placed in a prison to see what happens to "good people in a bad environment." Learn why the experiment had to be abandoned after six days due to the unforeseen severity of the effects on participants.

Stroop effect
http://www.dcity.org/braingames/stroop/index.htm
Take part in an online psychological experiment to see the Stroop effect in action.

Quote Attributions

opening quote

quote

Each chapter in *Psychology* contains quotes that relate to the topics covered. These quotes appear both within the main text and at the start of the chapters, and their attributions are detailed here. Quotes are listed in the order that they appear in the chapter, and the page numbers at the end of each attribution refer to the pages in this volume where the quote appears.

What Is Psychology?

Zimbardo, P. *Psychology and Life (12th edition)*. Glenview, IL: Scott, Foresman, and Co., 1988, p. 6.

Ancient Greek Thought

Thales. Cited in Aristotle, *De Anima, c.* 350 B.C., p. 10.
Heraclitis. Fragment DK22, B45, *c.* 500 B.C., p. 11.
Plato. *Republic*, Book IV, *c.* 360 B.C., p. 12.

Early Psychology

Porter, R. *Medicine: A History of Healing*. New York: Barnes and Noble, 1997, p. 16.
Porter, R. *The Greatest Benefit to Mankind: A Medical History of Humanity*. New York: Norton, 1999, p. 18, p. 19.
Freud, S. *New Introductory Lectures on Psychoanalysis*, London, U.K: Hogarth, 1933, p. 21.

Nature and Nurture

Mill, J. S. *Principles of Political Economy*. 1848, p. 22.
Galton, F. *Hereditary Genius*. 1869, p. 23.
Watson, J. B. *Behaviorism*. New York: The People's Institute Publishing Co., 1925, p. 25.
Breland, K. and Breland, M. "The Misbehavior of Organisms." *American Psychologist*, **16**, 1961, p. 26.

Beginnings of Scientific Psychology

Wundt, W. M. *Principles of Physiological Psychology*. New York: MacMillan, 1910, p. 30, p. 32.
Titchener, E. B. "Brentano and Wundt: Empirical and Experimental Psychology." *American Journal of Psychology*, *32*, 1921, p. 39.

Functionalism

Boring, E. G. *A History of Experimental Psychology*. New York: Century, 1929, p. 40.
James, W. "Does Consciousness Exist?" *Journal of Philosophy, Psychology, and Scientific Methods*, 1, 1904, p. 42.
Carr, H.A. *Psychology*, 1925, p. 44.

Gestalt Psychology

Wertheimer, M. *Lecture to the Kant Society*, Berlin, 1924, p. 47.
Köhler, W. "Gestalt Psychology Today." *American Psychology*, 1959, p. 49.

Psychoanalysis

Freud, S. *New Introductory Lectures on Psychoanalysis*, London, UK: Hogarth, 1933, p. 52.
Aristotle. *De Anima. c.* 350 B.C., p. 54.
Hesse, H. *Demian*. New York: Boni and Liveright, 1919, p. 56.
Klein, M. *Envy and Gratitude: A Study of Unconscious Sources*. London, U.K: Tavistock Publications, 1957, p. 58.
Lacan, J. *La Psychanalyse*. Paris: Presses Universitaires de France, 1958, p. 60.
Glover, E. "Some Recent Trends in Psychoanalytic Theory." *Psychoanalytic Quarterly*, **30**, 1961, p. 62.

Phenomenology and Humanism

Maslow, A. *Toward a Psychology of Being*. Princeton, NJ: New York, Van Nostrand, 1962, p. 66.
Maslow, A. H. Cited in B. Maslow, *Abraham H. Maslow: A Memorial Volume*. Brooks/Cole Publishing, 1972, p. 67, p.69.
Rogers, C. R. *On Becoming a Person: A Therapist's View of Psychotherapy*. Boston, MA: Houghton Mifflin, 1961, p. 70.

Behaviorism

Skinner, B. F. *Beyond Freedom and Dignity*. New York: Knopf, 1971, p. 74.
Thorndike, E. L. *Animal Intelligence: An Experimental Study of the Associative Processes in Animals*. New York: MacMillan, 1898, p. 75.
Watson, J. *About Behaviorism*. 1937, p. 76, p. 82.
Bergman, G. *Philosophy of Science*. Madison, WI: University of Wisconsin Press, 1956, p. 79.
Watson, J. B. *Behaviorism*. New York: The People's Institute Publishing Co., 1925, p. 81.
Koestler, A., *The Ghost in the Machine*. London, UK: Arkana, 1967, p. 83.
Kubrick, S. In an interview with Michel Ciment with reference to his movie *A Clockwork Orange*, 1971.
Tolman, E. "The Determiners of Behavior at a Choice Point." *Psychological Review*, *45*, 1938, p. 87.
Lieberman, D. A. *Learning: Behavior and Cognition*. Belmont, CA: Wadsworth Publishing Co., 1990, p. 88.

Neuropsychology

Damasio, A. *Descartes' Error : Emotion, Reason, and the Human Brain*. New York: Putnam, 1994, p. 90.
Broca, P. Cited in K. W. Walsh, *Neuropsychology: A Clinical Approach*. New York: Churchill Livingstone, 1978, p. 93.

Brain-imaging Techniques

Thales. Cited in Aristotle, *De Anima, c.* 350 B.C., p. 96.
Coveney, P. and Highfield, R. *Frontiers of Complexity: The Search for Order in a Complex World*. London: Faber and Faber, 1995, p. 96.
Cabanis, P. *Traite du physique et du moral de l'homme*, *(2nd memoir)*. 1802, p. 97.
Broadwell, R. *Neuroscience, Memory, and Language*. Washington, DC: Library of Congress,

1995, p. 99, p.102.

Sherrington, C. S. *Man on His Nature*. Cambridge, UK: The University Press, 1940, p. 100.

Cognitive Psychology

Neisser, U., *Cognitive Psychology*. New York: Appleton-Century Crofts, 1967, p. 104, p. 108.

Simon, H. and Kaplan, C. Cited in M. I. Posner, *Foundations of Cognitive Science*. Cambridge, MA: MIT Press, 1989, p. 105.

Flanagan, O. *The Science of the Mind*. Cambridge, MA: MIT Press, 1991, p. 107.

Eysenck, M. W. *Handbook of Cognitive Psychology*. Hillsdale, NJ: Laurence Erlbaum, 1984, p. 109.

Marr, D. *Vision: A Computational Investigation into Human Representation and Processing of Visual Information*. San Francisco: W. H. Freeman, 1983, p.116.

Gigerenzer, G., Todd, P. M., and the ABC Research Group. *Simple Heuristics That Make Us Smart*. New York: Oxford University Press, 1999, p. 117.

Psycholinguistics

Chomsky, N. Language and Freedom Lecture, 1970, at Loyola University, Chicago. Cited in N. Chomsky, *For Reasons of State*, New York: Pantheon Books, 1973, p. 118.

Smith, N. Cited in N. Chomsky, *New Horizons in the Study of Language and Mind*. New York: Cambridge University Press, 2000, p. 119.

Chomsky, N. *Minimalist Explorations*. Lecture given at University College, London, 1995, p. 120.

Schulman, H. *Priming*. At http://www.psy.ohio-state.edu/psy312/priming.html, 1997, p.121.

Lenneberg, E. *Biological Foundations of Language*. New York: Wiley, 1967, p. 123.

Jusczyk, P.W. *The Discovery of Spoken Language*. Cambridge, MA: MIT Press, 1997, p. 124.

Computer Simulation

Turing, A. "Computing, Machinery and Intelligence." *Mind Journal*, **59**, 1950, p. 126.

McCarthy, J. and Minsky, M. L. From the proposal for the 1956 Dartmouth summer research project on Artificial Intelligence, p. 127.

Anderson, J. A. *et al.* "Distinctive Features, Categorical Perception, and Probability Learning: Some Applications of a Neural Model." *Psychological Review*, **84**, p. 448.

Evolutionary Psychology

Dobzhansky, T. "Nothing in Biology Makes Sense Except in the Light of Evolution." *American Biology Teacher*, **35**, 1975, p. 134.

Darwin, C. R. *On the Origin of Species*. London, UK: J. Murray, 1859, p. 135.

Wilson, E. O. *Naturalist*. New York: Warner Books, 1994, p. 136.

Tooby, J. and Cosmides, L. *Experimental Psychology*. At http://www.psych.ucsb.edu/research/cep/primer.html, 1997, p.139.

Solso, R. L. Cited in R. L. Solso and D. W. Massaro (eds.), *The Science of the Mind: 2001 and Beyond*. New York: Oxford University Press, 1995, p. 142.

Nonwestern Theories of the Mind

Owusu-Bempah, K. and Howitt, D. *Psychology beyond Western Perspectives*. Leicester, UK: British Psychological Society Books, 2000, p. 144.

Nsamenang, B "Psychology in Sub-Saharan Africa." *Psychology and Developing Societies*, **5**. 1993, p. 146.

Heelas, P. and Lock, A. *Indigenous Psychologies: The Anthropology of the Self*. New York: Academic Press, 1981, p. 147.

Paranjpe, A. C. and Bhatt, G. S. "Emotion: A Perspective from the Indian Tradition." *In* H. S. R. Kao and D. Sinha (eds.), *Asian Perspectives on Psychology*. New Delhi, India: Sage Publications, 1997, p. 149.

Porter, R. *The Greatest Benefit to Mankind: A Medical History of Humanity*. New York: Norton, 1999, p.150.

Cross-cultural Psychology

Masumoto, D. *Cultural Influences on Research Methods and Statistics*. Pacific Grove, CA: Brooks/Cole Publishing, 1994, p. 152.

Guyll, M. and Madon, S. "Ethnicity Research and Theoretical Conservatism." *American Psychologist*, **55**, 2000, p. 155.

Uleman, J. "Spontaneous Versus Intentional Influences in Impression Formation." In S. Chaiken and Y. Trope (eds..), *Dual Process Theories in Social Psychology*. New York: Guilford Press, 1999, p. 156.

Kaplan, H. I. and Sadock, B. J. *Synopsis of Psychiatry: Behavioral Sciences, Clinical Psychiatry*. Philadelphia, PA: Lippincott, Williams, and Wilkins, 1994, p. 159.

Kardiner, A. *They Studied Man*. Cleveland, OH: World Publishing Co., 1961, p. 201.

Research Methods

Pavlov, I., *Conditioned Reflexes: An Investigation of the Physiological Activity of the Cerebral Cortex*. London, UK: Oxford University Press, 1927, p. 162.

Every effort has been made to attribute the quotes throughout *Psychology* correctly. Any errors or omissions brought to the attention of the publisher are regretted and will be credited in subsequent editions.

Set Index